Ancestral

Ancestral Feeling

*Postcolonial Thoughts on
Western Christian Heritage*

Renie Chow Choy

scm press

© Renie Choy 2021

Published in 2021 by SCM Press

Editorial office
3rd Floor, Invicta House,
108–114 Golden Lane,
London EC1Y 0TG, UK

www.scmpress.co.uk

SCM Press is an imprint of Hymns Ancient & Modern Ltd
(a registered charity)

HYMNS Ancient
&Modern

Hymns Ancient & Modern® is a registered trademark of
Hymns Ancient & Modern Ltd
13A Hellesdon Park Road, Norwich,
Norfolk NR6 5DR, UK

Cover photos: Cloister, Gloucester Cathedral; Portrait photographs
of author's grandparents (© Renie Chow Choy)

British Library Cataloguing in Publication data
A catalogue record for this book is available
from the British Library

ISBN 978-0-33406-090-1

Typeset by Regent Typesetting
Printed and bound by
CPI Group (UK) Ltd

Contents

For my parents

Most
For n
condu
ing ea
empe
stand
ity, f
cano
magr
pract
of fa
visite
est i
pers
Pant
but
mor
min
of C
Her
cent
ing
by
triu
and
is r
sur
inv
mir
art

doesn't necessarily have to understand sixteenth-century Sri Lankan Catholics and an English Anglican doesn't necessarily need to understand nineteenth-century Trinidadian Anglicans. Owing to the history of empire, Western Christianity has an explanatory power which Christianities of the 'Global South' do not, its history essential for explaining much about Catholic and Protestant dogma, polity and spirituality. The unsettling fact is that, despite my Chinese heritage, ignoring the history of China altogether would not leave any fatal gaps in my knowledge about such topics.

This is not a book I ever set out to write. As a historian of medieval Christianity, my specialism is European by nature and I would have been quite content carrying on writing books about Benedictine monks and Latin liturgy in Western Christendom. I would hope that most people understand why many ethnic minorities see racialization as the cause of the situations they face, but for my part I have not wanted to perpetuate the stereotype that ethnic minority historians can only ever write about race. Furthermore, I am no expert on critical race theory or postcolonial theory. Nor am I a theologian with expertise on non-Western ecclesiology, liberation theologies, black theologies and so on. But, restless with internal conflict, I write as a historian who feels guilt about my Europhile interests; insecurity because my white British students can often speak with greater personal knowledge about the things I try to teach than I can; indignation because the assertion I so commonly hear – that Christianity was revolutionary because 'There is neither Jew nor Greek, there is neither bond nor free, there is neither male nor female: for ye are all one in Christ Jesus' – seems ignorant and uninformed about historical realities.

This book concerns an impossible dilemma: on one hand, the colonizing assumptions behind the notion of 'Christian heritage'; on the other, the fact that millions around the world feel affinity for this same 'Christian heritage'. Inevitably, the arguments I present will invite critique that they do not sufficiently challenge the status quo: in the view of an external reviewer, they are too 'emollient'. For I am hardly proposing the downfall of the traditional historical enterprise. Admittedly, throughout this book I display a rather defeatist view regarding the inevitable centrality of Western Christian heritage: its literature, sacred art, music, architecture explain too much of the religion of millions across the globe. Thus, I focus on the 'ancestral feeling' that keeps ethnic minority Christians tied for ever to Europe – and I do not propose its suppression. I argue that notions of ancestral bond cannot be circumvented, because the language of family, generations, forefathers, progenitors, inheritance and heritage permeate nearly every page of Scripture from the Old Testament to the New, and Christians have never been able to think about faith as something other than 'received' and 'passed on'. But recognizing the manner in which the theological and historical enterprise has been held captive by imperializing assumptions, much of it expressed through the paternalistic language of 'lineage', how can I still tolerate my own elective affinity with Western Christian heritage? Is it possible, having encountered the national Charlemagne of the Panthéon, to esteem him still as a spiritual forefather?

This book is about the legacies of colonialism, and scholars have coined different terms to capture what is at stake. The most widely used term, 'postcolonialism', is also the one that is the most misunderstood. Most people seem to adopt 'postcolonial' for its mere temporal connotations, as in 'after colonialism'. So the assumption is that, with the world having been largely decolonized, we now live in the 'postcolonial era'. There are two things to be said about this. First is that the question of whether and when empire has ended is still the subject of much heated debate. As outlined by Sathnam Sanghera in his *Empireland*:

> Some posit it was the massacre in Punjab in 1919 when the British lost the moral argument, some say it was the 1930s when Gandhi gained traction against the British, some argue it was 1947 when the British formally withdrew from India, some pinpoint it to the handover of Hong Kong to the Chinese in July 1997, some gesture towards the Suez crisis of 1956, some insist it continues to exist in the remaining British Overseas Territories we still possess, which in 2020

consisted of Anguilla, Bermuda, the British Antarctic Territory, the British Indian Ocean Territory, the British Virgin Islands, the Cayman Islands, the Falkland Islands, Gibraltar, Montserrat, the Pitcairn Islands, South Georgia and the Sandwich Islands, the Sovereign Base Areas of Akrotiri and Dhekelia, St Helena, Ascension and Tristan de Cunha and the Turks and Caicos Islands.[3]

But, second, in its more precise, technical and potent usage, the term 'postcolonial' denotes an active reading posture that exposes 'the whole colonial syndrome' that has seeped into our language, thought and assumptions, often without our even noticing.[4] As a term that became established in critical literary theory in the 1980s following Edward Said's *Orientalism* (1978) and the work of the Subaltern Studies Group, it is not synonymous with 'anti-colonial': rather, its task is more intellectual, seeking to expose the effects of colonialism on ways of thinking, being, feeling for both colonized and colonizer.[5] In Sugirtharajah's words, a postcolonial reading focuses on exposing and critiquing 'the universalist, totalizing forms of European interpretation that were passed on to us', and must be a 'discursive resistance' not only to imperial ideologies and attitudes but also 'to their continual reincarnations' in fields of study as diverse as the historical, economic, scientific and theological.[6] For the aims of this book, I employ the term 'postcolonial' in this second sense.

Then there are a host of terms to describe the people who experience the tensions caused by imperial prejudice and oppression. In this book I adopt the house style of the British government's website (Gov.uk) and the Office for National Statistics, which recommend the use of the term 'ethnic minorities' to refer to all ethnic groups in the UK except the White British group.[7] But the term 'ethnic minorities' lacks the power that other terms have to expose dichotomies of power, such as 'colonized' and 'colonizers'. Some terms emphasize the sites on which these dynamics of power are played out: we are the 'Global South', the 'subaltern' ('below' and 'other', to indicate subordination and an inferior rank). Other terms focus on the effects caused by those in power acting upon those without power: we are the 'racialized', 'ethnicized', 'marginalized', 'minoritized'. Still other terms focus on the consequences of emigration and disruptions to identities, families and sense of belonging caused by these imbalances of power: we are 'hybrid', 'diasporic', 'migratory', 'bordered'.

Which of these above names for 'people of colour' can possibly capture the unique set of emotional, psychological and intellectual tensions that I wish to explore in this book? As it happens, the practice of naming – literally, the conferral of given names – are a rather helpful way of illustrating the problem I tackle in this book. I have always felt that the profusion of unique 'English' baby names emerging from the one tiny island of Hong Kong could itself sustain a lengthy monograph. As was the case in British colonies around the globe, missionaries and teachers in missionary schools typically gave children and young people their Christian names: Samuel, Philip, Paul, Jacob, Thomas, Mary, Elizabeth, Priscilla, and so on. But apart from the missionary influence, Westernization generally also inspired rather more eccentric naming: Rimsky, Marsilius, Winky, Pinky. Native English-speakers will react with mockery or bewilderment and the abundance of such names in East Asia – especially when set alongside the monosyllabic Chinese surnames – offers a source of perennial amusement and ridicule for expats. Such a response fails to appreciate that quirky 'faux-English' names are symptomatic of a debasing postcolonial predicament. Decades of colonial education have conditioned Hong Kongers to connect English names with learning and prestige. A name like 'Chow Shun-Man' (my Chinese name transliterated) doesn't exactly exude the same level of educational attainment, cultural sophistication and status that English names like Augusta, Victoria, Louis and Arthur do. But Hong Kongers are also aware that we were not accorded the same rights as the English, as exemplified in the 'British National (Overseas) nationality status', a 'nationality' which (until January 2021, precipitated by the dramatic unravelling of stability in Hong Kong) did not actually grant Hong Kong people the right to even reside in the UK. As with

English nationality, so with names. Many self-conscious Hong Kongers deliberately invent names that evoke Englishness but are not a straightforward copy, to emanate Western sophistication while acknowledging the reality of difference. A quick trick to make a male first name sound English without being a total copycat is to add 'son' to any syllable:[8] I know of an Addson, Kingson, Garson and Greenson. I also know of a Winchester, York, Aragon, Fancy, Pansy and Rainbow – not to mention the name conferred on me by my parents inside Hong Kong's Queen Mary Hospital, which I am told on a regular basis reminds British people of the UK's best-selling heartburn and indigestion tablet. Names are usually the first revelation of one's identity. If I have managed to convey how a simple name can reflect such complex questions of identity in the bearer, brought about by an English inheritance without the concomitant privileges of ethnicity or nationality, then I hope we can begin to get a sense of the topic I wish to broach in this book.

A note on Chinese terms

Chinese characters today exist in traditional and simplified forms, the former still in use in Hong Kong, Macau, Taiwan and many historic overseas Chinese communities outside Asia, and the latter associated with the reforms of the government of the People's Republic of China under Mao Zedong in the 1950s and 1960s. In this book I use the traditional form.

For transliteration of Chinese terms, I have followed the Yale romanization of Cantonese as standardized in Gerard Kok and Parker Po-fei Huang's textbook *Speak Cantonese* (1958) and still widely used today.

I have retained the most commonly recognized transliterations for key events and names of people and places (e.g. Shang Dynasty, Zhou Dynasty, Guangdong, Hong Kong, Confucius). Where a term is of distinctly personal interest to me, I have rendered it in the Cantonese of my mother tongue (e.g. 'Chow' in place of Zhou).

Notes

1 James Baldwin, speaking for the proposition 'The American Dream is at the expense of the American Negro', Cambridge Union, England, 17 February 1965. Printed in Raoul Peck (ed.), 2017, *I Am Not Your Negro: A Companion Edition to the Documentary Film Directed by Raoul Peck*, New York: Vintage International, p. 23.

2 Isabel Hofmeyr, 2002, 'How Bunyan Became English: Missionaries, Translation, and the Discipline of English Literature', *Journal of British Studies* 41(1), pp. 84–119 at 110.

3 Sathnam Sanghera, 2021, *Empireland: How Imperialism has Shaped Modern Britain*, London: Viking, pp. 33–4.

4 '... a *process* of disengagement from the whole colonial syndrome': Peter Hulme, 1995, 'Including America', *Ariel: A Review of International English Literature* 26 (1), pp. 117–23 at 120, emphasis in original.

5 The clearest and most accessible text in my opinion for outlining the intellectual influences, preoccupations and obligations of postcolonial studies is Leela Gandhi, 1998, *Postcolonial Theory: A Critical Introduction*, 2nd edn, London: Routledge.

6 R. S. Sugirtharajah, 1998, *Asian Biblical Hermeneutics and Postcolonialism: Contesting the Interpretations*, Sheffield: Sheffield Academic Press, around pp. 17–18.

7 www.ethnicity-facts-figures.service.gov.uk/style-guide/writing-about-ethnicity#ethnic-minorities-and-ethnic-groups (accessed 27.08.2021); https://style.ons.gov.uk/house-style/race-and-ethnicity/ (accessed 27.08.2021).

8 Joyce Man, 'Hong Kong Loves Weird English Names', *The Atlantic*, 1 October 2012.

Introduction

While I preoccupy myself with 'decentring Europe' from the Introduction to Church History course I lead, my friend in the USA is moving in the opposite direction: she is organizing a ten-day 'Christian heritage tour' to England for members of her Chinese American church. Prior to the shutdown of the travel and tourism industry caused by Covid, inbound religious tourism to the UK was experiencing an unprecedented boom; when the industry begins its recovery, my friend will still have many tour operators to choose from. She could choose from one of several tours to the UK operated by Faith Journey, which promises to 'bring into vivid focus the remarkable events and individuals that forever changed the religious landscape of the world'. An experience of 'true communion awaits' as tourists visit Canterbury where St Augustine first established a stronghold for Christianity in the British Isles; Norwich, inside the cell where St Julian spent two decades in prayerful seclusion; Dublin, to view the splendidly illuminated eighth-century manuscript of the Gospels, the Book of Kells; Iona, to attend morning Eucharist at the ancient abbey which played a crucial role in the Christianization of Scotland; Edinburgh, to the childhood home of John Knox, leader of the Scottish Reformation; Bristol's 'New Room', the world's oldest Methodist building. The website promises, 'We will not only be swept up by the beauty of the cities, villages and countryside of picturesque England and Scotland, we will also come away with ... a deep appreciation for the depth of dedication of those who led the way.'[1] Or my friend might prefer Pilgrim Tours, whose itinerary boasts stops at St Paul's Cathedral, the 'parish church of the British Commonwealth'; the Metropolitan Tabernacle, where Charles Spurgeon held his great revival meetings; Southampton, where the Mayflower sailed from England in 1620 and the birthplace of hymnwriter Isaac Watts; and Magdalene College in Cambridge, where C. S. Lewis was professor.[2] Or she might choose to join the 'God and Greater Britain Tour', during which tourists 'follow in the footsteps of many of the great heroes of the faith', including William Tyndale, Thomas Cranmer, Nicholas Ridley and Hugh Latimer, John Owen, John Bunyan, George Whitefield, John Wesley, John Newton, William Cowper, Charles Simeon, William Wilberforce, Charles Spurgeon, J. C. Ryle, Martyn Lloyd-Jones, C. S. Lewis and J. R. R. Tolkien. Tour itineraries even come with recommended devotional reading, like *The Christian in Complete Armour* by seventeenth-century Puritan divine William Gurnall, which accompanies a visit to the East Anglian village of Lavenham.[3] In the capital, my friend could sign up for walks led by Christian Heritage London, which serve, as its website indicates, quoting Hebrews 13.7, to help you 'Remember your leaders, those who spoke to you the word of God. Consider the outcome of their way of life, and imitate their faith.' The tours hit sites associated with Wilberforce, Spurgeon, Tyndale, Whitefield, Elizabeth Fry, John Newton and others who 'have inspired generations of believers internationally'.[4] If this abundance of choice is bewildering, she might seek advice from the Christian Heritage Network, which provides visitors 'with a guarantee of quality and values', ensuring that Christian tourists enjoy tours led by 'people who use Christian history to help us think about Christianity today' and 'to have real fellowship with fellow Christians'.[5]

The kind of tourists attracted to these sites may bemuse the British. Each year, the Welsh town of Llanover in Monmouthshire attracts between 1,500 and 2,000 Koreans visiting the chapel associated with Nonconformist minister Robert Jermain Thomas. Working for the London Mission Society, Thomas had spent only months along the Taedong river sailing towards Pyongyang and smuggling Bibles at each port stop before he was captured by the Koreans and executed in 1866. Today, a staggering one-third of South Koreans identify as Christian, of which 9 million are Protestant and 5 million Catholic, and more missionaries are sent abroad from South Korea than from any other country apart from the USA.[6] As a *Times* report explains, many Koreans credit the establishment of Protestantism in Korea to Thomas's distribution of Bibles, and regard him as their 'spiritual ancestor'. Among them is the Revd Peter Cho who describes how, when he first set foot inside the nineteenth-century chapel where Thomas's father had been minister, 'the tears didn't stop for an hour', and so moved was he by the sense of connection to Thomas that he ended up moving to Wales and becoming a minister in Caerphilly.[7] More sensationally, a *Daily Mail* article from 2012 announces, 'Forget Lourdes, go on a pilgrimage to Barnsley! Mining town hoping to become top destination for 70m Chinese Christians.'[8] The article explains that tourism chiefs in this South Yorkshire mining town are launching a major push to attract Chinese Christian tourists to the birthplace of famous nineteenth-century missionary to China, Hudson Taylor. John Foster, chairman of the Barnsley Work and Skills Board, explains that the rationale for this strategy is that 'More than 50 per cent of the overseas tourists visiting Britain are Chinese', many of them Christians who attribute their faith to the Chinese Overseas Mission Fellowship founded by Taylor. 'One kissed the ground outside Boots. They refer to Barnsley as their spiritual home', a group member of the Barnsley Work and Skills Board says. Astoundingly, Mr Foster muses, 'There are more Christians in China and the Far East who owe their heritage to James Hudson Taylor than there are people in Britain.'

If this is true, the insecurity that is regularly displayed by politicians about the threat to Great Britain's Christian heritage seems to be rather misdirected. For the 2015 General Election, UKIP published a pamphlet titled 'Valuing our Christian Heritage': laid over a photo of *Hymns Ancient and Modern*, the written message from Nigel Farage pronounces that 'we need a much more muscular defence of our Christian heritage'.[9] Then in her Christmas message in 2017, Prime Minister Theresa May aimed to unify a nation recovering from the shock of multiple terrorist attacks and the vote to leave the European Union, by imploring, 'Let us take pride in our Christian heritage and the confidence it gives us to ensure that in Britain you can practise your faith free from question or fear.'[10] More recently, Danny Kruger used his maiden speech in the House of Commons to lament that 'traditionally' there was a sense 'that our country is rooted in Christianity' but that 'Today those ideas are losing their purchase', and submitting, 'I know … that Christianity and the western past are badly stained by violence and injustice, but I am not sure that we should so casually throw away the inheritance of our culture.'[11] Steve Double, Conservative MP for St Austell and Newquay, sought to remind the British public on Premier Christian Radio that 'we are a nation that is very much built on Christian values and a very strong Christian heritage and we are very much building on that foundation from our history'.[12]

Expressed in terms of a national inheritance, these sentiments highlight a confusion over precisely *to whom* a 'very strong Christian heritage' belongs. The 2011 census found that the number of people professing to be Christian within England and Wales has fallen overall: the size of this group decreased 13 percentage points from 72% (37.3 million) in 2001 to 59% (33.2 million) in 2011 – and by all indications we can expect this downward trend to be confirmed when the results of the 2021 census are released. This means 4.1 million fewer people were identifying as Christian despite overall population growth.[13] Furthermore, among the Christian population within the whole of England, those identifying as white (English, Scottish or Welsh) fell from 32.5 million in 2001 to 27 million in 2011, a fall of 17%.[14] Now, if by *'our* Christian heritage' politicians have in mind white British nationals, then I agree the concern they express over the threat it faces and the need to protect it is merited. But, in fact, when looking across all other ethnic groups, the proportion of Christians in the UK actually increased between 2001 and 2011. The number of 'Other white' Christians increased from 1.3 million to 2 million, a growth of 50%, mostly reflecting migration from EU accession countries. UK ethnic minority groups show even greater increases: the number of black Christians (African/

Caribbean/other black) in England grew by 471,000 between 2001 and 2011, an increase of 58%; mixed-race Christians by 145,000, or 64%; and Asian Christians (Bangladeshi/Indian/ Pakistani/Other Asian in 2001, and including Chinese also in 2011) by 353,000, a staggering 390%.[15] Among foreign-born UK residents, the greatest proportion (3.6 million) identified as Christian, representing nearly half (48%) of the non-UK-born population. Over 1.8 million, or 53%, of foreign-born UK residents with Christian affiliation were recent arrivals, having immigrated during the period 2001 to 2011, as compared to those who had arrived before 2000.[16]

These statistics show that, despite political anxiety about its threatened survival, resident in the UK are in fact growing numbers of ethnic minority Christians who would very much affirm Christian heritage. That ubiquitous and seemingly innocuous personal possessive pronoun 'our' – as in '*our* Christian heritage' and 'the inheritance of *our* culture' – seems suddenly to disregard vast numbers of people, associating 'Christian heritage' with national history and traditions, and conjuring a picture of (to invoke the phrase used by Eliza Filby) that 'old trinity of Englishness, Anglicanism and Toryism'.[17] Indeed, upon hearing the phrase 'our Christian heritage', chances are one straightaway imagines pretty rural churches, abbey ruins, gothic cathedrals, the King James Bible, the Book of Common Prayer, boy choristers and charity schools. Christmas inspires particularly beloved and poignant evocations of national Christian heritage, with carol services by candlelight and children's nativity plays. To whom do these emblems of Christian heritage belong?

To illustrate what's at stake here, let me turn to 'England's Nazareth', the shrine of Our Lady of Walsingham. In 1061, the wealthy widow Lady Richeldis de Faverches had a vision of Angel Gabriel taking her in spirit to Nazareth, showing her the home of the Holy Family, and instructing her to build a replica in her manor at Walsingham Parva. The simple wooden house that she constructed soon became the focus of intense devotion to Our Lady, and Augustinian Canons in the twelfth century founded a priory nearby in order to care for the many pilgrims flooding to the site. By the fourteenth and fifteenth centuries, Walsingham rivalled Canterbury as a premier place of pilgrimage. As the pre-eminent shrine to Our Lady in England, a country which since the fourteenth century has been known by the title 'Dowry of Mary', Walsingham presents a particularly overt example of the close associations between Christian heritage and Englishness. Nearly every king and queen between Henry III to Henry VIII made pilgrimages to Walsingham, and the subsequent destruction of the shrine and priory during the Reformation has now become part of the national narrative about the restoration of England's architectural and cultural gems. Although vocal conservative evangelical protestors line the paths to protest against Marian processions, it remains the case that Walsingham is proudly advertised as a treasure of English heritage, with its medieval market town, historic pubs and hostelries, ancient farmland and early twentieth-century Marian shrine lovingly restored by Fr Patten, not to mention the 'tranquil atmosphere surrounding the ruins, wildflower meadows, river walks along the Stiffkey, and twenty acres of natural woodland carpeted with snowdrops in early spring', as one guidebook boasts.[18] Tokenism is not the answer I seek, but, absent a single photo of an ethnic minority individual in the brochure, I wonder whether there is room in this image of 'England's Nazareth' for the 15,000 people from the Tamil community who visit every year. Arriving from Sri Lanka, southern India, and all over Britain, the majority of the Tamils are Catholics, and some are Hindu, all drawn to the shrine to revere the Virgin Mary. Annually they represent the single largest pilgrimage group to the shrine. Why do our conceptions of Walsingham not immediately conjure images of this group?

Equally we might ask: why did a service at Westminster Abbey to mark the four-hundredth anniversary of the King James Bible not feature a single black person in the 'procession of the Bibles' when arguably it is predominantly black denominations who use the translation the most today? Or, why is it that we expect cathedral gift shops to stock royal family memorabilia, Union Jack cushions, Shakespeare and Jane Austen and Charles Dickens books, jams and marmalades, and bone china tea sets?

Will John Major's prediction materialize, when in 1993 he said that 'fifty years from now, Britain will still be the country of long shadows on county grounds, warm beer, invincible green suburbs, dog lovers and – as George Orwell said – old maids bicycling to Holy Communion through the morning mist'?[19] I can't comment on the former points, but I can say that the last will likely need a bit of tweaking: the National Parish Congregation Diversity Monitoring in 2007 found that in every adult age group, a black or black British adult is more likely to be a core congregation member of the Church of England than a white person of the same age.[20]

These examples point to two problems. First, the concept of 'Christian heritage' is not without racial or nationalistic implications, and raises questions about belonging: the 'our' in 'our Christian heritage' appears strongly reliant on conceiving the history of Christianity in terms of the history of the UK and Europe, in the tradition of Hilaire Belloc who notoriously pronounced in 1920, 'The Faith is Europe and Europe is the Faith.'[21] Second, the image of 'our Christian heritage' evoked by political discourse, state ceremony, tourist brochures, and gift shops does not make visible the many who would consider it 'theirs' as well. In this Introduction, I shall mention solutions proposed to the first of these problems only briefly, because it is more important that I spend time discussing why solutions to the first problem do not make the second problem go away.

First, with regard to the problem of Eurocentrism, most institutions of higher education have responded in recent decades with efforts to 'decolonize' the curriculum. Critiques of a Eurocentric mode of historiography are now so commonplace and well rehearsed that only a brief summary here is needed. These critiques aim to dismantle the metanarratives constructed from the perspective of the winners in history, the 'white male heroes' who constitute our Western intellectual canon. In Protestant historiography, this metanarrative results in curricular content which typically begins with early Christianity in the Middle East and North Africa, and then moves swiftly on to Rome and Latin Christianity, remaining within the orbit of Western Europe until the age of revival turns our attention to America, and with the world missions movement in the nineteenth and twentieth century we at last arrive at a 'global Christianity'. It's a syllabus that takes students of doctrine from the early Church Fathers to Augustine and Aquinas to Luther and Calvin and then to Jonathan Edwards and Karl Barth; a survey of worship that takes us from the Roman Rite to Gregorian chant to Bach and Palestrina to John and Charles Wesley. The glaring absence of women, the poor, the disabled, the queer, the enslaved, the colonized in such metanarratives has generated many correctives. One common corrective is to propose an alternative or revisionist canon, introducing works into the curriculum of non-Western provenance that are unknown or little known in the West. So for example, alongside Ambrose, Augustine, Bede, Anselm and Bernard of Clairvaux, we find in Sterk and Coakley's new anthology, the 'Chinese Christian Sutras', Agathangelos on the history of the Armenians, John of Ephesus on the evangelization of Nubia, the *Lives* of Mâr Yahbh-Allâhâ and Rabban Sâwmâ, the War Chronicle of Amda Tseyon, and the *Kebra Nagast*.[22] Another important way to challenge our Eurocentric preoccupations is to rethink Europe's primacy and self-sufficiency: for example, we might emphasize that Augustine was not European but African, or that the expansion of Christianity in the early Middle Ages was as much (if not more) 'eastward' as 'westward', or that church rituals depended on important oriental imports such as incense. Another approach is to ask how significant theologians dealt with their own contexts of empires and issues of power: for example, we should observe how Martin Luther's belief in the freedom of the Christian led him to resist temporal authority, or note John Wesley's insistence that the principal cause of human suffering is the economics of greed.[23]

These correctives signal truly important advances, but they are not without their problems, as recent scholarship has also acknowledged. For example, rewriting the canon can merely perpetuate metropole/periphery binaries and with it the continued marginalization of minority groups: adding an 'ethnic'/feminist/gay/disabled author to the syllabus is quite different from weaving their perspectives into the very heart of intellectual culture. Furthermore, decisions about who and what counts as 'historically important' are still controlled by academics working in the West or trained in the West, and non-European academics are still expected to imitate and respect Western academic conventions of research and writing. But the biggest deficiency with these correctives is that they do not actually confront the fundamental impasse, owing to the fact of Western imperialism, of the inescapability of the West. To use Elizabeth Fox-Genovese's phrase, though we may feel 'colonized in relation to that élite western culture', throwing out Western history 'does not solve [the] problem any more than expurgating all traces of western technology solves the problem of colonial peoples'.[24] To illustrate this situation, I would like to discuss the oft-repeated truism that Christianity 'is not a Western thing', an assertion made on the basis of statistical evidence showing that the vast majority of today's Christians live in the 'Global South', commonly defined as Africa, Asia and Latin America, as opposed to the 'Global North' of North America, Europe, Japan, Australia and New Zealand.[25] A 2011 study by the Pew Research Center on the size and distribution of the world's Christian population estimated that more than 1.3 billion Christians live in the Global South (61%), compared with 860 million in the Global North (39%).[26] At least in the USA, Africans, African Americans, Latinx and Asians have become the majority body in theological colleges.[27] That Christianity's centre resides in the Global South rather than the North is clear enough, but I want to discuss what these statistics reveal about the history of Christianity and how this history is viewed. In this regard, the Pew Forum study offers us a prime case study for exhibiting the nature of the dilemma to be tackled in this book.

The Pew Research Center's study begins with estimates that about half of all Christians worldwide are Catholic (50% of all Christians and 15.9% of the total world population), and more than a third are Protestant (37% of all Christians and 11.6% of the total world population). Orthodox communions comprise 12% of the world's Christians, or 3.8% of the total world population, and other Christian groups (such as the Church of Jesus Christ of Latterday Saints, Jehovah's Witnesses and the Christian Science Church) make up the remaining 1% of Christians, or 0.4% of the world population. The vast majority of global Christians are Catholic or Protestant, making up a total of 87% of Christians in the world. The Pew Forum study stresses the overwhelmingly 'Southern' axis of this population. For example, of the ten countries with the largest number of Catholics, five lie in the Global South. Almost 40% of the world's Catholics live in Latin America and the Caribbean; more than a quarter live either in the Asia-Pacific or in sub-Saharan Africa. For the Protestant population, after the United States, which holds 20% of the worldwide total, Nigeria is second, with nearly 60 million Protestants, or more than 7% of all Protestants worldwide. China has the world's third-largest Protestant population, approximately 58 million. Pentecostals, charismatics and evangelicals are termed 'movements' within the Protestant 'tradition' in the Pew Forum study. Estimates suggest that around 44% of the world's Pentecostals reside in Sub-Saharan Africa, 37% in the Americas and 16% in Asia and the Pacific. Almost half (49%) of all charismatic Christians in the world live in the Americas and nearly 30% of charismatics live in the Asia-Pacific region. Sub-Saharan Africa has both the greatest concentration of evangelical Christians (13% of Sub-Saharan Africa is evangelical) and the largest share of the world's evangelicals (38%). About 1 in 3 evangelicals live in the Americas (33%) and roughly 1 in 5 reside in the Asia-Pacific region (21%).[28]

So much for numbers. I want to draw attention to the interpretive angle running throughout the study to accompany these statistics on Christianity's overwhelming concentration in the Global South. Here are some examples of statements made in the study:

- 'There are more Catholics in Brazil alone than in Italy, France and Spain combined.'
- 'In 1910, about two-thirds of the world's Christians lived in Europe, where the bulk of Christians had been for a millennium.'

- 'The Protestant Reformation, which split Western Christianity and gave birth to Protestantism, took place in Europe in the 16th century. Today, however, only two of the 10 countries with the largest Protestant populations are European.'
- 'Nigeria now has more than twice as many Protestants ... as Germany, the birthplace of the Protestant Reformation.'
- 'China probably has more Christians than any European nation except Russia.'
- 'Despite Europe's historical links to Protestantism, its share of the global Protestant population (13%) is eclipsed by the share in sub-Saharan Africa (37%), the Americas (33%) and the Asia-Pacific region (17%). Only the Middle East-North Africa has a smaller share of Protestants (less than 1%) than Europe.'[29]

The insistently Eurocentric frame of reference for describing the expansion of Christianity in Africa, Asia and the Americas is suggestive of a wide range of motives and sentiments: triumph and satisfaction about the success of Western missions and evangelism; gratitude that Christianity survived the end of formal colonialism and thrives today in formerly colonized populations; vindication from the accusation that the South never wanted Christianity; apprehension about the forces from the Global South that will inevitably shape the Christianity of the Global North; and so on. My own interest in this Eurocentric frame of reference, however, is less ideological and more theoretical, and it is triggered by this statement appearing near the outset of the study: 'Clearly, Christianity has spread far from its historical origins.'[30] The statement acknowledges a basic, unavoidable fact, that Christianity, no matter how global in reach and how non-Western in demographic composition, is tied to Europe by a historic relationship. Thus, for example, when emphasizing the large populations of Pentecostals, charismatics and evangelicals in sub-Saharan Africa, the Americas, and the Asia-Pacific, the study takes pains to point out that Pentecostalism 'has roots' in the nineteenth-century Holiness Movement in Britain, and that modern evangelicalism is 'traced' to seventeenth-century Lutheran Pietism in Germany and Methodism in England.[31] To put it completely bluntly, *history* is the problem – that is to say, thinking historically ('historicizing') about the development of Christianity is the reason why Europe is inescapable.

'Roots' like these always pull the story of world Christianity back to Europe. These 'roots' are not simply descriptive: more forcefully, they possess an explanatory and even causal power, making sense of why a certain Christian group is here and not there, why it is mostly comprised of one ethnicity and not another, why it uses one version of the Bible and not another, why it constructs churches in one style and not another, why it tends to prefer one style of communion cup over another. And thus these roots represent 'Turning Points', as Mark Noll has called them: of the 13 'Decisive Moments in the History of Christianity', remarkably *ten* occur in Western Europe.[32] These 'critical turning points' explain 'why certain events, actions, or incidents may have marked an important fork in the road or signalled a new stage in the outworking of Christian history'. Astoundingly, after the first three turning points (fall of Jerusalem, Council of Nicaea, Council of Chalcedon), every single turning point thereafter refers to an event taking place in Europe or of European provenance: 'the monastic rescue of the Church' (Rule of Benedict); 'the culmination of Christendom' (Charlemagne); the Great Schism; the beginnings of Protestantism (Diet of Worms); 'A New Europe' (the English Act of Supremacy); Catholic reform and worldwide outreach (the founding of the Jesuits); the 'new piety' (conversion of the Wesleys); the French Revolution; the Edinburgh Missionary Conference; the Second Vatican Council; and the Lausanne Congress on World Evangelization. Noll has selected all of these events for their effect on global Christianity; it is telling that, beyond the sixth century, the centre of origination is consistently Western Europe. To understand global Christianity, in other words, one must always understand Western European Christianity first.

To repeat, historicizing is the problem – an issue that I shall outline with greater detail in the first two chapters. But for now it is important to note that this is the reason why works on church history trying to redress Eurocentrism by emphasizing Christianity's non-Western origins cannot make Europe's central role as progenitor of global Christianity go away. This is what I believe distinguishes the primary task of my book from many others, such as Vince Bantu's *A Multitude of All Peoples: Engaging Ancient Christianity's Global Identity*. Bantu begins by explaining the origins of the 'Western/white captivity of the church', a historical background that will be useful to summarize here.[33] With Constantine's ascension to power, Christianity became intimately linked with the aims and operations of the Roman imperial identity. During the fifth century, christological debates, as particularly crystallized at the Councils of Ephesus (431) and Chalcedon (451), ostracized the majority of Christians in Africa, Asia and the Middle East. The rise of Islam in the seventh century drastically weakened Byzantine, Persian and Near Eastern Christianity, and over the same period Western, Latin Christian power became ascendant, epitomized by the reign of Charlemagne and the Carolingian empire in the eighth and ninth centuries.[34] These, Bantu argues, are the 'roots of Western Christian identity politics' and the reason for the perception of Christianity as a Western or white religion.[35] Yet, he continues, the gospel had in the earliest centuries taken root across Africa, the Middle East and Asia. Therefore, the remaining three-quarters of Bantu's book covers early Christianity in the non-Western contexts of Africa, the Middle East and Asia: North Africa and the Nile Valley kingdoms of Egypt, Nubia and Ethiopia; Antioch and Palestine, and the Syriac-speaking Christian communities of Syria, Lebanon and Arabia, and the Caucasian Christianity in Armenia and Georgia; Persia and various regions in India, Central Asia and China. This is the 'global Christianity' that flourished until the Muslim conquests and until Western Christendom assumed the 'self-appointed role of world Christian patron', and which still survives today in the many forms of Eastern Christianity, including the Eastern Orthodox, Eastern Catholic, Oriental Orthodox and the Church of the East.[36]

At this point my project diverges. For while Bantu rightly traces these ancient churches of Eastern Christianity, I feel compelled to stay on the 'European track' if my goal is to understand the roots of my own denominational affiliation, and those of the greatest proportion of Christians globally today, brought into the sphere of Western Christianity by the fact of Western imperialism: Catholics, Anglicans, Baptists, Methodists, United Reformed, Pentecostals and so on. Within these traditions, the history of Christianity *must* largely be the history of Europe, and this is keenly felt in the theological influences, devotional literature, hymnic repertoire, architectural styles and so on which they have inherited and which feel the most familiar. Thus, I would agree with one reviewer's assessment of Thomas Oden's *How Africa Shaped the Christian Mind: Rediscovering the African Seedbed of Western Christianity* as 'naïve and hyperbolic', despite its educational value and progressive intentions.[37] Part of the naivety is that Oden is not arguing anything that has not already been a long-established part of church historical studies: that the earliest forms of Christianity can be traced to Africa, and that many of the religion's earliest and most seminal thinkers (Origen, Clement of Alexandria, Tertullian, Plotinus, Augustine and so on) were Africans. But more naive is Oden's apparent assumption that simply to acknowledge these facts is enough to claw back the effects of centuries of historical development – effects that not only diminished the influence of North African Christianity but in fact *Westernized* it. This last point is particularly pernicious and requires exposition. For example, in discussing early monasticism, Oden correctly asserts that 'the matrix in which monasticism was spawned was the Egyptian desert: Anthony, Pachomius, Evagrius of Pontus, John Cassian … well before Benedict wrote his monastic rule'. Therefore, 'It is hard to make a case for a viable European monasticism before it had appeared first in Africa, then to the Isle of Lérins, then to Marseilles, Liguria and Montecassino. Antony, Pachomius and Marcarius of Africa preceded the patterns that later developed in Provence and the Po Valley.'[38] But does he realize that our view of Egyptian desert monasticism is largely dependent on European monasticism? That our knowledge of Egyptian monasticism comes from second-hand reports by

Western monks like Caesarius in Lérins and Marseilles and Benedict in Montecassino? That most of the earliest extant texts of Egyptian monastic rules were copied and produced in European monasteries like Corbie, Tours, Fleury and Trier? Likewise, Oden stresses that 'from Tertullian first came the formal Latin language of *trinitas* and from Cyprian came the advancement of conciliar method, and from Augustine the most brilliant forms of interior psychological analyses in late antiquity'. He goes on to emphasize, '[T]hese achievements were made in Africa by Christians whose lives had been formed in the indigenous worshiping communities of Africa.'[39] But does he realize that the works of Tertullian come down to us in manuscripts, none older than the late eighth century, and even the very earliest produced in monasteries in present-day France, Germany, Spain and Italy?[40] With Augustine we have an even clearer example of a writer who, though North African in life, must be considered European in legacy. Only two North African manuscripts with works by Augustine have survived. The older of the two, dating to around the fifth century, was transported through Italy to the monastery of Corbie in Northern France, and from there to Paris in the seventeenth century before finally resting in St Petersburg. Other manuscripts datable to the sixth and seventh centuries were all produced in Italy, France and Spain. By far the greatest source of our knowledge of Augustine comes from authors who compiled his works or extensively quoted Augustine in their own writings to consolidate dogma in such areas as the Trinity, grace, the sacraments and the Church: for example, the extensive compilations of Augustine's works made by Prosper of Aquitaine in the fifth century come from Italy; Cassiodorus's commentary on the Psalms included extensive quotations from Augustine's Psalms commentary and was produced in Italy; Bede's commentaries on the Pauline epistles consist largely of quotations from Augustine's works, and was produced in England.[41] And for all the fame of Augustine's *Confessions*, it may come as a surprise that only very few manuscripts of it were produced before the ninth century. The oldest complete text of Augustine's *Confessions* is dated to the sixth century to an abbey in Nonantola; the earliest reliable witnesses to the text were produced in ninth-century French monasteries.[42] Thus, though it is of course true that Augustine was African, the manuscripts and texts from which our knowledge of Augustine emerges are a product of Western Christendom, his immense intellectual legacy forged in the centres of devotion and learning in Western Europe. Regrettably, it is therefore naive to think that simply recalling his North African birthplace will solve the problem of Western dominance in the history of Christianity. Though it is no doubt crucial to recognize Africa's fundamental role in shaping earliest Christianity, it remains the case that many of the theologians Oden has listed in his appendix which await 'discovery' will have to be discovered via Europe – in its monasteries and the manuscripts they preserved, and in editions and translations produced by European scholars.

What this points to is the inescapable pervasiveness of Europe which has touched so much of Christianity, even the things we try to label 'non-European'. For this reason, even the most well-intentioned pleas from Christian theologians and historians to 'decolonize the curriculum' fail to pinpoint the actual impasse. A few examples follow. In *Whose Religion Is Christianity?: The Gospel Beyond the West*, Lamin Sanneh insists that much of contemporary Christianity has been freed from Western Christendom's 'global, imperial mandate' and is no longer 'a religious expression of Europe's political reach and economic and security interests'.[43] Yet even if he can point to successful ways in which 'indigenizing the faith meant decolonizing its theology',[44] it appears one cannot so easily decolonize Christian *history*, as Sanneh himself inadvertently makes clear in a later section of his book entitled 'The River and its Tributaries'. Here the 'river' denotes Catholic and Protestant origins in Europe, and the tributaries are the 'Catholic and Protestant soundings', indigenized responses and local idioms which assumed their own 'internal logic', particularly through the use of native languages. By the use of this image, however, no matter what he would assert about Bible translation as 'shelter for indigenous ideas and values', the English and Latin Bibles from which translations were required in the first place take historical, chronological precedence as the 'source' from which the 'tributaries' flow.[45]

Andrew Walls comes closer to an effective diagnosis of the problem preoccupying me.[46] Examining the reasons for our general reluctance to consider the part that the non-West plays 'in the total story of the faith', he cites the example of the traditional Scottish church history syllabus used when he was a student and observes that the selection of events and persons studied represents influences bearing on his confessional tradition. 'The geographical bias starts early; early church syllabuses tend to lose interest in the Greek-speaking church ... The reason is, of course, that Scottish, German, and American Christianity were more directly affected by events in the Latin-speaking area.' He then analyses the 'lurking dangers, both historical and theological', to this mindset:

> One is that we think by study of our own tradition we are doing church history. We are not – we are doing *our* church history. If this is the only lens through which we study Christian history, we have bypassed the story of the whole people of God in favour of clan history.

He proposes several remedies, the most powerful of which in my judgement is the re-conception of the significance of elements within the church history syllabus. He uses the example of the significance we assign to the Reformation of the sixteenth century, which in the West is considered a watershed moment. Yet, in the total history of Christianity its significance may not be so 'defining'. For one thing, from the point of view of Africa and Asia, the missionary movement, Catholic and Protestant, has been a single story since the sixteenth century, the Catholic Reformation and the Evangelical Revival alike necessary to it. In other words, although in the West it is possible to recount Catholic and Protestant histories separately from one another, in many parts of the world it is not. Furthermore, he asks us to stop relying on the assumption that Christianity exists in the three modes of Roman Catholic, Protestant and Orthodox, because these categories reflect events in Western history. They have in the West a significance that they cannot have in the non-Western world: a large segment of African Christianity, Walls observes, cannot be called either Catholic or Protestant in any meaningful sense: 'it is simply African'. So he concludes that 'if we are to acquire historical understanding of Christianity as a non-Western religion, the re-conception of the categories by which Christians have been described will be required'.[47]

Walls provides an effective appraisal of the historiographical challenge. But whether or not we would be willing to redefine and reconceive the significance of 'turning points' or 'decisive moments' (such as, as he suggests, the Reformation) is another question, and interest in doing so is significantly hampered by one crucial addiction we all have when it comes to narrating Christian history. That is, as Walls points out, our tendency to want to study *our* church history, which I shall describe as our attachment to the notion of religious ancestry or, to use the phrase of Hervieu-Léger in her classic work to which we will turn later, a 'lineage of belief' and a 'symbolized genealogy'.[48] Walls himself exhibits no immunity from this language that so powerfully holds us captive to the West. 'It is natural and right to seek to understand one's own tradition; *it is the means to know who one's ancestors are.*' And his warning against doing 'clan history' suggests that Walls still works from the model of 'ancestry': 'our version may be copied by people who have different ancestors', he says of Christians in the non-West whose histories are not necessarily explained with recourse to the same historical figures and events.[49] One set of ancestors for the West and another for the non-West.

This is a problematic assumption. Walls' logic is that though the categories Catholic, Protestant and Orthodox will continue to indicate organization and affiliation, yet 'it is likely that they will become less and less useful as descriptors'.[50] I am not convinced this is necessarily so, because our descriptions of religious habits are still best understood with recourse to historic origins: historic origins explain why, for example, 'bishop' can have completely different meanings depending on where in Africa you live, why some Africans pray in English and others in French and others in tongues, why some Africans observe the sabbath and others don't. No matter how much we may try to re-evaluate the significance of events that influenced denominational development (the 'turning points' which are so important in a 'clan history'), the fact remains that explanations for why certain practices have taken hold among individual groups and locales require reference to European developments. To illustrate, let me dissect Walls' proposal that a history of 'African Christianity' should be neither Protestant nor Catholic, but simply 'African', and point out the dangers of this myopic regionalism. Today, over 15 million Southern Africans identify as 'Zionist', including 1 in 3 South Africans and 1 in 2 Swazis. Their roots are directly traceable to Dr John Alexander Dowie, a Scotsman born in Edinburgh and raised in the traditions of congregationalist Holiness Christianity and nonconformity. Dowie founded an evangelical faith-healing church in the inner-city slums of Melbourne in 1880s colonial Australia; from here the movement he started migrated to a utopian settlement called Zion City near Chicago, Illinois in the 1890s, thence to the Boer and British farms of the Transvaal in the 1900s, to the black townships of Johannesburg in the 1920s–40s, and finally to the kingdom of Swaziland in the mid-century.[51] I grant the many advantages with calling Southern African Zionists an 'African-initiated church', but equally there are dangers with the classification of 'African Christianity' as somehow distinct from the Anglosphere. Cabrita pleads for a move away from tribal analysis towards an entangled and global history, by which she means a 'transatlantic lens', not one simplistically Afrocentric, asserting, 'scholars have largely failed to understand African and American Zionists as two products of a single Protestant Christian tradition', treating the evangelical divine healing movement in the USA in near total isolation from its worldwide context, and rarely considering the role of divine healing in the spread of global Christianity. In fact, the Zionist movement was – like Protestantism and evangelicalism more broadly – 'constituted by North American and European trade, military expansion, and missionary networks across the imperial world, including to South Africa, Australia, and India'.[52]

The major problem with speaking as though there can be one lineage for Western Christianity and a different one for African Christianity is that it does not recognize the 'elective affinities' global Christians possess in addition to their ethnic affinities. I speak from personal experience. Kind friends and colleagues frequently try to make me feel 'included' in conversations about the history of Christianity by directing the conversation to the 'Nestorian Church' present in China in the seventh century, which is supposed to prove that Christianity is not a Western thing. The disappointment is palpable when I reply that the Church of the East, though important in its own right, doesn't explain why there are so many Christians in China today or the kind of Christians they are. Instead, to understand contemporary Christianity in East Asia, I have to go via the 'usual route' of Europe: I have to understand such European topics as the distinction between Catholicism and Protestantism, the modern missionary movement, and the reaction against Western missions leading up to and during the Communist Revolution, the establishment of the Three Self Patriotic Movement using concepts first articulated by Anglosphere missionaries Henry Venn, Rufus Anderson and John Livingstone Nevius. Chinese Christians today certainly find references from the history of Western Christianity (hymns, art, architecture, literature) more familiar than those from Syriac Christianity. If genealogical language must be used – as even Walls uses – the line of descent goes, for most ethnic minority Christians, via Western Europe and the Anglosphere.

The relationship between Western Europe and the expansion of global Christianity is one of the lasting legacies of imperialism, especially as it concerns the British Empire, at its height the largest empire in history. As Sanghera argues in *Empireland*, to acknowledge imperial legacies does not mean one is somehow unpatriotic or anti-British. It only means recognizing that much of contemporary Britain is rooted in its imperial past, explaining the fact of global diasporas, British exceptionalism, the concentration of financial wealth in the City of London, the wealth of many families and institutions around the nation. Empire also explains the millions of people around the world who profess affinity for Britain – people for whom English and Her Majesty and Pears soap and roast beef all arouse a sense of familiarity. And it explains the multiculturalism of Britain itself: many centuries of imperialism tied the colonized to Britain, brought them to Britain as immigrants, and ultimately made them citizens. 'The ties were deep', writes Sanghera, 'and if we acknowledge this simple fact as a nation it would transform all conversations about multiculturalism.' Conceptions of national identity must embrace this simple truth, he writes: 'that black and Asian people had been made citizens through the imperial project'. Immigrants from former British colonies are not 'aliens and interlopers' but are here because of 'long-standing historical ties'. As Ambalavaner Sivanandan, Director of the Institute of Race Relations, once put it, 'We are here because you were there', a sentiment echoed by the historian David Olusoga who, in response to a racist remark, tweeted, 'If you don't want Nigerians in the UK all you need to do is go back to the 19th century and persuade the Victorians not to invade Nigeria.'[53]

The imperial explanation for Britain's racial diversity applies equally to Christianity. Empire explains Christianity's racial diversity – why there are Christians in Nigeria, Kenya, Uganda, the Bahamas, Jamaica, India, Malaysia and my own birthplace of Hong Kong. Empire also explains Christian Britain's racial diversity – why there are Nigerian, Kenyan, Ugandan, Bahamian, Jamaican, Indian, Malaysian, and Hong Kong Christians in Britain. And empire explains why my parents became Christians in Hong Kong, why I know my way around an English Bible and hymnal, why I employ certain English phrases in my prayers, why I know what generally happens at a church committee meeting, why I understand the function of the altar and lectern in a church, why I instantly recognize what a tea towel is doing atop a child's head in December.

Empire, to borrow the words of Sanghera, 'exists as a legacy in my very being'.[54] That this legacy is inscribed into my very being means not only a familiarity with, or a recognition of, the practices and traditions of Western Christianity, but also good will and affection towards it, like the feelings of recognition that a black British or British Asian person might possess for

Worcestershire sauce or Imperial Leather soap or the red telephone box or left-handed traffic. Thus when Wordsworth invokes 'ancestral feeling' to inspire love and pious sentiment for the nation's inheritance of steeple-towers, spires and ancient minsters, he is only thinking of 'English hearts', but today Christians who have been touched by colonialism and globalization will also be 'feeling ancestral', enacting what Santa Ana has termed 'self-placement' in the history of English Christianity.[55]

This book examines the 'ancestral feeling' for Western Christian heritage which, for many ethnic minority Christians, is a product of the influence of Christianity in former colonies and should be considered an under-acknowledged imperial legacy. I address the postcolonial critique that imperialism is conquest not only of land but also, and in a manner still operative today, of history. I argue that the notion of 'religious ancestry' is a prime mechanism in which Christian historiography achieves this hegemony. But I also address the irony that, while 'Christian heritage' is laden with colonial assumptions and imperializing effects, yet global majority Christians continue to feel great attachment to it and claim it as their own. I therefore vehemently argue against a remedy that would propose: 'Christianity is not only Western. So let Western Christians have their Western church history. Now let us find some Chinese church history for the Chinese; let us now find some African church history for the Africans.' Such a position only serves to divide, alienate, marginalize and tribalize, and it is a thin disguise for exclusionary habits. The fact is that – like the racial diversity in the metropole which is the direct product of a relationship with the colonies – empire also cultivated among diverse people a sense of 'ancestral feeling' towards Western Christianity. Ethnic minority Christians feel an elective affinity with Christian heritage and, because it concerns matters of faith, instinctively presume that it is *our* heritage too. What is required is an 'inclusive memory' which actively fosters a sense of belonging for Christians of all ethnic and cultural backgrounds who, as a result of historic global processes, have come to identify deeply with Western Christian heritage.[56]

Therefore despite its hegemonizing dangers when applied to Christian heritage, this book chooses to indulge in 'ancestral feeling'. I apply Wordsworth's phrase positively, informed by an important and oft-cited study conducted by psychologist Peter Fischer and his team, which found positive psychological effects from thinking about ancestors.[57] Fischer's study was rooted in the hypothesis that because our ancestors generally managed to overcome a multitude of personal and societal problems such as disease, war, loss of loved ones, or economic hardship, thinking about them should remind us of their sacrifices, perseverance and success, and in turn induce increased levels of control, motivation and capacity for approaching problems. The team devised four studies to test the psychological effects of 'ancestor salience', that is, thinking about concrete ancestors (parents/grandparents) and abstract ancestors (those we do not personally know or who died before we were born). The studies provided evidence that: (1) Thinking about concrete and abstract ancestors increases our own expectations about our performance; this effect can be partially explained by the fact that thinking about ancestors also increases how much control we think we have over our lives; (2) Participants who thought about their ancestors performed better in an intelligence task (attempted to solve more test questions and solved more of them correctly) than participants who thought about their last shopping trip; and (3) The positive psychological effect of thinking about ancestors does not depend on whether participants ever met their ancestors or not, whether participants think about positive or negative aspects of their ancestors, or how participants feel about themselves. The researchers concluded that remembering ancestors provides people with a positive psychological resource and increases problem-solving abilities and intellectual performance: this is the 'ancestor effect'. The study concludes that 'whenever people are in a situation where intellectual performance is extraordinarily important, for example, in exams or job interviews, they have an easy technique to increase their success'.[58]

The 'ancestor effect' offers a justification for this book: contemplating the lives of our ancestors is clearly a healthy thing.

I'm under no delusions that thinking about religious ancestors who inspire me (a ninth-century monk, a fourteenth-century cleric, a nineteenth-century missionary) is the same – and would produce the same empirical results – as thinking about my biological ancestors. But I am interested to discover whether 'ancestor salience', proven to be such a powerful tool by virtue of its affective and relational effects, might offer a corrective to the central exclusionary practice I wish to oppose, which is the segregation of Christian (Western) heritage and ethnic (non-Western) heritage into distinct spheres. The central thesis to be explored in this book is that blurring the boundary between the two inheritances, intentionally fostering 'ancestral feeling' – both for one's ethnic inheritance as well as religious – is one possible way to enhance inclusion and reinforce a sense of belonging among ethnic minorities in the study of European historical subjects. History-making activities have particular significance for ethnic minority Christians who must do the extra – and unnatural – work not required of white Christians, the work of 'self-placement': to somehow insert their story inside a European history in order to make sense of why the latter is personally relevant. History is not only an act of inter-pretation but also of identifications with the past, of having or making a sense of intimate connection, and just as the past that inspires genealogists is those dimensions that are connected to their personal identity, so the same goes for Christian history as it relates to the personal identity of Christians.[59]

Thinking about ancestors is a deeply personal affair. Tell-ing the story of my biological ancestors comes close to writing a memoir, which, for obvious reasons, is widely considered the most emotionally trying of all literary genres. But thinking about *religious* ancestors is an equally personal and therefore emotionally laden task. It means announcing my particular affinities and idiosyncratic tastes – what kind of sacred music I like, which saints I wish to emulate, what kind of theology I like to read – and thereby exposing myself to caricature and judgement. The personal nature of this endeavour means that my book can only concern those topics about which I can speak from experience. I am therefore confined to the geographic regions which have, for me specifically, generated the biggest questions about Christian heritage as imperial legacy: this means the history of Christianity in England, and the forms of Protestant Christianity that were transported to British colonies, including the city of my birth and early upbringing, Hong Kong, and the country where I spent my youth, Canada.

The book's main argument can be summarized as follows. For the majority of global Christians, thinking historically about the origins of their Christian affiliations renders Western Christianity categorically inescapable. Therefore, historical thinking itself represents the fundamental problem since it makes the West (England specifically in this book) inescapable. It follows that we must find a way to think about the history of Western Christianity that promotes an inclusive memory and fosters belonging. My study begins with an analysis about how 'religious ancestry' as a concept serves the aims of empire. Chapter 1 discusses the origins of ancestral thinking in Christian thought, the process by which this way of thinking became associated with English national identity, and how this thinking shaped ideas about the relationship between metropole and colonies. Chapter 2 explains why critical theorists have condemned the Christian conception of history – and genealogical thinking in particular – as problematic in its supersessory assumptions and exclusionary effects. I analyse the ways in which 'religious ancestry' requires ethnic minority Christians to look with deference to Europe, to covet and study the European inheritance, to adopt a chronology of historical development to which we are perpetually absent until brought into the metropolitan view by the processes of imperialism. Chapter 3 attempts to address these consequences by bridging the divide between 'religious' and 'ethnic' ancestry. I suggest what can be gained by thinking about my religious ancestry through my family's genealogical record. I make recourse primarily to the arguments of Hervieu-Léger as well as recent insights from ethnography about the restorative potential of intergenerational narratival writing. Applying the theoretical frameworks established in Chapter 3, the remaining chapters take an autobiographical turn. Chapters 4–6 represent an effort to understand Christian religious heritage in light of themes emerging in my own family history. Chapter 4 explores how my mother's stories of poverty and hardship affect my relationship to the Western Christian literary and musical canon. Chapter 5 explores how my nostalgia for home, intensified by my family's diasporic realities, affects the way I experience ecclesiastical heritage sites in England such as abbey ruins. Chapter 6 explores the goal of upward social mobility which has undergirded the migrations in my father's family, and discusses the dilemma, particularly in regard to the accusation of racial betrayal, of using Christian heritage as cultural capital to serve intergenerational aspirations. These three chapters confront the three main sites at which religious history meets my family history: the canon, heritage places and cultural capital.

Ultimately, this book expresses my hope that Christianity in England can distribute an inheritance to those in its former empire who claim descent. By this I do not mean that English Christianity alone guards the assets and treasures for which the Global South thirsts; I *do* mean that Christianity in England has a power, precedence and prestige owing to an entrenched way of viewing history which considers it the progenitor of many varieties of global Christianity. Just as many people from former colonies feel they have a rightful claim to British citizenship by virtue of their membership within the empire, so do many ethnic minority Christians assume English Christian heritage to be their proper possession, and I would like to lay claim to this inheritance that has been dominated by a white-majority culture. Yet if one looks at conceptions of Christian heritage through the prism of identity and belonging, one is immediately struck by the gulf that separates the assumptions of the white British from ethnic minority Christians. The National Trust – which protects many historic sites of Christian interest – has a membership that is less than 1 per cent black.[60] The national past – 'our Christian heritage' – like all aspects of heritage, as Patrick Wright has noted, seems 'to be identifiable as the historicised image of an instinctively conservative establishment'.[61] Thus Conservative MP Lord Cormack's definition of 'heritage' not as significant places and things but as 'certain

sights and sounds' implies that heritage is inherent and incom-
municable, something with which 'one must have grown up in
the midst of ancestral continuities': the sights and sounds of
'the Eucharist in a quiet Norfolk Church with the mediaeval
glass filtering the colours, and the early noise of the harvest-
ing coming through the open door; or of standing at any time
before the Wilton Diptych'.[62] I could go on: the sight of church
steeples, the sound of church bells, the smell of climbing roses
on a church wall. Of such cultivated senses, Stanley Baldwin
said: 'These are the things that make England, and I grieve for
it that they are not the childish inheritance of the majority of
the people today in our country.'[63]

Are they not? If so, it is not for lack of appreciation by the
majority, but because Stanley Baldwin implies that this heritage reflects quintessentially English sensibilities, the property
of the well-established, landed class who, out for a walk on
an autumnal evening, would be moved by the smell of 'that
wood smoke that our ancestors ... must have caught on the
air when they were coming home with the result of the day's
forage'.[64] The irony of this, as Corinne Fowler has pointed out,
is that heritage sites attract nostalgia for an era when Britain
was connected with colonized countries across the globe – a
fact that is forgotten at best, covered up at worst, in the discourse on 'our Christian heritage'. In this country we continue
to think of the colonial action as having taken place elsewhere,
off stage.[65] So naval battles were fought in far-away oceans;
sugar was planted and harvested in exotic islands; tea was
picked in the Orient – and the Christianization of dark, brown,
yellow-skinned people occurred in the heat of the Tropics. Yet
it was this global empire that, having evangelized the people of
Asia, Africa and the Americas, galvanized them to believe they
were part of the Christianity of England. We need to see the
legacies of empire through a single frame. We ought not to be
satisfied with the assumption that Christians from the colonies
have only changed the face of Christianity in England by
making it more ethnically diverse: we must also insist that the
impact be historiographical, necessitating an adjustment to the
definition of 'heritage'. For the vast majority of the white British

public, England's Christian heritage might denote cassocks and stained glass and church bells, but for Christians from former British colonies – statistically more evangelical and charismatic – this heritage is impregnated, enlivened, activated by something more *a*historical and expressed in more devotional terms. Some of my ethnic minority students say that Christian heritage for them means Scripture, justice, morality, humility; Christians from former colonies are much more likely to interpret the historical marks that English Christianity has left on them in terms of worship, doctrine, ethics, mission, evangelism. And these aspects in turn make the 'national heritage' of things like medieval manuscripts and Norman baptismal fonts take on religious – as opposed to national or ethnic – significance. Thus, claiming 'Christian heritage' as something that primarily pertains to those with white British ancestry has as much logic as claiming the same for British weather, and does as much damage as claiming the same for civility.[66]

Christianity in this country has paid a high price for its associations with national and ethnic identity, and its failure to understand how much it represents 'home and family' to diasporic people.[67] The undervaluing of members of the 'Windrush Generation' when they arrived from the colonies to the metropole included the undervaluing of their commitment to English Protestant Christianity – to the Anglican, Methodist, Baptist and other traditions. It has often been the case that 'white Christians' did not take seriously the role that England has played in the lives of those Christianized under its influence, and have not entirely understood the depth of identification with Western Christianity as a forebear in the family of faith. The answer to postcolonial dilemmas is therefore not to foist a separate lineage upon ethnic minority Christians who have been touched by empire; the answer must lie in stripping the '*our*' in 'our Christian heritage' of its nationalistic and racial connotations.

Notes

1 https://myfaithjourneys.com/protestant-tours/england-scotland/ (accessed 17.08.2021).

2 www.pilgrimtours.com/britain-tours/english-heritage-8.html (accessed 17.08.2021).

3 www.englishchurchhistorytour.com/about (accessed 17.08.2021).

4 www.christianheritagelondon.org/index (accessed 17.08.2021).

5 christianheritagenetwork.org.uk (accessed 17.08.2021). Quoted in https://baptisttimes.co.uk/Articles/561248/New_Christian_heritage.aspx (accessed 17.08.2021).

6 Mark Greaves, 2014, 'Welsh martyr who brought the Scriptures to the shores of Korea'. www.thetimes.co.uk/article/welsh-martyr-who-brought-the-scriptures-to-the-shores-of-korea-b8tm3ondzlc] (accessed 17.08.2021).

7 Greaves, 'Welsh martyr who brought the Scriptures to the shores of Korea'.

8 Rob Cooper, 19 January 2012, 'Forget Lourdes, go on a pilgrimage to Barnsley! Mining town hoping to become top destination for 70m Chinese Christians', *Mail Online* [online]. Available at: www.dailymail.co.uk/news/article-2088212/Barnsley-Lourdes-Chinese-Christians-Yorkshire-town-launch-bid-attract-millions-tourists-Far-East.html (accessed 17.08.2021). There is now a heritage trail around Barnsley which features locations associated with his life and family: www.visit-barnsley.com/the-james-hudson-taylor-trail.

9 UKIP Policies for Christians, 'Valuing our Christian Heritage' [online]. Available at: www.support4thefamily.org/UKIPChristian_Manifesto-1.pdf.

10 24 December 2017, 'Prime Minister Theresa May's Christmas Message 2017' [online]. Available at: www.gov.uk/government/news/prime-minister-theresa-mays-christmas-message-2017 (accessed 17.08.2021).

11 29 January 2020, 'Danny Kruger – 2020 Maiden Speech in the House of Commons' [online]. Available at: www.ukpol.co.uk/danny-kruger-2020-maiden-speech-in-the-house-of-commons/ (accessed 17.08.2021).

12 Cara Bentley, 18 February 2020, '"We've seen an erosion of the Christian heritage of our nation quite enough" says MP following latest challenge to prayers in Parliament', Premier Christian News [online]. Available at: https://premierchristian.news/en/news/article/we-ve-seen-an-erosion-of-the-christian-heritage-of-our-nation-quite-enough-says-mp-following-latest-challenge-to-prayers-in-parliament (accessed 17.08.2021).

13 Office for National Statistics, '2011 Census: Key Statistics for England and Wales, March 2011' [online]. Available at: www.ons.

gov.uk/peoplepopulationandcommunity/populationandmigration/
populationestimates/bulletins/2011censuskeystatisticsforenglandand
wales/2012-12-11 (accessed 17.08.2021).

14 Council for Christian Unity/Church of England, 2014, 'Changes
in the Ethnic Diversity of the Christian Population in England between
2001 and 2011, East Anglia Region', Table 2, p. 5 [online]. Available
at: www.churchofengland.org/sites/default/files/2017-10/east_anglia.
pdf (accessed 17.08.2021).

15 Office for National Statistics, '2011 Census'. But note that,
in 2011, the ONS census re-positioned the 'Chinese' tick box from
'Any other ethnic group' to 'Asian/Asian British'. This means that the
statistics for Asian groups are not strictly comparable between 2001
and 2011, and the change of categorization explains the 8% fall in
Christians identifying as 'Chinese and Other' between 2001 and 2011, a
statistic captured in the Council for Christian Unity/Church of England
but not explained.

16 Office for National Statistics, '2011 Census analysis: Ethnicity and religion of the non-UK born population in England and
Wales: 2011' [online]. Available at: www.ons.gov.uk/peoplepopula
tionandcommunity/culturalidentity/ethnicity/articles/2011census
analysisethnicityandreligionofthenonukbornpopulationinenglandand
wales/2015-06-18 (accessed 17.08.2021).

17 Eliza Filby, 2015, *God and Mrs Thatcher: The Battle for Britain's
Soul*, London: Biteback Publishing, p. 113. See also James Crossley,
2014, *Harnessing Chaos: The Bible in English Political Discourse since
1968*, London: Bloomsbury. And recently, see especially Anthony G.
Reddie, 2019, *Theologising Brexit: A Liberationist and Postcolonial
Critique*, London: Routledge.

18 Heritage House Group, 'Walsingham Abbey: A Guide to the
Priory and Abbey Grounds, Shirehall Museum and Bridwell', back
cover.

19 Speech to the Conservative Group of Europe, 22 April 1993, as
quoted in Corinne Fowler, 2020, *Green Unpleasant Land: Creative
Responses to Rural Britain's Colonial Connections*, Leeds: Peepal Tree
Press, p. 46.

20 For example, among over-64s in the black population, 1 in 11
was a core congregation member of the Church of England, but 1 in 14
among white people of the same age group. 'Celebrating Diversity in
the Church of England: National Parish Congregation Diversity Monitoring' [online], p. 14. Available at: www.churchofengland.org/sites/
default/files/2017-10/celebratingdiversitygsmisc938_0.pdf (accessed 17.
08.2021). The report following diversity monitoring conducted in 2014
did not include this data.

21 Hilaire Belloc, 1920, *Europe and the Faith*, London: Constable
& Co, *passim*.

22 Wayland Coakley and Andrea Sterk (eds), 2004, *Readings in World Christian History*, Maryknoll, NY: Orbis. See also Dale T. Irvin and Scott W. Sunquist, 2001 and 2012, *History of the World Christian Movement*, 2 vols, Maryknoll, NY: Orbis.

23 See Pui-lan Kwok, Don H. Compier and Joerg Rieger (eds), 2007, *Empire: The Christian Tradition. New Readings of Classical Theologians*, Minneapolis, MN: Fortress Press, chapters by Deanna A. Thompson on 'Martin Luther', pp. 185–200, and Theodore W. Jennings Jr, 'John Wesley', pp. 257–70.

24 Elizabeth Fox-Genovese, 1986, 'The Claims of a Common Culture: Gender, Race, Class and the Canon', *Salmagundi* 72 (Fall), pp. 131–43 at 135–6.

25 Probably first taking hold in public consciousness with Philip Jenkin, 2002, *The Next Christendom: The Coming of Global Christianity*, Oxford: Oxford University Press.

26 The Pew Forum on Religion and Public Life, Pew Research Center, December 2011, 'Global Christianity: A Report on the Size and Distribution of the World's Christian Population' [online]. Available at: www.pewforum.org/2011/12/19/global-christianity-exec/ (accessed 17.08.2021).

27 Willie James Jennings, 2020, *After Whiteness: An Education in Belonging*, Grand Rapids, MI: Eerdmans, p. 6.

28 Pew Forum, 'Global Christianity'.

29 Pew Forum, 'Global Christianity'.

30 Pew Forum, 'Global Christianity', p. 13.

31 Pew Forum, 'Global Christianity', p. 69.

32 Mark Noll, 2012, *Turning Points: Decisive Moments in the History of Christianity*, 3rd edn, Grand Rapids, MI: Baker Academic.

33 Vince L. Bantu, 2020, *A Multitude of All Peoples: Engaging Ancient Christianity's Global Identity*, Downers Grove: IVP Academic: phrase used on p. 6 and *passim*.

34 Bantu, *A Multitude*, chapter 1.

35 The title of chapter 1.

36 Bantu, *A Multitude*, p. 70.

37 Thomas Oden, 2007, *How Africa Shaped the Christian Mind: Rediscovering the African Seedbed of Western Christianity*, Downers Grove, IL: InterVarsity Press. Reviewed by *Publishers Weekly*, 1 December 2007 [online]. Available at: www.publishersweekly.com/978-0-8308-2875-3 (accessed 17.08.2021).

38 Oden, *How Africa Shaped the Christian Mind*, p. 54.

39 Oden, *How Africa Shaped the Christian Mind*, p. 59.

40 See http://tertullian.org/manuscripts/index.htm.

41 Clemens Weidmann, 2012, 'Augustine's Works in Circulation', in Mark Vessey, (ed.), *A Companion to Augustine*, Chichester, West Sussex: Wiley-Blackwell, pp. 431–50.

42 Gert Partoens, 2020, 'Manuscript Transmission, Critical Editions, and English Translations', in Tarmo Toom (ed.), *The Cambridge Companion to Augustine's 'Confessions'*, Cambridge: Cambridge University Press, pp. 245–62.

43 Lamin Sanneh, 2002, *Whose Religion is Christianity?: The Gospel Beyond the West*, Grand Rapids, MI: Eerdmans, pp. 22–3.

44 Sanneh, *Whose Religion*, p. 22

45 Sanneh, *Whose Religion*, p. 108ff.

46 Walls, Andrew, 2002, 'Eusebius Tries Again: The Task of Reconceiving and Re-visioning the Study of Christian History', in Wilbert R. Shenk (ed.), *Enlarging the Story: Perspectives on Writing World Christian History*, Eugene, OR: Wipf and Stock, pp. 1–21.

47 Walls, 'Eusebius Tries Again', pp. 7, 12–13.

48 Danièle Hervieu-Léger, 1993, *La religion pour mémoire*, Paris: Cerf, trans. Simon Lee, 2000, *Religion as a Chain of Memory*, Cambridge: Polity.

49 Walls, 'Eusebius Tries Again', p. 7.

50 Walls, 'Eusebius Tries Again', p. 13.

51 Summary follows Katharina Wilkens, 2020, Review of Joel Cabrita, 2018, *The People's Zion: Southern Africa, the United States, and a Transatlantic Faith-Healing Movement*, in *African Studies Review* 63(1), pp. E29–E31.

52 Joel Cabrita, 2018, *The People's Zion: Southern Africa, the United States, and a Transatlantic Faith-Healing Movement*, Cambridge, MA: Harvard University Press, p. 3.

53 Ian Sanjay Patel, 2021, *We're Here Because You Were There: Immigration and the End of Empire*, London: Verso; Sathnam Sanghera, 2021, *Empireland: How Imperialism has Shaped Modern Britain*, London: Viking, p. 69.

54 Sanghera, *Empireland*, p. 14.

55 As quoted on p. ix: William Wordsworth, 1814, *The Excursion*, Book Sixth, lines 6–8, 17–29, in Ernest De Selincourt and Helen Darbishire (eds), 1959, *The Poetical Works of William Wordsworth, Vol. 5: The Excursion; The Recluse*, 2nd edn, Oxford: Oxford University Press, pp. 186–7; Jeffrey Santa Ana, 2015, *Racial Feelings: Asian America in a Capitalist Culture of Emotion*, Philadelphia, PA: Temple University Press, p. 466.

56 The term comes from Antonella Poce, Maria Rosaria Re, Fulvia Strano, *Inclusive Memory: How to Promote Social Inclusion, Well-Being and Critical Thinking Skills within a Museum Context*, in Thomas Kador and Helen Chatterjee (eds), 2020, *Object-Based Learning and Well-Being: Exploring Material Connections*, London: Routledge, chapter 4.

57 Peter Fischer et al., February 2011, 'The Ancestor Effect: Think-

ing about our Genetic Origin Enhances Intellectual Performance', *European Journal of Social Psychology* 41(1), pp. 11–16.

58 Fischer et al., 'The Ancestor Effect', p. 15.

59 Paul Ashton and Hilda Kean, 2012, *Public History and Heritage Today: People and their Pasts*, Basingstoke: Palgrave Macmillan, pp. 29, 31.

60 *Business Live*, 28 November 2008, 'National Trust bringing history to everyone' [online]. Available at: www.business-live.co.uk/ lifestyle/national-trust-bringing-history-to-everyone-3953788. Cited in Fowler, *Green Unpleasant Land*, p. 127, fn 16. In response to my request for information from English Heritage, I was informed that it does not gather data about the ethnic profile of its members.

61 Patrick Wright, 2009, *On Living in an Old Country: The National Past in Contemporary Britain*, updated edn, Oxford: Oxford University Press, p. 43. To see this at work, one may read Roger Scruton's 2012, *Our Church: A Personal History of the Church of England*, London: Atlantic Books, and then follow up with reviews by Terry Eagleton, Diarmaid MacCulloch and Simon Jenkins who accuse Scruton of, respectively, making 'God an Englishman', of 'loving Jesus with an air of superiority' and of 'nostalgic nationalist piety'.

62 Wright, *On Living in an Old Country*, pp. 77–8, 81, quoting Patrick Cormack, 1976, *Heritage in Danger*, London: New English Library, p. 14.

63 Stanley Baldwin, 1927, *On England, and Other Addresses*, London: Allan, p. 7, quoted in Wright, *On Living in an Old Country*, p. 78.

64 Baldwin, *On England*, in Wright, *On Living in an Old Country*.

65 Fowler, *Green Unpleasant Land*, p. 127.

66 Yet a study conducted by Ingrid Storm suggests there are certainly people for whom Christianity functions primarily as a proxy for white British identity. See Ingrid Storm, 2011, 'Ethnic Nominalism and Civic Religiosity: Christianity and National Identity in Britain', *The Sociological Review* 59(4), pp. 828–46.

67 This statement and what follows is taken from a letter written by Dr Jane Williams in support of my appeal against the decision of an admissions authority not to award my daughter a place at our preferred Church of England school. At the risk of sounding melodramatic, her letter has been received by my family and by me with the sort of weight befitting a family heirloom, because it reads as a personal tribute to the history, sacrifices, hopes and prayers of my daughter's grandparents and so accurately expresses what is at stake in these dilemmas. I wish to take this opportunity to publicly express my gratitude to Dr Williams by dedicating this Introduction to her.

I

'Religious Ancestry': Christian Historiography and English Imperialism

He remembering his mercy hath holpen his servant Israel:
as he promised to our forefathers, Abraham and
his seed for ever.

(Magnificat)

For Christians, the language of descent within the family of God is the default mode for thinking about confessional faith and history. Yet it is precisely this genealogical orientation which prompts the accusation that the Christian view of history is fundamentally ideological and embroiled in issues of power and domination. Therefore the inclination to talk about faith as an 'inheritance' and 'heritage', though second nature for Christians, requires close scrutiny. This chapter discusses: (1) the origins of ancestral thinking in Christian thought, (2) the process by which this way of thinking became associated with English national identity; and relatedly, (3) how the language of Christian heritage shaped ideas about the relationship between metropole and colonies, and therefore in what way the notion of Christian ancestry exists as an imperial legacy today.

To understand the centrality of genealogical concepts in the Christian approach to historicizing, we should begin with the letter of St Paul to the Romans. In Romans 4 and 9—11, Paul makes the claim that Abraham can justifiably be called the 'ancestor' of Gentiles who profess faith in Christ, employing a rationale that has been understood in various ways.[1] One view is that Paul, by establishing faith as the basis of salvation, installs Abraham as the father of Christ-followers on the grounds that he is a prototype of faith, exemplar of salvation by faith without works. A related view stresses Paul's attack on an essential component of first-century Jewish self-understanding: by claiming that Abrahamic ancestry can be 're-assigned' to Gentile Christ-followers, Paul explicitly rejects the Jewish assumption that covenant privileges are strictly associated with ethnic Israel and therefore unavailable to Gentiles. Another view interprets Paul as proposing for Gentiles only an imagined kinship to Abraham, while reserving ethnically and ritually derived conceptions of Abrahamic ancestry for the Jewish community, so that Jews continue to relate to God as they always have, with a separate but parallel line of relationship to Christ for Gentiles.[2] There are many more possible readings of Romans and what concerns us here is not which one is best but how they all highlight Paul's preoccupation with patrilineal descent, an emphasis expressed most clearly in Galatians 3.7 (NIV): 'Understand, then, that those who have faith are children of Abraham.' Romans, Galatians, 1 Corinthians and Philippians 3 consistently promote this rhetoric of identity: Christ-believing Gentiles receive an entirely new founding ancestor, and with it a stock of experiences appropriated from Jewish culture and history, the 'Abrahamic *mythomoteur*' to use Robert Foster's term.[3]

Christian historicism fundamentally rests on the belief that Christians are joined to Jews by an ancestral relationship. Whichever term has been used to describe this belief – supersessionism, covenant theology, replacement theology, fulfilment theology – and whichever way it has been variably denounced, the fact is that Christians feel that Jewish history and the history of Israel have something to do with them.[4] Paul's teaching trained Christians to consider it possible to insert themselves into the composite of ethnic, racial and ritual dimensions which constituted the Jewish people; he taught Christians that 'faith' could transcend these specific definitions of the 'people of God' and that the set of instructions and promises delivered to the Jewish people could be 'inherited' by Christians. Using arboreal imagery, Paul represented patriarchs and prophets as the trunk on to which Gentile believers in Christ have recently been grafted.[5] With this move, Paul permitted the fleshly, ethnic descendants of Abraham to be redefined in allegorical and figural terms as descendants by virtue of faith and by grace rather than literally and physically. Ethnic status is translated into a spiritual community, and the physical sign (genealogical descent from Abraham) is given allegorical meaning (spiritual genealogy). Paul seemed even to suggest, according to Boyarin, that the *true* meaning of physical genealogy is spiritual genealogy; a promise, one once made to Abraham, is now fulfilled in those who, although in some cases Abraham's physical heirs, discover their more fundamental genealogy to lie in their common faith.[6] Therefore, Christians can readily interpret any references to forefathers, inheritance, heritage and so on in the Old Testament as having something to do with them. A classic example is Psalm 16.6 ('The lines are fallen unto me in pleasant places; yea, I have a goodly heritage', AV), or Psalm 90.1 ('Lord, thou hast been our dwelling place in all generations', AV), or the whole of Psalm 78, which Christians tend to interpret as the heritage of blessing that comes from faith, passed down from generations of God-fearing Israelites to the Church and future generations. This is why Christians can pray the Magnificat and thank God for his mercy 'promised to our forefathers, Abraham and his seed forever' with a sense of personal devotion. Christians can even read the famous 'begats' employed in the genealogical lists of Genesis, Numbers, Ruth, Chronicles, Ezra and Nehemiah, despite their literal meaning to the ethnic Jewish community and use in the justification of priesthood, as somehow fundamental to Christian identity.[7] For Christians, genealogies (particularly the two in Matthew and Luke) recounting generations of Jewish ancestors not only confirm that Jesus came from the line of David and by fulfilling prophecy has a legitimate messianic claim, but also identify the lineage of faith from which Christians descended. The Epistle to the Hebrews displays the historical thinking resulting from this logic. Chapter 11, the 'Faith Hall of Fame' as popularly known, marks a turning point in the early Christian appropriation of biblical history, as the writer lays hold of key figures and events in Jewish history and makes them pertinent to Christian faith and history. Hebrews 11 'functions as a genealogy which legitimates the Christian audience by providing them with a biblical ancestry', identifying a list of important ancestors from whom Christians can rightfully claim to be descendants: Abel, Enoch, Noah, Abraham, Isaac, Jacob, Joseph, Moses' parents, Moses, Gideon, Samson, David …[8]

Notwithstanding the warning in the Pastoral Epistles of the dangers of debating or discussing genealogies,[9] genealogy is foundational to Christian historiography. Referring to the legalization of Christianity in AD 313 which gave rise to the first systematic histories from a Christian perspective, Howard Bloch asserts, 'From the fourth century on, the defining mode of universal history was that of genealogy.'[10] The 'universal history' to which he refers were attempts to produce a history of the world as chronologically and geographically global as the resources available to the chronicler allowed. For medieval Christian chroniclers, this generally meant beginning with creation and the forms of ancient history provided in the Hebrew Scriptures and the 'epitomes' of Greek and Roman historians, which they then updated to their own time, often with a general focus on their local context as well as some awareness of broader events in world history.[11] Christian writers considered the universal histories they wrote to be 'salvation history'.[12] The first significant work of Christian chronography, Eusebius' fourth-century world chronicle (often called Eusebius-Jerome because it is known to us in the form of Jerome's Latin translation), merges the historical accounts found in the Hellenistic, pagan tradition of Olympiad chronicles with the genealogies and king lists of the Old Testament, beginning with the birth of Abraham.[13] By making Abraham the starting point for his dating system, Eusebius makes it clear that this forefather is the 'founding ancestor' of world civilizations.

Genealogical thinking, a way of historicizing that assumes succession from an original source to the thing generated or begotten, of which Eusebius-Jerome's chronicle was an early example, became entrenched in the genre of the 'chronicle epitome' adopted by historians in the Middle Ages.[14] The most influential of these works organized and sequenced historical events according to Augustine's 'six ages of the world', which became the normative structure for chronicles written in the Latin world. In Bede's universal chronicles, for example, events are dated according to the first age from Adam to Noah (ten generations); the second from Noah to Abraham (ten generations); the third from Abraham to David (14 generations); the fourth from David to the Babylonian exile (17 generations); and the fifth age to the birth of Christ (14 generations).[15] Although counting by generations is 'suspended' in the sixth age (because it is not known when the sixth age will end), the continuity of style implies that the sixth age works by the same principle of generation as the previous five. Thus, just as the first five ages of Bede's chronicle contain records such as 'Tanaus became the first ruler of the kingdom of the Scythians', 'Vizoues was the first to reign over the Egyptians', 'Belus was the first to rule the Assyrians', and so on, so the sixth age is structured in much the same way: Bede describes Mark as the first Gentile to be made bishop, Philip the first of all emperors to be a Christian, Orosius the first to bring the relics of Stephen to the West, Palladius as first bishop of the Irish, and so on.[16] This narrative style, preoccupied as it is with identifying founding fathers, betrays an unmistakable 'genealogical consciousness', as noted by Hans Hummer. Hummer shows how, for early medieval Frankish chronicles, the progress of the world proceeds along generational lines, first through the primordial trunk of biblical father-to-son generations and then by a combination of overlapping royal, priestly, imperial, episcopal and filial successions.[17] In this way, the order of history was made visible 'in the lines of generational descent and in the succession of empires', extending to the kings and bishops contemporaneous with the chronicler. Early medieval chronicles such as the Chronicle of Fredegar, the *Liber historiae Francorum* and the Royal Frankish Annals thus 'remained deeply enmeshed in the chronological scheme and organizational "grid" of genealogy'.[18] Hummer therefore uses words like 'primordial trunk' or 'main stream' to denote the way biblical genealogy undergirded early medieval historiography in the Frankish realm: the 'generational progression of history' can be seen 'most obviously in the unbroken line of descent from Adam to Jesus, but also in the successions of kings, emperors, judges, priests, and bishops'.[19] As Bloch similarly explains, 'History as procreation' is 'an extension of Creation, its direction a lineage from Adam – through Noah, Abraham, Solomon, and David – to Christ', who produces issue through the apostles, saints, bishops, priests and kings.[20] Within this genealogical mode, salvation history could admit a remarkably wide horizon: Old Testament genealogy provided the chrono-logical and theological scaffold upon which to place not only Christian saints, clerics and kings, but also figures from Greek mythology, Germanic gods, Scandinavian heroes and barbarian rulers.[21] This approach to narrating world history by using biblical genealogy as the reference point for all other histories became even more explicit in the twelfth century. In Peter of Poitier's *Compendium Historiae in genealogia*, the genealogy of Christ serves as the timeline on which the histories of other dynasties mentioned in the Bible (Egyptians, Babylonians, Persians etc.) and the lineage of Jewish high priests and judges are paralleled and synchronized. Peter of Poitiers' later, updated version shows the line of the popes as the *linea Christi*, and this line becomes the extended time axis along which Roman and Holy Roman emperors and other ruling dynasties are placed. Medieval universal chronicles often took the form of 'genealogical rolls', portable documents of considerable physical length, professionally executed and illuminated. One famous example is Matthew Paris' *Chronica Majora*, which featured diagrams showing the descent of Christ from his Old Testament ancestors followed by the succession of popes, emperors and kings, with each lineage traced in an unbroken, vertical line, punctuated by small roundels function-ing as historical markers. Even as late as the fifteenth century, the six ages framework was still being used to organize and visualize historical data. Rolevinck's *Fasciculus Temporum* utilized two timelines, an *anno mundi* timeline and an *anno ante Christi nativitatem* timeline, which morphed into a single *anno Christi* timeline after the Nativity. Before the Nativity, the history features a lineage of Christ's biological ancestors depicted in roundels; after the birth of Christ, the lineage continues with Christ's successors, the popes. To give historical data chronological structure and meaning, medieval chronicles relied on genealogy, both as physical descent from Abraham to Christ and as spiritual descent from Christ down to contemporary times.

As the cases above show, the Christian universal chronicle made genealogy the dominant mode of historical thinking for over a thousand years.[22] Christian historiography in the Western Middle Ages relied on a paradigm 'characterized by linearity, temporality, verticality, fixity, and continuity', producing a form of thinking about history which 'derives its legitimacy from a connection to origins'.[23] Precisely because it can transcend facts of genetics, medieval genealogy has been described as a 'mental structure'[24] or a *Denkform*.[25] Christian genealogical thinking required a very particular sort of skill: the ability to use historical data as a form of self-relation apart from biological bloodline. For although genealogy in universal chronicles began with blood relations (Adam, Noah, Abraham, David, Solomon), it extended beyond the simply biological.[26] Christian chronicles envisioned events in Western Christendom (empire, saints, bishops/popes, finding of relics, missions, founding of abbeys etc.) as occurring along a temporal continuum *in linea Christi*, traceable to Christ and through him to Abraham.

During the Early Modern period, new textual genres enabled by the invention of the printing press, like newspapers, diaries, plays, almanacs, antiquarian history and topography, eclipsed the chronicle by robbing it of its commemorative, communicative, historical and recreational functions.[27] The Protestant Reformation had much to do with the decline of universal chronicles. Produced in monasteries and recording above all the lives and deeds of bishops, popes, saints, kings and aristocrats for the sake of commemorative intercessory prayer, the universal chronicle became synonymous with 'superstition' and 'monkery', and a symbol of a corrupt and defunct church.[28]

In England, Protestantism radically challenged the assumption that history was an ally of the Christian Church: while the passage of time, historical precedence and, crucially, the succession of generations could previously be viewed as the guardians of orthodoxy, now they sowed distrust. In his *The True Ancient Roman Catholike* (1611), Robert Abbot attacked Catholic authors claiming to have the 'infallible assurance' that, after over a thousand years, the Roman Catholic faith in England was identical to the one propagated by Gregory I and Augustine. Laurence Humphrey proclaimed that the word of Christ 'is our antiquity', thereby denouncing histories written by Catholics.[29] Emerging Protestant historiography elevated Scripture as the yardstick against which the historical Church's legitimacy should be judged. Yet this new historical model was, ironically, equally genealogical in orientation. In rejecting a genealogy based on a lineage of bishops, kings and saints, the Protestant Church put another genealogy in place, based on the idea of the persecuted elect who faithfully receive and guard the message passed through the generations in the face of worldly corruption. This approach was especially – even uniquely – conspicuous in England, where the development of Protestant historiography led to the creation of a singular interpretation of English national history which reconfigured, repurposed and revitalized genealogical thought.[30] During the sixteenth and seventeenth centuries, a sizeable group of scholars, theologians, polemicists and historians (John Bale, John Foxe, William Harrison, Matthew Parker etc.) strove to demonstrate the apostolic origins of the Church of England, a pure form of Christianity which had been transferred intact to England well before the intrusion of the Church of Rome in the late sixth century. Even if we disregard the legend that the Lord himself had walked upon England's mountains green in the form of the Holy Grail, what is left still provides an extraordinary lineage: Joseph of Arimathea, along with some half-dozen apostles including Simon Zelotes, St Peter and St Paul had all, according to the histories written and endorsed by English Protestant scholars, visited these shores and established Christianity in England. Though unattested by historical sources before the sixth century, King Lucius of the Britons was also said to have converted to Christianity in the second century, replacing paganism with a system of proto-archbishoprics and bishoprics under an early – and thus uncorrupted – pope, Eleutherius.[31] Protestant historians employed this lineage to prove that an indigenous Christianity had been founded in England well before the mission in 596 of Augustine. The sixteenth-century churchman John Bale asserted that Augustine, as a missionary for and from the Roman church, had only brought contamination – a 'Romish monk ... not of the order of Christ as was Peter, but of the superstitious sect of Benedict [of Nursia], there to spread abroad the Romish faith and religion', a truly foolish endeavour, 'for Christ's faith was there long afore'.[32]

The 'recitation of lineage and longevity', to borrow Felicity Heal's phrase, was for the newly formed Protestant Church in England not just about constructing a rival genealogy.[33] Positing the existence of a true lineage in the 'order of Christ' also represented an attack on the false lineage of errant believers. The apocalyptic struggle between the true, spiritual Protestant Church and the corrupt, worldly Catholic Church was waged as much on the historiographical battlefield as the doctrinal and ecclesiastical, largely a matter of assigning the proper ancestors from which English Christianity ought to claim descent. Certainly the most influential apocalyptic writer in this vein was John Foxe, the author of *Acts and Monuments*, usually called the *Book of Martyrs* (1563). The work portrays the battle between Satan and the elect over the beliefs and practices of the Roman church, but what is most important are the *martyrs* who result from this battle. As Minton has argued, just as the cult of martyrs was important to Eusebius in the fourth century because of 'the need to be able to see the post-Constantinian church as the heir of the Church of the martyrs', so it was for Foxe.[34] Martyrs emerging from the bloody reign of Mary proved that the nascent Church of England could rightfully claim descent from the martyrs described in 'the Judges, Kings, Maccabees, and the Acts of the Apostles after Christ's time', who had exhibited steadfast faith, resistance against corruption and courage in the face of death.[35] The suffering and death of the faithful presented proof of an unbroken lineage from the Old Testament to the apostolic Church to the Protestant Church in England.

Protestant apocalyptic historiography has therefore been regarded by cultural theorists as one of the contributing factors to the formation of English nationalism. A history of the true Church required discerning the correct lineage, identifying the proper forebears and rejecting the corrupt descendants of Rome, and such a history consequently rested on a portrayal of England as an elect nation, preserving pure faith over and against the forces of spiritual deceit and worldliness. The medieval notion of election had been based on Augustine's idea of the pilgrimage of the citizens of the *civitas Dei* towards God, a journey that the English people took with the entire Church catholic. But Edwin Jones has argued that, after the break with Rome and the Henrician Reformation, the English turned inward, relying on a definition of 'election' that stressed the English nation's separation and distinction from others. The English Reformation, he argues, emphasized not the universal but the national, as demonstrated by the foundation of an established 'Church of England' and the consolidation of a powerful nation-state.[36] Whether the national church really did act as a vehicle of a new, self-conscious and triumphalist patriotism based on the belief that England possessed a divine and exclusive 'manifest destiny' has been the subject of rigorous and heated debate. But at the very least, the campaign to 'nationalize' the Church was so effective that John Aylmer could pronounce in 1559 that 'God is English', an assertion he made to rouse 'true Englishmen in readiness, courage, and boldness'. Latimer likewise declared, 'Verily God hath shewed himself God of England, or rather the English God'; Lyly remarked 'The Living God is only the English God'; and Matthew Parker took for granted an 'Almighty God is so much English as he is'.[37]

The pressing question, however, is how Protestant England's view of its religious lineage, and the particular form of English nationalism it engendered, relate to British imperialism. Two influential sixteenth-century clerics-cum-explorers, Richard

Hakluyt and Samuel Purchas, both believed in Britain's place as an elect nation, but did not feel it was this status that underpinned colonial annexations.[38] Hakluyt's tireless promotion of the English colonization of North America stemmed from his views about civil life rather than Christianity: none of his major reflections about his explorations so much as touched on the relationship between true and false churches, the doctrine of salvation or the role of the English as divine agents in an apocalyptic age. Purchas took greater interest in England's place in the apocalyptic battle within sacred history, but expressed the impossibility of creating a unitary empire to encompass the entirety of the Three Kingdoms as well as their American plantations within a singular identity based on English Protestantism. Both clerics were clear on their approach to exploration and colonization: Britain was not a millennial vehicle or even a community defined by any precise definition of Protestantism which could be sufficient basis for imperial annexations. Even John Winthrop, the first governor of the Massachusetts Bay Colony, facing the indigenous peoples of New England, admitted that Christianity alone could not be adequate justification for claims to title and possession of land. John Locke pronounced that no European, 'not even the English', could be allowed any right of possession 'on grounds of religious belief alone': the charter for settlement was only legitimate if it took place in 'vacant places'. Thus the argument from vacancy (*vacuum domicilium*) or absence of ownership (*terra nullius*) became a standard rationale for the British dispossession of indigenous peoples in North America, Australia and Africa from the seventeenth century until well into the nineteenth century.[39]

The particular concept of religious ancestry which emerged from imperial annexations based on vacancy is one of the most profound legacies of the British Empire. Thomas Paine, writing *Common Sense* in 1776 and looking out towards the 'empty land' of America, declared, 'The Reformation was preceded by the discovery of America; As if the Almighty graciously meant to open a sanctuary to the persecuted in future years.'[40] He had seen the Atlantic colonies play host to a wide range of dissenting and separatist traditions: settler colonies under the one imperial umbrella of Great Britain had to accommodate English Anglicans, Welsh Nonconformists, Irish Catholics, Scottish and Irish Presbyterians, Baptists, Quakers and others.[41] English colonies were not, as those of Catholic kingdoms such as Spain, Portugal, and France were, set up to receive direct support from a centralized religious institution. The established church in England not only refrained from sending huge numbers of clergymen to the colonies but also lacked religious orders like the Dominicans and Franciscans and Jesuits.[42] Instead, religious provision for settlers in the early British Empire depended on chaplains, societies and subsidies, and in most colonies resident, territorial bishops were not installed until the 1840s. Thus Hilary Carey argues, 'At all times, it is important not to exaggerate the extent of state-supported religion in the British empire.'[43] Thus, even as English Protestants indulged in their inheritance as 'a chosen generation, a royal priesthood, an holy nation, a peculiar people', such lofty pedigree did not necessarily extend to the colonies, where religious provision was left substantially to disparate sects and denominations.[44] Not surprisingly, the legends about the role of Peter, Paul, Simon Zelotes and King Lucius in establishing Christian Britain – stories which were so important to the self-understanding of English Protestants – figured hardly at all in the colonies: the Christianity of the colonies did not replicate the ecclesiastical preoccupations of the motherland.

Instead, the voluntary principle that undergirded Christianity in English colonies introduced a different sort of ancestral relationship, and profoundly affected how the association between colony and metropole would be conceived. By the turn of the nineteenth century, 'Christendom' as the bond of Catholic faith uniting European nations was clearly no longer tenable. Instead, the more important spiritual bond was that which existed between England and the New World, and the term 'Christendom' increasingly encompassed the Christian Church worldwide with its many divisions and denominations.[45] Today, for example, the vast majority of the churches which in total endow Jamaica with the world record of 'more churches per square mile than anywhere else in the world' are Protestant, comprising Baptist, Anglican, United Church, Presbyterian, Methodist, Moravian, Brethren, Church of God and other Pentecostal groups. The presence of each group in Jamaica is the outcome of highly specific historical developments that relate to imperialism, slavery, migration, mission and sectarianism. This is the reason why Hilary Carey's book *God's Empire*, which concerns religion and colonialism in the nineteenth-century British world, must employ the structure it does, examining British missionary involvement in the colonies strictly by denomination: Anglicans, Catholics, Evangelical Anglicans, Nonconformists, Presbyterians. By 1901 these groups represented an overseas British Christian world of around 10 million people. Yet for all their variety, these 'Christian seedlings' were joined by one common link: they were planted by the British.[46] Thus is it the case that, when speaking of the varied confessional histories throughout the colonies of the British Empire, we tend to think in terms of 'ecclesial ancestry': descent of disparate groups from a common origin, an ancestral tie owing to a series of 'accidents' of political or geographical nature, related to imperialism.[47] In this sense, the unavoidable fact which tends to cause some degree of sheepishness, that the worldwide Anglican Communion is primarily the result of historic imperial ties, is not restricted only to Anglicanism but also symptomatic of all Protestant denominations. The Protestant paradigm reconstructed 'Christendom' as a spiritual brotherhood derived from common descent, its diversity and global reach fuelled by the spirit of progress.[48]

In this regard, it is interesting to note that the *Oxford History of Protestant Dissenting Traditions*, though very recently published in 2020 and claiming to adopt a progressive organizing structure, seems to underestimate how dependent it is on the very conventional configuration of 'ancestral' ties between England and the colonies. Indeed, John Coffey explains that the series will follow a narrative structure tracking 'diffusion and migration': 'In this model, Protestant Dissenting traditions originating in England are on the move, first to Wales and Ireland, and then to the American colonies and beyond.' And so the governing motif first 'traces the emergence of Dissenting denominational traditions within England'; then it 'explores how traditions of Protestant Dissent developed elsewhere in the British Atlantic world'; finally it will 'show how traditions of Protestant Dissent were transmitted beyond the West, being reconfigured in Africa, Asia, and South America'. The author recognizes the same question about 'religious ancestry' with which I am concerned, though employing a technological image in place of the biological: 'This raises difficult questions about … what connection there is between twenty-first-century global Protestantism and early modern English Dissent. Does global Protestantism run on software designed in seventeenth-century England?'[49] Coffey answers, generally, in the affirmative. There is the textual legacy, with seventeenth-century English texts like the Westminster Confession of Faith and the Westminster Shorter Catechism and Bunyan's *Pilgrim's Progress*, translated into 200 languages, which continue to exert wide influence among Dissenting traditions. Practices like baptism by immersion, and principles like civil and religious liberty, freedom of conscience and religious pluralism, all come from the Dissenting tradition which originally emerged in seventeenth-century England. The author cannot but notice that there are 'now more Presbyterians in South Korea than in Scotland, more Baptists in Brazil than in Britain, more Methodists in Zambia than in Wales'. In a strikingly frank admission, he continues: 'Protestant Dissenting traditions have enjoyed disproportionate cultural influence across the Anglophone world, and were dispersed around the globe by generations of Protestant missionaries and indigenous evangelists.'[50] These statements are impossible to dispute, and they betray how very dependent we are on the narrative of 'diffusion and migration' from England as the place of origin and forebear of legacies that have shaped the globe.

In summary, I have outlined in this chapter why the language of descent is the default mode for thinking about the history of Christianity, and how this language reinforces English exceptionalism, in particular:

1 the appropriation of Jewish ancestry by Christians, producing a notion of religious heritage that is highly spiritualized;
2 the mobilization of religious ancestors to legitimize the English national church;
3 the dependence on the language of ancestry to describe the relationship of Dissenting traditions and denominations in the colonies to the metropole.

I could illustrate the complex dynamic between these three points by way of Henry William Tucker, nineteenth-century prebendary of St Paul's Cathedral, honorary secretary of the Church Missionary Society and former secretary of the Society for the Propagation of the Gospel. In 1886, he wrote, 'In all these lands, whither the Anglo-Saxon race drifts and settles, Christianity, imported, perhaps with all its differences and divisions, from Great Britain, will supply the people with spiritual life.'[51] What stands out from this statement is that despite 'differences and divisions', everyone must still trace their supply of spiritual life back to the 'Anglo-Saxon race'. The claim is bold. Not only does Tucker claim spatial universalism (from the one origin to 'all these lands'), but he also claims a temporal universalism: no matter the differences and divisions of sect and tradition in the colonies, *all* can trace their lineage back to England. Another minister preaching at a meeting of the Baptist Missionary Society, W. L. Watkinson, put it in even more audacious terms in 1897:

> *England stands much in the same position that Israel did.* It is the spiritual centre of the world. As Palestine came between Egypt and Assyria, so this island comes in a wonderful manner between the old world and the new. God gave spiritual gifts in a remarkable degree to Israel; the revelation of Himself, the knowledge of His law, the sense of eternity … God in His government has also given to us special powers for the diffusion of the Gospel.[52]

The spatial and temporal hegemony so clearly assumed by Tucker and Watkinson – an assumption about what is original and what is new – has today become the target of strident post-colonial critique.

Notes

1 What follows is largely from Christopher Zoccali, 2016, 'Children of Abraham, the Restoration of Israel and the Eschatological Pilgrimage of the Nations: What Does it Mean for "In Christ" Identity?', in Brian Tucker and Coleman A. Stohl (eds), *T&T Clark Handbook to Social Identity in the New Testament*, London: Bloomsbury T&T Clark, pp. 253–72. For a personal take, see the discussion by Giles Fraser, *Chosen: Lost and Found between Christianity and Judaism*, particularly chapter 4, 'Romans', pp. 93–133.

2 Zoccali, 'Children of Abraham', with reference to Ernst Käsemann, 1971, *Perspectives on Paul*, Philadelphia, PA: Fortress Press; Michael Cranford, 1995, 'Abraham in Romans 4: The Father of All Who Believe', *New Testament Studies* 41(1), pp. 71–88; Terence Donaldson, 1997, *Paul and the Gentiles: Remapping the Apostle's Convictional World*, Minneapolis, MN: Fortress Press; Caroline E. Johnson Hodge, 2007, *If Sons, then Heirs: A Study of Kinship and Ethnicity in the Letters of Paul*, Oxford: Oxford University Press.

3 Robert Foster, 2016, *Renaming Abraham's Children: Election, Ethnicity, and the Interpretation of Scripture in Romans 9*, Wissenschaftliche Untersuchungen zum Neuen Testament 2/421, Tübingen: Mohr Siebeck.

4 On these terms, see Gavin D'Costa, 2019, *Catholic Doctrines on the Jewish People after Vatican II*, Oxford: Oxford University Press.

5 John Dawson, 2002, *Christian Figural Reading and the Fashioning of Identity*, Berkeley, CA: University of California Press.

6 Daniel Boyarin, 1994, *A Radical Jew: Paul and the Politics of Identity*, Berkeley, CA: University of California Press.

7 Matthew A. Thomas, 2010, 'Genealogy, Genealogies: Hebrew Bible/Old Testament', in *Encyclopedia of the Bible and its Reception* [online], Berlin, Boston: De Gruyter. Available from: www-degruyter-com/document/database/EBR/entry/MainLemma_5937/html (accessed 17.08.2021).

8 Pamela Eisenbaum, 1997, *The Jewish Heroes of Christian History: Hebrews 11 in Literary Context*, Atlanta, GA: Scholars Press. In this way could Jewish forefathers 'begat' Christian descendants.

9 1 Timothy 1.4 and Titus 3.9 dismiss those who teach false doctrine and devote themselves to 'myths' and 'genealogies'. It is unclear precisely which 'genealogies' are being castigated. Perhaps the writers warn against speculation regarding the content of Old Testament

genealogies like that found in some Jewish Pseudepigrapha or in esoteric rabbinic interpretations of the genealogies in Chronicles; alternatively Gnostic enumerations of aeons, as mentioned by Irenaeus, may be the target. See Allison C. Dale Jr, 'Genealogy, Genealogies: New Testament', in *Encyclopedia of the Bible and its Reception* [online].

10 Howard Bloch, 1983, *Etymologies and Genealogies: A Literary Anthropology of the French Middle Ages*, Chicago, IL: University of Chicago Press, at p. 37.

11 Graeme Dunphy, 'World chronicles', in Graeme Dunphy and Cristian Bratu (eds), *Encyclopedia of the Medieval Chronicle* [online]. Available at: http://dx.doi.org.ezphost.dur.ac.uk/10.1163/2213-2139_emc_SIM_02577> (accessed 17.08.2021).

12 Bloch, *Etymologies and Genealogies*, pp. 37–8.

13 Richard W. Burgess and Michael Kulikowski, 2013, *Mosaics of Time. The Latin Chronicle Traditions from the First Century BC to the Sixth Century AD, Vol. 1: A Historical Introduction to the Chronicle Genre from its Origins to the High Middle Ages*, Turnhout: Brepols, pp. 119ff.

14 Burgess and Kulikowski, *Mosaics of Time*, pp. 31–2, 191–2.

15 Bede, *De temporum ratione*, chapter 66, ed. Charles W. Jones, 1978, Corpus Christianorum Series Latina 123B, Turnhout: Brepols. See James T. Palmer, 2014, 'The Ends and Futures of Bede's *De temporum ratione*', in Faith Wallis and Peter Darby (eds), *Bede and the Future: Studies in Early Medieval Britain and Ireland*, Farnham: Ashgate, pp. 139–60. See also the helpful tables in Peter Darby, 2012, *Bede and the End of Time*, Farnham: Ashgate, pp. 21, 224–5.

16 Faith Wallis, 1999, *Bede: The Reckoning of Time*, Translated Texts for Historians 29, Liverpool: Liverpool University Press.

17 Hans Hummer, 2018, *Visions of Kinship in Medieval Europe*, Oxford: Oxford University Press, p. 283.

18 Hummer, *Visions of Kinship*, p. 283.

19 Hummer, *Visions of Kinship*, p. 288.

20 Bloch, *Etymologies and Genealogies*, p. 38.

21 Walter Pohl, 2016, 'Genealogy: A Comparative Perspective from the Early Medieval West', in Erik Hovden, Christina Lutter and Walter Pohl (eds), *Meanings of Community Across Medieval Eurasia*, Leiden: Brill, pp. 232–72.

22 Bloch, *Etymologies and Genealogies*, p. 37.

23 Bloch, *Etymologies and Genealogies*, p. 93.

24 Howard Bloch, 1986, 'Genealogy as Medieval Mental Structure and Textual Form', in Hans Ulrich Gumbrecht, Ursula Link-Heer and Peter-Michael Spangenberg (eds), *La littérature historiographique des origines à 1500, vol. 1: Partie historique, Grundiss der romanischen Litteraturen des Mittelalters 11/1*, Heidelberg: Carl Winter, pp. 135–56.

25 Kilian Heck and Bernhard Jahn, 2000, 'Genealogie in Mittelalter

und Früher Neuzeit. Leistungen und Aporien einer Denkform', in Kilian Heck and Bernhard Jahn (eds), *Genealogie als Denkform in Mittelalter und Früher Neuzeit*, Tübingen: Niemeyer, pp. 1–9.

26 Zrinka Stahuljak, 2014, 'Genealogy', in Elizabeth Emery and Richard Utz (eds), *Medievalism: Critical Terms*, Cambridge: D. S. Brewer, pp. 71–8.

27 Daniel Woolf, 2000, *Reading History in Early Modern England*, Cambridge: Cambridge University Press, cited in Alexandra Walsham, 2018, 'Chronicles, Memory and Autobiography in Reformation England', *Memory Studies* 11(1), pp. 36–50.

28 Walsham, 'Chronicles, Memory and Autobiography in Reformation England', p. 37.

29 Felicity Heal, 2005, 'Appropriating History: Catholic and Protestant Polemics and the National Past', *Huntington Library Quarterly* 68(1–2), pp. 109–32.

30 'This concern for the origins of a particular Protestant church does seem to be a largely British phenomenon': Felicity Heal, 2005, 'What Can King Lucius Do for You? The Reformation and the Early British Church', *The English Historical Review* 120(487), pp. 593–614, at 597. See also Avihu Zakai, 1992, *Exile and Kingdom: History and Apocalypse in the Puritan Migration to America*, Cambridge: Cambridge University Press, pp. 12–55.

31 Daniel Woolf, 2012, 'Historical Writing in Britain from the Late Middle Ages to the Eve of Enlightenment', in José Rabasa et al., *The Oxford History of Historical Writing: Volume 3: 1400–1800*, Oxford: Oxford University Press, pp. 473–95.

32 John Bale, *Actes of the Englysh Votaryes*, quoted by and adapted from Glanmore Williams, 1970, *Reformation Views of Church History*, Cambridge: James Clarke, p. 39.

33 Heal, 'What Can King Lucius Do for You?', p. 597.

34 Gretchen Minton, 2002, '"The Same Cause and like Quarell": Eusebius, John Foxe, and the Evolution of Ecclesiastical History', *Church History* 71(4), pp. 715–42.

35 John Foxe, *The Actes and Monuments*, published in The Unabridged Acts and Monuments Online (1583 edition), 2011, Sheffield: HRI Online Publications [online], p. 5. Available at: www.dhi.ac.uk/foxe/ (accessed 17.08.2021).

36 Edwin Jones, 1998, *The English Nation: The Great Myth*, Stroud, Sutton Publishing.

37 Patrick Collinson, 1988, *The Birthpangs of Protestant England: Religious and Cultural Change in the Sixteenth and Seventeenth Centuries. The Third Anstey Memorial Lectures in the University of Kent at Canterbury, 12–15 May 1986*, New York: St Martin's Press. The entire book is relevant but quotations here are from p. 4.

38 What follows is from David Armitage, 2000, *The Ideological*

Origins of the British Empire, Cambridge: Cambridge University Press, chapter 3 on 'Protestantism and Empire: Hakluyt, Purchas and Property'.

39 Armitage, *Ideological Origins of the British Empire*, p. 97.

40 Thomas Paine, *Common Sense; Addressed to the Inhabitants of America*, quoted in Armitage, *Ideological Origins of the British Empire*, p. 69.

41 Carla Pestana, 2011, *Protestant Empire: Religion and the Making of the British Atlantic World*, Philadelphia, PA: University of Pennsylvania Press.

42 Pestana, *Protestant Empire*, p. 74.

43 Hilary Carey, 2011, *God's Empire: Religion and Colonialism in the British World, c.1801–1908*, Cambridge: Cambridge University Press, p. 54.

44 1 Peter 2.9.

45 Mary Anne Perkins, 2004, *Christendom and European Identity: The Legacy of a Grand Narrative since 1789*, Berlin: Walter de Gruyter, pp. 41–3.

46 Carey, *God's Empire*, p 71.

47 See the comments of Martyn Percy, 2006, *Clergy: The Origin of Species*, London: Continuum, pp. 179–80.

48 Perkins, *Christendom and European Identity*, chapter 2, 'Protestantism and Anglicanism in the 19th century: The challenge to Europe-as-Christendom', pp. 36–51.

49 John Coffey, 'Introduction', in John Coffey (ed.), 2020, *The Oxford History of Protestant Dissenting Traditions, Volume I: The Post-Reformation Era, 1559–1689*, Oxford: Oxford University Press, pp. 1–38 at 34–5.

50 Coffey, 'Introduction', pp. 34, 37.

51 Henry William Tucker, 1886, *The English Church in Other Lands or the Spiritual Expansion of England*, p. 214, as quoted in Carey, *God's Empire*, p. 30.

52 Various, 1924, *Missionary Sermons: A Selection from the Discourses Delivered on Behalf of the Baptist Missionary Society on Various Occasions*, p. 42, quoted in Perkins, *Christendom and European Identity*, pp. 251–2, emphasis mine.

2

'Religious Ancestry':
The Postcolonial Critique of
Christian Historiography

God is decreeing to begin some new and great period in
his Church ... [W]hat does he then but reveal Himself to
his servants, and as his manner is, first to his Englishmen;
I say as his manner is, first to us, though we mark not the
method of his counsels, and are unworthy.

Milton, *Areopagitica*, November 1644

... descendants of the conquered, like me, always carry
two bags: one containing the conqueror's history,
the other that of the conquered. Descendants of the
conquerors ... only have to worry about the first bag.

Mihir Bose, 'The backlash against colonialism holds lessons
in guilt and gratitude', *Financial Times*, 1 January 2021

In 1842, John Conybeare addressed the theme of 'Christian
colonization' in a sermon he preached in the Chapel Royal at
Whitehall on behalf of the Society for the Propagation of the
Gospel. Suggesting that, just as a citizen of a country belonging
to the former Roman Empire 'prides himself on his ancestral
participation in their dominion', so it would be with the sons
and daughters of the British Empire in the far-flung colonies of
the world:

But the descendants of British Colonists, if we do our duty
by them now, will be able to point to a more imperishable
record of their connexion with the home which sent them

forth. In some far distant age, when time shall have blotted out from their statute-books the traces of British law, and even effaced from their language the impress of British literature, still there will remain to them an heir-loom of their mother-land, over which time shall have no power; still British Christianity shall bind them by the chains of reverential love, by the sympathies of a common worship, by the fellowship of an unearthly communion, to the generations which have gone before. Still they will look back with grateful affection and patriotic pride to the mighty mother of empires, who was the parent not only of their national but of their moral growth ... they will not forget the memory of their first teachers, but will celebrate your Christian wisdom and parental forethought.[1]

Today we may deride such a brazen display of jingoism, but on closer inspection I dare say Conybeare would feel that his prediction has proved correct. The infantilizing and paternalistic language used for describing the historic links that tie Christians of the global South to England has by no means been abolished, and expressions of 'gratitude' coming from the colonized for the role empire played in their salvation are still oddly common. If this were only a problem with poor choice of words, it would be relatively easy to solve. But the depth of 'reverential love' and 'grateful affection' which many ethnic minority Christians feel for their religious inheritance is deep and sincere, and what is more, the parentage for which thanks is felt is not just towards the British alone but to the whole 'extended family' that comes with such parentage – that is, to use Conybeare's crucial phrase, the link 'to the generations which have gone before'.

To illustrate what I mean, let me turn to Richard Foster's very popular *Streams of Living Water: Essential Practices from the Six Great Traditions of Christian Faith*. A much-loved and accessible approach to the history of Christianity complete with timelines, summaries about 'critical turning points in Church History', and dictionary-like entries on 'notable figures and significant movements in Church History', the book distils six dimensions of faith and practice that Foster argues are discernible from the Christian past: the Contemplative Tradition (prayer-filled life); the Holiness Tradition (virtuous life); the Charismatic Tradition (Spirit-empowered life); the Social Justice Tradition (compassionate life); the Evangelical Tradition (word-centred life); and the Incarnational Tradition (sacramental life). Foster introduces his book by saying, '[M]any are the lives that illustrate these themes: Abraham, Sarah, Jacob, Moses, Ruth, David, Hannah, Samuel, Isaiah, Jeremiah, Mary, Peter, Elizabeth, Paul, Tabitha, Lydia, John',[2] and it is clear that we are supposed to read the chronologically ordered lists of 'Notable Figures' in each tradition as coming from the same spiritual lineage as these biblical characters. For example, the 'Contemplative Tradition' begins with Jesus of Nazareth and John the Apostle, and then places subsequent figures along the same timeline (Antony of Egypt, Pachomius, Gregory of Nyssa, Benedict of Nursia, John Climacus, Maximus the Confessor, Cuthbert, Benedict of Aniane, Simeon the New Theologian, Antony of Kiev, Aelred of Rievaulx, Clare of Assisi, Gregory Palamas, Julian of Norwich, Catherine of Siena, John of the Cross, Brother Lawrence, and so on), thereby encouraging us to consider them all as members in a single lineage of spiritual giants. Laudably, Foster has excavated non-Western figures in each stream which even ecclesiastical historians in the West would have trouble recognizing (e.g. Euthymius the Great, fourth-century Armenian abbot; Nicodemus the Hagiorite, eighteenth-century Greek monk; Seraphim of Sarov, eighteenth-century Russian Orthodox mystic; Toyohiko Kagawa, twentieth-century activist and evangelist). Still, this is an undeniably Western family tree. After accounting for all the 'Notable Figures and Significant Movements in Church History' which are of Middle Eastern, North African and Greek provenance, as well as those of later Russian and North American provenance, prominent personalities and significant movements originating from Western Europe still account for well over half of the total 243 figures and movements listed.[3] The book is now available in eight languages including Chinese and Korean. Informed by Foster that this is their religious heritage, Chinese and Korean Christians eagerly read the biographies of these ancestors with 'reverential love' and 'grateful affection'. Wordsworth writing in 1814 is only thinking of 'English hearts' when he describes an 'ancestral feeling' of gratitude for the Church's heritage; he has not entertained the possibility that a non-Englishman might also one day know something of this feeling. Hence a deep chasm between the 'ancestral feeling' of the English colonizer, and the 'reverential love' and 'grateful affection' of the colonized.

To understand the reason for this, we need to turn not just to the colonization of land but to another form of colonization, an *ongoing* legacy of imperialism that continues to perpetuate inequalities today, and that is the colonization of history. A conception of time that relies on tracing descent from origins explains not only the inescapable Eurocentrism of our histories but also the bond of attachment that keeps us tied to Europe. Indeed, neglecting this fact is the reason why contemporary correctives to the problem of Eurocentrism in the history of Christianity (revising or diversifying the canon, etc.) seem to me rather like treating the symptoms rather than the cause. Indeed, works of theological scholarship offering new postcolonial paradigms may be effective as far as theologizing is concerned but offer little help where historicizing is concerned.

Let me take as my first example Sang Hyun Lee's *From a Liminal Place: An Asian American Theology*.[4] In this book, Lee takes as his starting point the idea that the Asian American experience is the postcolonial condition of marginality (being excluded) and liminality (being located at the periphery or edge of a society). For Lee, God himself is liminal, 'being in between two or more worlds'.[5] Observing that Jesus was a Jewish Galilean and conducted his public ministry among Galileans, a marginalized people, Lee argues that God became incarnate *as* a Galilean because liminality is central to his Godself; Jesus' assumption of a liminal situation in time is a reiteration of the liminal experience within the Trinity. Lee's central thesis is that Asian Americans, unlike the white majority, are uniquely situated to perpetuate the divine activity of liminality and participate in God's work because their social condition mirrors

Trinitarian social life. Lee exhorts Asian American Christians to embrace their peripheral positions in society and possibilities for 'liminal creativity'. His arguments ought to make me feel better about my situation, but why (speaking for myself only) am I not convinced? Lee's strategy for resolving the tensions faced by Asian Americans is to do what theologians do, applying a doctrine of God to a contemporary situation or dilemma. But when it comes to the critique of Eurocentrism, the problem with a wholly theological approach is, of course, that the dilemma is *historical*: God may very well be 'liminal', but the historic Christianity that communicated him was anything but. And though the Christ of the New Testament might have been the Galilean 'stranger', Christ comes down to me from Late Antiquity, the Middle Ages and the modern period through the established, imperial, and dominating power of Western Christendom.

Asserting that Christ was a Jew or a Galilean, 'peripheral' and 'liminal', does not make the problem of Christianity's historic ascendancy through Western Europe go away. An even clearer example illustrates this difficulty. Kamudzandu's *Abraham as Spiritual Ancestor: A Postcolonial Zimbabwean Reading of Romans 4* makes the argument – central to the language I'm trying to problematize in this book – that Paul turns Abraham into a *'genealogical metaphor so as to reinforce the inclusion of other people besides Jews'*.[6] Abraham serves as a model not of the believer's saving faith but of God's method of operation, which is to fulfil his promises by incorporating peoples into the blessings bestowed on founding ancestors. In Kamudzandu's reading, the crucial idea in Romans 4.1–25 is thus not how Abraham was justified but rather whose father he is and in what way his children are related to him. Kamudzandu argues that Paul transforms the dominant 'imperial' ancestry of the day, exemplified in the figure of Aeneas (ancestor of Greeks and Romans), into an inclusive spiritual ancestry through the figure of Abraham.[7] By creatively reconstructing 'Abraham the Jew' rather than 'Aeneas the Roman' as the proper ancestor of people of faith, Paul subverts imperial power and shows postcolonial Christians how to embrace their own histories to innovatively define relationships of spiritual kinship. This means the Shona people can reconstruct their own cultural heroes (such as Nehanda and Chaminuka) as spiritual ancestors – and thus his argument for a 'cross-cultural appropriation of the role of ancestors'.[8]

I daresay some may find this reading not only *not* post-colonial but fundamentally colonial. As Jennings has argued in his influential book *The Christian Imagination: Theology and the Origins of Race*, supersessionist readings of any sort – either ones which displace Israel within the economy of salvation or, as in Kamudzandu's work, ones which reinterpret Abraham as the forebearer of all people of faith – rely on the same colonizing logic. A supersessionst reading '[jettisons] Israel from its calculus of the formation of Christian life', replacing Israel with the Church; in so doing it positions Christian identity fully outside the identities of Jews and makes its own election and inclusion the primary matter.[9] The logic at work here is the same as what would later be used by Europeans in their acts of racializing and colonizing the people they encountered: 'they positioned themselves as those first *conditioning* their world rather than being conditioned by it'.[10] Thus before the scientific concept or social principle of race had even emerged as a 'fully formed "racial optic" on the world', writes Jennings, 'it was a theological form' first.[11] And so,

> in the age of discovery and conquest supersessionist thinking burrowed deeply inside the logic of evangelism and emerged joined to whiteness in a new, more sophisticated, concealed form. Indeed, supersessionist thinking is the womb in which whiteness will mature.[12]

In Western Europe, the Christian theological imagination was 'woven into processes of colonial dominance'. Wherever it went in the modern colonies, Christianity relied on a warped sense of hospitality: losing total sense of having ever been the 'Gentile', instead 'It claimed to be the host, the owner of the spaces it entered'.[13] When they encountered people in Africa and the Americas, Europeans did not understand themselves as the 'lost sheep of Israel' but instead as Israel itself, the direct recipient of divine election addressing other people as Gentiles. European Christians ought to have understood themselves in the divine story in the form of humble and desperate petitioners, like the centurion and the Canaanite woman.[14] Instead:

> The colonialist moment helped to solidify a form of Christian existence that read this text as though we were standing with Jesus looking down on the woman in her desperation, when in fact we, the Gentiles, are the woman, not we, a generic humanity, but we, those who are outside Israel.[15]

The danger in thinking that doctrinal and exegetical solutions alone have emancipatory effects is that it ignores how Christian theological concepts have themselves been encased in imperializing logic, and overlooks their complicity as agents of marginalization and racialization. As Jennings argues, we must refuse this process of disassociation and dislocation, between abstract thinking versus situated historical thinking: we must observe 'the points of a history in which the Christian theological imagination was woven into processes of colonial dominance'.[16] Kamudzandu's proposal of 'spiritual ancestry' (that Abraham is as much the ancestor of the Zimbabwean as of the Englishman) is powerless as a postcolonial response when one acknowledges the fact that it was precisely this supersessionist thinking which lay behind the imperial project in the first place. Such a proposal is akin to me joining the Christian Heritage London tour around the British Museum to view, as advertised, 'items associated with actual Bible characters' – Abraham, Hezekiah, Daniel, Esther, Nehemiah – but completely overlooking the sheer force of British supremacy which secured not only the possession of the antiquities themselves, but also my interest in them, as one whose knowledge about 'Bible characters' is derived from a childhood in a British-ruled territory.[17] Spiritual ancestry cannot be naively understood in the abstract, because the concept has been 'woven into processes of colonial dominance': the religious ancestors revered by colonizers, from Abraham and St Paul to Augustine and

Tyndale, far from being 'liminal' or 'marginal', are part of the established cultural memory of the colonizers, rendering Europe the unescapable point of reference not just in space but in time.

To explain how 'history' can be colonized, and specifically how Western Europe benefits from it, one must note that modern imperialism came to maturity around the same time G. W. F. Hegel advanced his philosophy of history. Rejecting dichotomies between the world above and the world below, pure ideas and their earthly reflections, theory and practice, spirit and flesh, Hegel argued that the spirit of the world (*Geist*) unveils itself through human consciousness as manifested particularly through art, religion and philosophy, and in this way is materialized *in* history itself. The history of humanity is like a tree unfolding itself gradually, evolving when a new idea is nurtured in the environment of the old, the new overtaking the old while preserving its essence and raising it to a higher level.[18] History is therefore developmental, its progress proceeding dialectically, sequentially and epochally towards the end result of a full actualization of the 'Spirit'.

Hegel's ideas were applied to the study of church history by a nineteenth-century German émigré to the United States, Philip Schaff. Alongside the historical works he wrote and edited (*Ante-Nicene Fathers* and the *Nicene and Post-Nicene Fathers*; *History of the Christian Church*; *Creeds of Christendom*), Schaff also thought at length about the task of writing church history. In his *Principles of Protestantism* and *What is Church History?*, Schaff argued that the primary goal in the study of church history is to discern its 'organic development'. He used the term 'subjective Christianity' to denote the 'life of the God-man in his Church' (in contra-distinction to truth as objectively present in Christ and the Scriptures), describing it as:

> a process, a development, which begins small, and grows always larger, till it comes at last to full manhood in Christ, that is, till the believing human world may have appropriated to itself, both outwardly and inwardly, the entire fulness of

objective Christianity, or the life of Christ. In this view, the word of God also was not once understood by the church from the beginning, in all its depth and comprehension, but gradually always more and more with the advancing age of the church.[19]

Organic development, Schaff wrote, is what Scripture refers to as the kingdom of God being like 'the small mustard seed that gradually becomes a great tree' and like 'leaven, that works and spreads till the whole lump is leavened'. St Paul 'is full of the idea of a constantly advancing development on the part of the Church. He speaks of the whole building of the saints, as *growing* to a holy temple in the Lord.'[20] The expression *organic* implies that the stages of development, like the members of a living body, are indissolubly bound together and 'It is only the entire history of the church, from her commencement in the congregation at Jerusalem to her consummation in the general judgment, which can fully represent her conception.'[21] Thus his controversial claim that Protestantism must not be grounded in the rejection of Catholicism any more than Christianity rejected Judaism. Rather, like the relationship of Christianity to Judaism, Protestantism was the next stage in the organic development of the Church: for Schaff the Reformation was the 'the legitimate *offspring*, the greatest act of the Catholic church'.[22] Using typically Hegelian language, Schaff writes that the Church is an organic development in which each new stage 'grow[s] forth from the trunk of history, in regular living union with its previous development'.[23] Protestantism 'is the principle of movement, of progress in the history of the church'.[24]

The metaphor of a seed growing into a tree regularly features in nineteenth-century writing on the history of Christianity. It is the most vivid illustration of genealogical thinking, which takes its object of investigation (the Church) to be an internally unified subject, growing over time, but always remaining true to its own nature, as an acorn seed can grow into an oak tree but can never become an apple tree.[25] In England, theologians who, like Schaff, had also been influenced by continental Romantic idealism, developed the image into a full-blown ecclesiological theory – the so-called 'Branch Theory' – which became so influential that it is still the default position held by many Anglicans today.[26] Nineteenth-century Tractarians, including John Henry Newman, developed the concept of the Church as internally connected like branches of a tree.[27] William Palmer popularized the theory which identified Roman Catholicism, Greek Orthodoxy and Anglicanism as the three main branches of the Church.[28] 'Branch Theory' advanced the arguments of Tractarians advocating closer relations with the Roman and Eastern churches, on the grounds that the Church of England had grown through the same trunk via the apostolic succession of bishops and maintaining of the ecumenical creeds. Christopher Wordsworth, canon of Westminster and later bishop of Lincoln, published a catechism 'concerning the Church, and our own Branch of it', in which he argued that 'the members of any particular or national Church' could rightly be called Catholics, and that there were Italian Catholics, Greek Catholics, French Catholics and English or Anglo-Catholics. But, he was clear:

> ... the Church of Rome is *part* of the Catholic Church, as the other Churches before mentioned are; but neither the Church of Rome, nor the Church of England, nor the Greek Church, nor any other *particular* Church, is *the* Catholic or Universal Church, any more than a *Branch* is a *Tree*, or a *Hand* is the *whole Body*.[29]

Today, whether consciously or not, much of the Protestant approach to the history of Christianity relies on essentially the same paradigm. I myself use these diagrams to explain denominational relationships emerging from the history of Christianity:

A 'tree diagram'

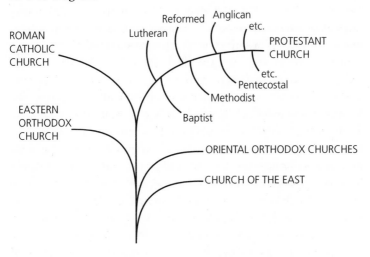

A 'timeline'

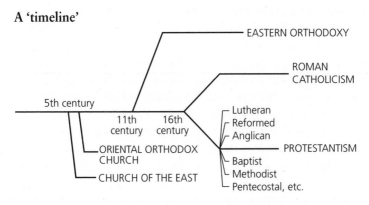

These diagrams fail dismally on countless points: for instance, they leave off innumerable movements and groups, depict schisms as sharp and clear-cut, and fail to portray the various reunions and communions which have today been re-established across divisions. Moreover, the diagrams are embarrassingly biased and clearly derived from Protestant ecclesiological assumptions, especially the view of the Church as an essentially unified entity beginning with a single trunk, growing with time into branches and stems. Yet despite our best attempts we always fall back on diagrams like these, for our instinct is to view our denominational affiliations 'genealogically', to trace the 'ancestral lineage' from which our confessional identity has issued. A good example can be found in the charts on 'American Denominational Families' appended to *From Aldersgate to Azusa Street*, used by the author to prove that many denominations – and, by extension, a large population of world Christians – trace their 'ancestry' to the Wesleys and Methodism.[30] This way of visualizing the history of Christianity unmasks our continued dependence on nineteenth-century historical frameworks such as the Branch Theory and idea of 'organic development'.

What becomes quite clear is how prominent Western Europe is in this linear, developmental (seed to tree) conceptualization of church history. Granted, 'early Christianity' begins in Palestine, and events like the Councils of Nicaea and Chalcedon occur in the East, and certainly Eastern Christianity, Oriental Orthodox Churches, and the ancient Church of the East retain its presence. But not only does the Latin Church give birth to the vast majority of confessional traditions with which the world's Christians identify today, but in fact the basic schematization of church history itself identifying 'forks' along the road (which result from the early church councils, the eleventh-century 'Great Schism', the Protestant Reformation, denominationalism) relies on Western periodizations and Western assumptions about which junctures constitute significant changes and developments. Jan Patočka points out that this way of plotting events depends on an essentially Eurocentric framework, and that 'history as a specific continuum, phrased in the way we have become used to: antiquity, Middle Ages, and so forth, this is specifically European'. What is more, 'we project it onto those other civilizations. We use this European standard for them and we cannot do otherwise. For this reason, and in this sense, we say that history is the history of Europe.'[31]

Likely as a reaction to the accusation that 'history is the history of Europe', some scholars have tried recently to argue that the thing binding these branches together is not just the

mere 'historical accident' of European imperialism but something much more essential, theological and ecclesiological and,
therefore, timeless. For example, Guillermo René Cavieses
Araya argues against the view of the 'Anglican Communion as
a federation of Churches held together only by their common
historical ancestry' rather than as an ecclesiastical body with
a common identity and sacramental life.[32] He wants to show
that it is possible to 'formulate a (new) ecclesiology of the
Anglican Communion, capable of usurping the current view
of global Anglicanism as an accident of history, loosely bound
by a common ancestry'. He uses three examples – the Anglican
Churches of Japan, Malawi and Chile – to showcase Anglican
ecclesiological identities that have developed outside the main
sphere of influence of the British Empire, and in areas where
the spread of the English language did not play a major role
in their development and growth. Rejecting the idea that their
commonalities stem from historic events and a set of doctrines
that were issued historically (e.g. Chicago, Lambeth Quadrilat-
eral, the 39 Articles of Religion), Araya asserts that the basis
of the Anglican Communion lies instead on 'a particular and
contemporary embodiment of the vision and comprehension
of the Church ... which the Apostles and the earliest fathers
of the Church envisioned'.[33] Yet, though this argument works
well as a plea for appreciating the unique ecclesiological identity of the Anglican Communion, it does not work well as a
study in history. For all of Araya's valiant efforts to deny the
centrality of an Anglocentric 'common ancestry', we would
still have to refer to the tree diagram above to understand what
the 'Anglican' in the 'Anglican Church' of Japan, Malawi and
Chile even refers to. It soon emerges that the stubborn culprit
we must blame for making Europe the 'common ancestor' for
most things and, moreover, for making Japan, Malawi and
Chile not even appear on the radar until the twentieth century,
is, in fact, the very act of *historicizing*.

Historicism has therefore attracted serious critique by postcolonial theorists. The most influential is Chakrabarty's analysis
in *Provincializing Europe: Postcolonial Thought and Historical Difference*, in which he bluntly defines 'historicism' as that

which 'came to non-European peoples in the nineteenth century as somebody's way of saying "not yet" to somebody else'.[34] Chakrabarty defines 'historicism' as a mode of thinking with the following characteristics:

> It tells us that in order to understand the nature of anything in this world we must see it as an historically developing entity, that is, first, as an individual and unique whole – as some kind of unity at least in *potentia* – and, second, as something that develops over time. Historicism typically can allow for complexities and zigzags in this development; it seeks to find the general in the particular, and it does not entail any necessary assumptions of teleology. But the idea of development and the assumption that a certain amount of time elapses in the very process of development are critical to this understanding.[35]

Historicism, the premise that peoples occupied different positions on a universal path of progress (in Chakrabarty's book, capitalism, modernity and rationalism, but applicable across any subject), has relegated colonial subjects to a state of deferred arrival, of perpetual belatedness, of the perpetual need to 'catch up'. Chakrabarty describes this as a '"first in Europe, then elsewhere" structure of global historical time'.[36]

As we have seen, the modus operandi in the discipline of church history is avowedly historicist: it takes its object of study (the Church or Christianity) to be internally unified and sees it as something developing over time, a development commonly conceived in terms of the kingdom of God, or missions and evangelism, or revival and reform. This, as Hayden White has pointed out, requires a certain mindset which privileges emplotment and narration in order to characterize events as 'elements in a matrix of causal relationships' and to show the 'process of development leading from one situation to some other situation by appeal to general laws of causation' – even if the one thing we can count on is that historians will disagree over every aspect of the telling of the plot.[37] This 'historical consciousness' extols Europe as the site on which many events crucial to the development of Christianity occurred: military campaigns, annexation of temporal power and ideas of sacral kingship, doctrinal debates and pronouncements, clerical and episcopal structures, technological advances, the Renaissance, the Enlightenment, dissent, toleration, modernity, liberalism, and so on. And so the Christian in, say, India, finds with his conversion to Christianity that he has suddenly gained 15 centuries of history to learn if he wishes to understand why he prays the way he does, or why his church looks the way it does, or why he sings the hymns he sings.

This is simply the effect of, to borrow Chakrabarty's phrase, an 'objectifying relationship to the past', necessary if one wants to understand his or her confessional lineage.[38] By 'objectifying' here, I mean taking the history of Christianity as an internally unified object of study developing and evolving over time, which presents our relationship to the past in terms of outgrowth from origin, evolution from the prototype, derivation from precedent – or, in the words we have been using, descendant from ancestor.

Thus, in an important essay, Dirlik argues that the problem is not the spatial location of history – of Europe as 'centre' and the need to 'de-centre' it and 're-centre' history elsewhere – but rather the status of history as a basic way of knowing the past.[39] Although the effort to be inclusive or to look for other histories are by no means insignificant, none of these endeavours to redress Eurocentrism can be confused with the abandonment of it. For we have failed to look for Eurocentrism where it is really embedded: not in the exclusion of others but within history itself as an undertaking. Dirlik argues:

> The distinguishing feature of Eurocentrism is not its exclusiveness but rather the reverse: its inclusiveness ... History, along with other social sciences systematized in the nineteenth century, articulates a new mastery over the world ... It is a history that takes entire societies and the whole world in all its aspects as its domain, and seeks to classify and explain them holistically and systematically.[40]

We have already seen this at work in the tree diagrams and time charts mentioned in this chapter, which take in one swoop the many movements, events and figures in the history of Christianity and classify them systematically along a single continuum. Therefore, a 'thoroughgoing critique of Euro-centrism leads inescapably to a conclusion that the project of overcoming Eurocentrism calls not for alternative histories but, in Nandy's words, *alternatives to history*'.[41] There is no solu-tion to the problem of Eurocentrism other than the undoing of history itself, because history *is* the reason for my perpetual belatedness as a colonized person: it is *historicizing* itself which makes me 'late', and which makes me always have to go via Europe. The point is stressed by a story James Baldwin has told about an experience taking a retreat in a remote Swiss village in the Bernese Alps over the winter of 1951–52. As the first black person the villagers had ever seen, he was made to feel a spectacle, and it did not matter that he was an accomplished poet and highly respected intellect. He reflects on the irony of his situation:

> [The villagers] move with an authority which I shall never have; and they regard me, quite rightly, not only as a stranger in their village but as a suspect latecomer, bearing no cre-dentials, to everything they have – however unconsciously – inherited. For this village, even were it incomparably more remote and incredibly more primitive, is the West, the West onto which I have been so strangely grafted. These people cannot be, from the point of view of power, strangers any-where in the world; they have made the modern world, in effect, even if they do not know it. The most illiterate among them is related, in a way that I am not, to Dante, Shake-speare, Michelangelo, Aeschylus, Da Vinci, Rembrandt, and Racine; the cathedral at Chartres says something to them which it cannot say to me ... Out of their hymns and dances come Beethoven and Bach. Go back a few centuries and they are in their full glory – but I am in Africa, watching the conquerors arrive.[42]

Fundamentally, the purpose of postcolonial theory is to expose the ongoing legacies of empire in our patterns of thought, including the way in which homogenizing, centrist, linear historicism confines the subaltern to a perpetual state of belatedness through the notion of inheritances and heritage. Genealogies therefore represent the antithesis of the postcolonial project, and a significant dimension of postcolonial theory rests on the poststructuralism of Foucault who, in 'Nietzsche, Genealogy, History', completely inverts the literal meaning of the term 'genealogy'.[43] Foucault's genealogy is a tool for critique and for dismantling history as traditionally understood and done. He rejects the essential nature of identity and aims to expose the haphazard manner by which truth and knowledge are forged, thereby rejecting the very search for origins. Opposed entirely to the aims of a literal genealogy, Foucault proposes instead that:

> The search for descent is not the erecting of foundations: on the contrary, it disturbs what was previously considered immobile; it fragments what was thought unified; it shows the heterogeneity of what was imagined consistent with itself.[44]

This postmodern genealogy vehemently opposes a traditional genealogy which treats an object as a fundamentally unified, historically developing entity, the progress and complexities of which we can track over time, finding always how one thing has led to the next. In Foucault's rendering, a true, critical genealogy must show no such continuities: its job is to undermine the very idea that an object can be traced to origins, or that its legitimacy derives from a connection to origins.

Foucault's use of 'genealogy' is distinctively philosophical and usually limited to academics who enjoy the difficult demands of poststructuralist theory. But his critique of traditional genealogy has been influential, and passionately shared by Deleuze and Guattari who declared, emphatically: '*We're tired of trees. We should stop believing in trees, roots, and radicles. They've made us suffer too much.*'[45] In their view, thought patterns relying on tree diagrams and arborescent images are harmful. They want to dismantle our genealogical patterns of thought by replacing our reliance on arboreal imagery with a different one: the rhizome, in other words bulbs and tubers (as in a potato), which are 'absolutely different from roots and radicles'.[46] A rhizome is envisaged as a dense and tangled cluster of interlaced threads or filaments, any point in which can be connected to any other. As Tim Ingold explains:

> Whether the image is botanically accurate need not concern us here. It has the virtue of giving us a way of beginning to think about persons, relationships and land that gets away from the static, decontextualising linearity of the genealogical model, and allows us to conceive of a world in movement, wherein every part or region enfolds, in its growth, its relations with all the others.[47]

With no points or positions of its own, and existing only in multiplicity, a rhizome is a protest against 'arborescent systems' which are 'hierarchical systems with centers of significance and subjectification', and in this way 'The rhizome is an antigenealogy'.[48] Insisting that the tree has dominated Western thought to the detriment of social realities, the authors offer the rhizome as a relational – rather than hierarchical – model which better captures lived experiences and how identities emerge and change in response to social landscapes, rather than received as 'inheritance'.[49] Instead of thinking of people as passing along a line of transmission, we should think of them as passing along lines of movement and exchange at the places where their respective paths cross or commingle.[50] 'Throughout their lives', as Bird-David puts it, persons 'perpetually coalesce with, and depart from, each other'.[51]

I am very much convinced by the merits of this reconceptualization, but not very much by the vocabulary required. As we have already established in the previous chapter, too much in theology and ecclesiology depends on the language of 'ancestry': we could not realistically be expected to start calling Abraham our 'rhizome' instead of our ancestor, effective though it may be for removing supersessionist and hegemonizing connotations.

But though I will not be embarking on a programme to replace my Wordsworthian 'ancestral feelings' for Augustine, Benedict, Luther and Bach with 'rhizomatic feelings', still I cannot ignore the postcolonial problems associated with genealogy which have been highlighted both by theoretical critique and by my own lived experience. Is there a way to retain genealogical consciousness, the language of inheritance and ancestral feeling, while discarding the assumptions of linear descent, originary movement, historical development and essential unity, all of which work in continued favour of the colonizer and keep the colonized trapped in a state of perpetual lateness? My next chapter considers this question, beginning with the thought that, as a person of Chinese heritage reared in a Confucian tradition, 'ancestral feeling' dominates my mindset and way of life.

Notes

1 William Conybeare, *Sermons Preached in the Chapel Royal at Whitehall, During the Years 1841, 1842, and 1843*, quoted in Hilary Carey, 2011, *God's Empire: Religion and Colonialism in the British World*, pp. 321–2. The old Banqueting House was fitted as a Chapel Royal following a fire in 1698, and remained in use as a chapel until 1890.

2 Richard J. Foster, 1998, republished 2001, *Streams of Living Water: Essential Practices from the Six Great Traditions of Christian Faith*, New York: HarperCollins, p. xvi.

3 Foster, *Streams of Living Water*, 'Appendix B: Notable Figures and Significant Movements in Church History', pp. 303–78.

4 Sang Hyun Lee, 2010, *From a Liminal Place: An Asian American Theology*, Minneapolis, MN: Fortress Press.

5 Lee, *From a Liminal Place*, p. x.

6 Israel Kamudzandu, 2010, *Abraham as Spiritual Ancestor: A Postcolonial Zimbabwean Reading of Romans 4*, Leiden: Brill, p. 45.

7 See particularly Kamudzandu, *Abraham as Spiritual Ancestor*, chapter 4 on 'Ancestry and Descendancy in Romans 4'.

8 Kamudzandu, *Abraham as Spiritual Ancestor*, pp. 3, 5, 9.

9 Willie James Jennings, 2010, *The Christian Imagination: Theology and the Origins of Race*, New Haven, CT: Yale University Press, p. 33. Jennings goes on to say that this created a 'conceptual vacuum that was filled by the European'.

10 Jennings, *The Christian Imagination*, p. 60, emphasis mine.

11 Jennings, *The Christian Imagination*, p. 58.

12 Jennings, *The Christian Imagination*, p. 36.

13 Jennings, *The Christian Imagination*, p. 8.

14 Jennings, *The Christian Imagination*, p. 261.

15 Jennings, *The Christian Imagination*, p. 262.

16 Jennings, *The Christian Imagination*, p. 262.

17 Christian Heritage London: www.christianheritagelondon.org/index. For an overview of the issue of the removal of cultural artifacts ('looting') from the Middle East during the colonial period, see Salam Al Quntar, 2017, 'Repatriation and the Legacy of Colonialism in the Middle East', *Journal of Eastern Mediterranean Archaeology & Heritage Studies* 5(1), pp. 19–26.

18 J. L. Talmon, 1967, *Romanticism and Revolt: Europe 1815–1848*, London: Harcourt, pp. 86–87; Margaret Meek Lange, 2021, 'Progress', *The Stanford Encyclopedia of Philosophy* (Summer 2021 edn) [online]. Available at: https://plato.stanford.edu/entries/progress/.

19 Philip Schaff, 1846, *What is Church History: A Vindication of the Idea of Historical Development*, Philadelphia, PA: J. B. Lippincott and Co, reprinted in Charles Yrigoyen Jr and George M. Bricker (eds), 1979, *Reformed and Catholic: Selected Historical and Theological Writings of Philip Schaff*, Pittsburgh, PA: Pickwick Press, pp. 17–143 (page citations are to original edition), p. 97.

20 Schaff, *What is Church History*, p. 87, emphasis in original.

21 Schaff, *What is Church History*, p. 91.

22 David R. Bains and Theodore Louis Trost, 2015, 'Philip Schaff: The Flow of Church History and the Development of Protestantism', *Theology Today* 71(4), pp. 416–28 at 419, emphasis mine.

23 Philip Schaff, 1844, *Das Princip des Protestantismus*, trans. John Nevin, in Bard Thompson and George H. Bricker (eds), 1964, *The Principle of Protestantism*, Philadelphia, PA: United Church Press, here quoted in Bains and Trost, 'Philip Schaff', p. 419.

24 Schaff, *Das Princip des Protestantismus*.

25 Schaff, *What is Church History?*, p. 91.

26 See Stewart Brown, Peter Nockles and James Pereiro, 2017, *The Oxford Handbook of the Oxford Movement*, Oxford: Oxford University Press.

27 John Henry Newman, 1898–1900, *Parochial and Plain Sermons*, 8 vols, London: Longmans, Green & Co., vol. IV, pp. 169–70, as discussed in Brown et al., *Oxford Handbook of the Oxford Movement*, p. 223.

28 William Palmer, 1842, *A Treatise on the Church of Christ*, London: Rivington, as discussed in Brown et al., *Oxford Handbook of the Oxford Movement*, p. 321.

29 Christopher Wordsworth, 1843, *Theophilus Anglicanus; or,*

Instruction for the young student, concerning the Church, and our own Branch of It, London: Rivington, p. 7, as discussed in Brown et al., *Oxford Handbook of the Oxford Movement*, p. 218, emphasis in original.

30 'Appendix: American Denominational Families', in Henry H. Knight III (ed.), 2010, *From Aldersgate to Azusa Street: Wesleyan, Holiness, and Pentecostal Visions of the New Creation*, Eugene, OR: Pickwick, pp. 365–68.

31 Jan Patočka, 2002, *Plato and Europe*, trans. Petr Lom, Stanford, CA: Stanford University Press, p. 222, quoted in Mary Anne Perkins, 2004, *Christendom and European Identity: The Legacy of a Grand Narrative since 1789*, Berlin, Walter de Gruyter, p. 151.

32 Guillermo Rene Cavieses Araya, 2019, 'A (New) Ecclesiology of the Anglican Communion: Rediscovering the Radical and Transnational Nature of the Anglican Communion', unpublished PhD thesis, University of Leeds, p. 442, and pointing to the discussion by Ephraim Radner, 'Children of Cain: The Oxymoron of American Catholicism', in Ephraim Radner and Philip Turner (eds), 2006, *The Fate of Communion: The Agony of Anglicanism and the Future of a Global Church*, Grand Rapids, MI: Eerdmans, pp. 25–56.

33 Araya, 'A (New) Ecclesiology', p. 11.

34 Dipesh Chakrabarty, 2000, *Provincializing Europe: Postcolonial Thought and Historical Difference*, Princeton, NJ: Princeton University Press, p. 8.

35 Chakrabarty, *Provincializing Europe*, p. 23. See extended and important 'A Note on the term "Historicism"' including footnote 67 with extensive bibliography.

36 Chakrabarty, *Provincializing Europe*, p. 7.

37 Hayden White, 1973, *Metahistory: The Historical Imagination in Nineteenth-Century Europe*, 40th Anniversary Edn 2014, Baltimore, MD: Johns Hopkins University Press, p. 12.

38 Chakrabarty, *Provincializing Europe*, p. 252.

39 Arif Dirlik, 2002, 'History Without a Center? Reflections on Eurocentrism', in Eckhardt Fuchs and Benedikt Stuchtey (eds), *Across Cultural Borders: Historiography in a Global Perspective*, Lanham, MD: Rowman & Littlefield, pp. 247–84, at 248.

40 Dirlik, 'History Without a Center?', p. 252.

41 Dirlik, 'History Without a Center?', p. 277, referring to Ashis Nandy, 1995, 'History's Forgotten Doubles', *History and Theory* 34(2), pp. 44–66.

42 James Baldwin, 1955, 'Stranger in the Village', in *Notes of a Native Son*, republished 2017, London: Penguin, p. 168–9.

43 Michel Foucault, 'Nietzsche, Genealogy, History', first published in 1971, *Hommage à Jean Hyppolite*, Paris: Presses Universitaires de France, trans. and repr. in Paul Rabinow (ed.), 1991, *The Foucault*

Reader, rev. edn, London: Penguin. For the term 'genealogy', Foucault referred to Friedrich Nietzsche's *Zur Genealogie der Moral* (1888), which accuses the 'English psychologists' of employing 'genealogy' to explain the historical development of morality – i.e. of relying on Platonist, Hegelian, positivist and utilitarian narratives. Nietzsche argues that a true and effective genealogy will detect the innovations and inventions of the powerful which constitute those things we misunderstand as normative. This is the accepted reading of Nietzsche, but Jacqueline Stevens, 'On the Morals of Genealogy', *Political Theory* 31(4) (2003), pp. 558–88, has argued that Nietzsche is not advocating but, rather, mocking the genealogical approach and that Foucault (and therefore all subsequent works calling themselves Foucaultian and genealogical) fetishized the concept by evacuating 'genealogie' of its old meanings and redefining it as something entirely different.

44 Foucault, 'Nietzsche, Genealogy, History', in Rabinow, *The Foucault Reader*, p. 82.

45 Gilles Deleuze and Félix Guattari, trans. Brian Massumi, 1988, *A Thousand Plateaus: Capitalism and Schizophrenia*, London: Athlone, p. 15, emphasis mine.

46 Deleuze and Guattari, *A Thousand Plateaus*, pp. 6–7.

47 Tim Ingold, 2000, *The Perception of the Environment: Essays on Livelihood, Dwelling and Skill*, London: Routledge, p. 140.

48 Deleuze and Guattari, *A Thousand Plateaus*, pp. 18, 12, 23, emphasis mine.

49 See the remarks of Patricia A. McAnany, 1995, *Living with the Ancestors: Kinship and Kingship in Ancient Maya Society*, revised edn 2013, Cambridge: Cambridge University Press, p. xxviii.

50 Ingold, *Perception of the Environment*, p. 145.

51 Nurit Bird-David, 1994, 'Sociality and Immediacy: Or, Past and Present Conversations on Bands', *Man*, New Series 29(3), pp. 583–603 at 597, quoted in Ingold, *Perception of the Environment*, p. 145.

3

The Ancestor Effect

Our family is pure and splendid;
humbly we inherit the blessings of our ancestors.

門第清華, 敬承先澤

Around the same time that David 'our spiritual ancestor' lived in the Middle East *c.* 1000 BC, ancestor veneration as a virtue and obligation was being promoted in China by a man whom those sharing my maiden surname 周 consider their ethnic ancestor, the Duke of Chow.[1] Helping his brother overthrow the corrupt Shang dynasty and found the Western Chow (=Zhou) dynasty, the Duke of Chow is credited with inaugurating a golden era of Chinese civilization, and establishing many of the social and political ideals that were to pervade Chinese imperial society and epitomize classical Chinese religion and cultural accomplishment. An archetype of rectitude, the Duke of Chow created a system of rituals for the harmonious ordering of society, at the heart of which was the duty of all the living to honour their ancestors. Adopting the Duke of Chow as his personal hero and inspiration, Confucius (551–479 BC) proposed an ethical philosophy based on these principles of proper etiquette and conduct (禮, *li*) aimed at regulating group life, and in particular kinship groups. He articulated an intra-family hierarchy which obliged children to honour and obey their parents, and the living to honour their ancestors. The latter obligation was fulfilled by presenting ritual offerings to the tablets or images of individual lineage ancestors at the household altar, by honouring collective ancestors at the ancestral clan hall, and by participating in communal rituals held at ancestral graves on specific dates, such as the Qingming tomb-sweeping festival. This ethical system made the cherishing of ancestors, and of the rituals to honour them, central to the cultivation of character, virtuous leadership and the maintenance of goodness.[2]

I dreaded Friday evenings growing up. While friends gathered for sleepovers with pizza, ice cream and films, I had to go straight home after school to complete an hour of Chinese character memorization, quickly gulping down my dinner before being promptly driven back to school for three hours of 'Chinese school'. Needless to say, not much learning was retained, but one lesson does remain: I learned I had an illustrious surname, Chow 周, one of the oldest among Chinese surnames, and the name of the most culturally significant of all dynasties in China's history and also, in power for around eight centuries from *c*. 1046 to *c*. 256 BC, the longest-ruling of all. I was told that anyone bearing the surname could consider him- or herself a descendant of so distinguished a family line. The origins of my lineage are the stuff of legend. According to Chinese mythology, a concubine of the legendary emperor Ku (帝嚳) in the twenty-fifth century BC called Jiang Yuan (姜嫄) was impregnated by a god after stepping in his footprint. Ashamed, she abandoned the baby, Hou Ji (后稷), in the wilderness, where various types of birds and forest animals sheltered and suckled him. Obtaining a position in the royal court, Hou Ji became a hero of agriculture, successfully developing over a hundred herbs and crops such as beans, rice and gourds, introducing millet to the Chinese as a staple grain and disseminating agricultural knowledge and practices in China. Twenty-six generations later, around the late twelfth or early eleventh century BC, his descendant, Gu Gong Danfu (Old Duke Father Dan 古公亶父), is said to have led his clan (still then going by the name of Ji) in a southward migration to the northern portion of Qishan and Fufeng counties in the present-day Shaanxi province of western China. Here, his clan expanded farming practices, established agriculture as the basis of nation-building, consolidated political power and even built a palace in the Chow Plain (Zhouyuan 周原) area, the association with which led the clan to adopt the name of Chow, 周.

'Old Duke Father Dan' assumed the name Chow Tai-Wong (周太王), and during the late Shang dynasty his grandson Chow Man Wong 周文王 (=Zhou Wen Wang in Mandarin, c. 1152–1056 BC) became a powerful count who fathered 18 sons, among them the famed Duke of Chow and his brother Chow Mou Wong 周武王 (=Zhou Wu Wang in Mandarin). In 1046 BC, Chow Mou Wong overthrew the Shang dynasty, thereby establishing the venerable Chow (=Zhou) 周 dynasty.[3]

I find it ironic that my paternal grandparents, peasant rice farmers who I daresay epitomized both the agricultural talents associated with Hou Ji and the noble virtues associated with the Duke of Chow, were among the most destitute of all people globally in the early 1900s. People like them could not be expected to boast a traceable lineage – their lives are lost to time, the stories and even the names of their parents and *their* parents having evaporated without notice like the sweat on their bodies from rigorous work in the fields. Their histories are not like those of prominent families, whose ancestors had passed imperial exams and were esteemed philosophers and civil servants, and who therefore became the founding ancestors of lineages recorded in *juhk póu* 族譜, or genealogy records. Yet, by a stroke of luck, my very distant grand-uncle discovered a genealogy book during the demolition of his father's home, possibly compiled by a clan chief in the early 1900s. Just before his death, he showed the book to another distant uncle, who copied parts of it and subsequently showed it to my parents – the only copy of the genealogy that we know of now. It tells of my direct ancestors, beginning with an unnamed founder who, due to hardships caused by climate and political unrest in the fourth year of the reign of the emperor Taizu of Song 宋太祖, that is, c. AD 972, had moved his family from Nanxiong to a district of Foshan prefecture in Guandong province called Nanhai 南海. With this act, he became a 'founding ancestor' of a new lineage. The book records the names, birth and death dates and burial locations of generations of Chow males and their wives and concubines, written in calligraphy and the literary style of Classical Chinese (古文) in use from the Chow dynasty in the twelfth century BC to the close of the

Han dynasty in the third century AD. There is no doubt as to the purpose of this *juhk póu* in the view of its compiler: the genealogy record provides evidence of the blessings of land, descendants and longevity enjoyed by the Chow line; it highlights the strict expectation to respect filial piety with utmost attention and to commit one's heart and strength to observing ancestral rites (especially on the days of Tomb Sweeping and the Winter Solstice); it emphasizes the duty to keep records so that the inheritances of land, homes, water wells, burial plots and shrines, as well as of good character and virtue, can be passed down intact from our founding ancestors to 'tens of thousands of generations' to come. Indeed, rootedness to land represents an unremitting theme in this genealogical record. Twenty generations after the founding ancestor first brought his branch of the Chow household to Foshan 佛山 in the tenth century, a Chow Man Jiu appears in the record as my ancestor who, some time between 1578 and 1637, settled in Luopo (羅鄱村), the rural village from which the Chow family would not depart for over 300 years, until the upheavals in China during the first half of the twentieth century caused a large diaspora to other parts of Asia and around the world. It is the village that my paternal family still call our *heung ha* 鄉下, ancestral village or native place.

Over the past two decades, the genealogy industry has enjoyed a rapid expansion: products and services have proliferated to meet the exponential growth in demand for ancestry research. The growth is facilitated by improved digitization of family records and driven both by reality television shows and trends in academia like the ever-increasing prominence of social and popular histories. Hard-won improvements in social and civil rights have helped to democratize the family ancestry industry from a service for an élite interested in heraldry and peerage to a common pursuit that can admit of a wide range of people from all walks of life.[4] Notably, it is the children of immigrants who are often particularly keen to pursue research into family histories. Settler immigrants in the Anglosphere (the USA, Canada, Australia, New Zealand) often wish to discover their ties to the UK, but for those whose families were displaced and stories lost by colonial processes, researching genealogy can often prove a fruitless task – and this is regrettable. Discussing the concept of the 'intergenerational self', Barnwell emphasizes the constitutive importance of inherited family knowledge which should normally be left intact: 'our sense of self is not tied solely to personally experienced events ... it is constructed from both personal history and the social cultural history in which our personal history is embedded'. Citing the work of Fivush, Bohanek and Duke at the Emory University Family Narratives Lab, Barnwell notes the positive correlation between children's knowledge of their family histories and their emotional resilience. A child's resilience is shown to derive directly from the stories that emplace them in time and space: 'By anchoring oneself in family history, one has a sense of place and security that may facilitate self-confidence and self-competence.'[5] Barnwell points to other studies and theories of collective memory (e.g. Mannheim and Halbwachs) which demonstrate the positive correlation between a healthy sense of self and the intergenerational transmission of shared knowledge.[6] Yet migration and displacement often sever these necessary intergenerational connections, disrupting the process and unmooring the self. Rediscovering one's 'roots' therefore does not always mean straightforward ancestry research, but also reconstructing severed connections to a land and past generations: 'If a family history and identity is not inherited it can be actively researched and collected, and an intergenerational self *composed retrospectively* via life writing and storytelling,' Barnwell writes.[7]

The appeal of genealogical research lies in the possibility of rooting one's sense of self in place and time, or what Ricoeur has called 'recognizing oneself in one's lineage'.[8] In this chapter, I would like to argue that both ethnic and religious genealogy offer the possibility of *'recognizing oneself in one's lineage'*. The dimensions of the past which inspire genealogists are those which are connected to their personal identity, and the same goes for Christian history as it relates to the personal identity of Christians. Of course I am not suggesting that a physical kinship of blood is the same as the spiritual ancestry posited by Christian theology and ecclesiology. But I would like to propose that kinship based on faith produces a similar effect as genealogical narratives about family, in that they are both what Richard Niebuhr has called 'internal history'. In proposing a 'historical method of Christian faith', Niebuhr draws a distinction between 'the outer history of things and the inner history of selves':

> It appears, first of all, that the data of external history are all impersonal: they are ideas, interests, movements among things ... Internal history, on the other hand, is not a story of things in juxtaposition or succession; it is personal in character. Here the final data are not elusive atoms of matter or thought but equally elusive selves ... In external history we deal with objects; in internal history our concern is with subjects.[9]

Niebuhr observes that in external history, the 'value' of a historical event or factor is measured by the effect it has on other events or factors; in internal history, on the other hand, 'value means worth for selves' – its relationship to one's self: 'whatever cannot be so valued is unimportant and may be dropped from memory'. He continues with an illustration:

> Here the death of Socrates, the birth of Lincoln, Peter's martyrdom, Luther's reform, Wesley's conversion, the landing of the Pilgrims, the granting of Magna Charta are events to be celebrated; this history calls for joy and sorrow, for days of rededication and of shriving, for tragic participation and for jubilees. *The valuable here is that which bears on the destiny of selves; not what is strongest is most important but what is most relevant to the lives of 'I's' and 'Thou's'.*[10]

In internal history, we measure the worth of events and factors not by their effect on other historical events but 'by their relevance to the destiny of the self'.[11] Niebuhr draws this contrast between external and internal history in order to make a point about the locus of revelation: Christianity is historical, yes, but it is not 'history as seen by a spectator'. Rather, the constant reference in Christianity is 'to subjective events, that is to events in the lives of subjects'.[12] But as I have already pointed out in the previous chapter, this spiritualization, the dissociation of 'internal history' from external historical data, is hopelessly naive if abstracted from the 'event' of empire and colonialism. The challenge, then, is how to make the Eurocentric 'timeline' of events in church history join up with the events of my life. If I can measure the worth of historical events not objectively but subjectively – that is, if, rather than only passively observing how my own history intersects with the history of Christianity and Europe, I instead wilfully tell the story of the latter in terms of the former – would it be possible for my story no longer to be consigned to perpetual lateness? Since this is a problem which 'bears on the destiny of selves', the question must fundamentally pertain to *narrative*, the stories we tell about ourselves.

The genre of the 'intergenerational narrative' or 'relational autobiography' has received much scholarly interest recently precisely because of its capacity to undermine the linearity and over-simplifications of strict genealogies and to acknowledge the tensions that arise from a postcolonial, postmodern condition. Histories that embrace anecdotal and personal experience and connect autobiographical elements to wider socio-political events and matters can better negotiate 'the complexities of lived moments of struggle, resisting the intrusions of chaos, disconnection, fragmentation, marginalization, and incoherence'.[13] As I wish to argue, a 'retrospective knowledge' that emphasizes the 'intergenerational self' can also help one address the burden of feeling simultaneously heir to – and excluded from – Western Christian heritage. In the rest of this chapter, I would like to explore the possibility that deploying the language of ancestry and exploiting the intergenerational framework, conflating both the biological and the spiritual as *one* story rather than two (flesh versus spirit), can address the postcolonial condition. I wish to consider what happens when I try to read my spiritual ancestry with my family ancestry in mind; what I propose is a genealogical, yet decidedly *non-linear*, approach.

I must indicate clearly what I do *not* mean by my attempt to tie religious ancestry with one's literal, biological ancestry. First of all, I acknowledge the reality that genealogy, as a hobby, is more easily enjoyed by privileged groups in society. As Nathan Lents notes for the USA, for example, wealthy white Christians with long roots in the country can more easily access their ancestral history than many African Americans for whom genealogical research could reveal not much more than the fact that, five or six generations ago, an ancestor was abducted, bound and transported to the USA to be sold into slavery. Many recent descendants of immigrants from Latin America, Asia, Africa and the Middle East also struggle to produce fruitful genealogical research from regions without well-preserved archives, which in turn furthers the perception that immigrants are not part of the pure ancestral stock of their adopted homelands.[14] Diasporic peoples are often the groups most attracted to genealogical studies, but *least* able to benefit from it: theirs are disrupted histories, lost histories, erased histories.

More problematically still, the use of genealogy to promote a connection between race and divine election for the purpose of asserting ethnic or genetic supremacy has a long and disturbing history in Western Europe. The naive remark some Christians make that we only need to know one thing about our ancestry, and that is that we are all children of Adam and Eve, completely fails to take into account how this logic – one which imposes onto biblical genealogy a contemporary application – has been used and where it has taken us. Debate rages today about whether or not 'race' is a modern invention, but racist ideologies are clearly evident in early medieval Europe through, for example, the attempt to assign continents to the descendants of Noah. Indeed, though medieval writers believed all races to be part of God's creation and descendants of Adam and Eve, yet they understood some to be worse than others, especially the descendants of Ham, the cursed son of Noah. In the seventh century, Isidore of Seville created a tripartite diagram commonly known as the 'T-O' map to show how Noah's descendants repopulated the earth: Europe is populated by the descendants of Japheth, Asia by Shem, and Africa by the cursed Ham. Over the course of the following centuries, the racial identities of Shem, Japheth and Ham settled onto the geographical designations of Asia, Europe and Africa, so that the blackness of Africans became linked with the curse of Ham. The entire medieval genre of *mappae mundi* is founded on this racial configuration, reflecting an ideology in Western thought which considered some races more deformed and sinful than others.[15] We need only acknowledge here the unspeakable horrors committed in the name of Christianity on the basis of these racial constructs. At times the results have been less evil but the ideology just as dangerous. Alan Koman claims that hundreds of millions of people alive today have genealogical links to the 24 prominent European men and women he lists – such as the most recently deceased among them, Sir John Stewart of Balveny, first Earl of Atholl (d. 1512) – through whom they are also the direct descendants of saints. By his calculations, 122 European saints are the direct ancestors of a vast number of Europeans and Americans today.[16]

Let me be absolutely clear that the ideological conflation of faith and ethnicity, and of religious genealogy with family ancestry, in order to serve nationalist, racist or supremacist agendas, is categorically *not* what my project proposes to do. On the contrary, the fact is that my religious genealogy (European) and family genealogy (Chinese) are usually confined to entirely separate spheres, the subject of distinct discourses, and perceived as having nothing to do with each other – unlike what can be said of the swathes of ethnically white Europeans and Americans whom Koman claims can trace, with convenient coherence, both their ethnic and religious lineage to medieval saints. For me the task of melding together my religious and ethnic heritage therefore represents a task in joining up two fragmented and disjointed parts of my identity. To fuse into a more coherent whole the memory of my non-Western biological ancestors with my Western religious heritage means to articulate an intergenerational family history which can help me claim a right to the Christian heritage of the West – effectively to write my non-Western family lineage into a Western religious lineage. The classic work first published in 1993 as *La religion pour mémoire* by Hervieu-Léger, an anthropologist of religion, is fundamental to my proposal here. Her much-cited thesis centres on the observation that all religions require collective memory for their survival, whereby groups and individuals must see themselves as part of a chain of memory, a 'lineage of belief'.[17] In traditional societies, this collective memory was contained within the structures, language and everyday observances. But with modernity – defined by Hervieu-Léger as urbanization, individualization, rationalization, pluralization and institutional differentiation – societies no longer function as sites of collective memory that reproduce what is inherited. Instead, modern societies cause the fragmentation and 'crumbling' of collective memory: 'The fact of being able to *differentiate* between a family memory, a religious memory, a national memory, a class memory and so on is already a token of having left behind the pure world of tradition.' Hervieu-Léger points to the '*differentiation* of total society memory into a plurality of *specialized* circles of memory'.[18] The issue with today's plural societies is not the amount or type of information available, but whether people have the ability to organize it healthily 'by relating it to a lineage to which they spontaneously see themselves as belonging'. The problem of transmitting knowledge and memory from one generation to the next, she continues, 'is structurally linked to the *collapse of the framework of collective memory which provided every individual with the possibility of a link between what comes before and his or her own actual experience*'.[19] In her view, secularization in modern societies should not be attributed to a loss of belief, but to a broken chain of memory. 'Elective fraternities', the recasting of memory and reinventions of tradition which restore a chain of memory, can compensate for the collapse of traditional vehicles for carrying collective memory.[20] Elective fraternities emerge where the imperative to re-establish identity is especially pressing. Thus, she speaks of 'ethno-religion' as the chain of memory reinvented, founded on choice and dependent on the strength of emotional ties. The support that her ideas lend to my experiment comes into focus when she argues that the convergence between the ethnic and the religious can be easily made because they share the same genealogical outlook:

> The particular attraction that operates between what is ethnic and what is religious springs from the fact that the one and the other establish a social bond on the basis of assumed genealogy, on the one hand, a *naturalized genealogy* (*because related to soil and to blood*), and a *symbolized genealogy* (*because constituted through belief* in and reference to a myth and a source), on the other.[21]

So the convergence between the naturalized genealogy based on blood and the symbolized genealogy based on the myth of shared origins allows a social group to 'imaginatively project a lineage of belief', a chain of memory.[22] For a diasporic group existing in a plural, postmodern society of fragmented and hybrid identities, such convergence represents a crucial act of reintegration and offers the possibility for the group to 'write itself into a history that bypasses itself'.[23] This possibility is precisely what I seek to discover in the second half of my book. 'What matters here', writes Hervieu-Léger, 'is not the actual substance of belief but the ingenuity, the imaginative perception of the link' which binds an individual to a lineage of belief:[24] here, we can certainly hear the echoes of Niebuhr's '*not what is strongest is most important but what is most relevant to the lives of "I's" and "Thou's"*'. Hervieu-Léger thinks of this in utopian terms: the making of memory, the construction of an 'imagined continuity', can push beyond the social conventions of the present, standing in protest against the 'misfortunes, the dangers, and the uncertainties of the present' which are caused by fragmentation, heterogeneity and hybridity.[25] In MacNeill's analysis:

> They allow the rootless oblivious individual to reposition himself or herself within a wider society through chains of memory. These chains of memory link the individual biographical memory to newly-made community collective memories which, in turn, are connected to the collective

memory of the whole society. 'The personal narrative is bridged to the grand narrative' for it answers the human need for coherence between the history of mankind and the destiny of the individual. Utopias work *ad intra* and *ad extra*.[26]

Hervieu-Léger's arguments permit me to explore how ethnic (naturalized) genealogy and religious (symbolized) genealogy 'combine in re-establishing a sense of "we" and of "our" which modernity has once fractured and created a nostalgia for'.[27] It is a clear signal that there is a way forward to challenge the identitarian and exclusivist assumptions behind the '*our*' when 'our Christian heritage' is invoked.

Moving on to the application of this theory to 'our Christian heritage' and genealogical consciousness, the first thing we will note is that where ethnic ancestors have been discussed with regard to religious dimensions, they – the biological ancestors of 'soil and blood' – have usually materialized as 'problems' in Christianity's encounter with native communities and practices.[28] The 'problem' of ancestors refers, of course, to the practice of ancestral veneration common in many cultures, including my own Chinese tradition which I described at the beginning of this chapter. In the encounter between Christianity and the Chinese people during the seventeenth and eighteenth centuries, it was the rites of ancestor veneration that generated the most explosive debate, known as the Chinese Rites Controversy, and which continues to be seen today as one of the great failures in the history of Sino-European relations.[29] Matteo Ricci (1552–1610) and the Jesuits viewed these rites as purely honorary and ceremonial, arguing that the Confucian emphasis on filial piety through offering meats and bowing before ancestral tablets was compatible with Christian belief. In doing so, they gained much respect and many converts among the Confucian literati. However, the Dominicans and Franciscans took the opposite view, with Juan Bautista Morales arguing that because ancestral rites were offered to the spirits of one's ancestors, they therefore involved idolatry and superstition. Controversy erupted and continued, involving as many as eight popes and several European universities. Pope Clement XI's decree in 1704, confirmed by the subsequent bulls *Ex Illa Die* (1715) and *Ex Quo Singulari* (1742), decisively banned ancestral rites. Many Jesuits refused to heed the bulls, leading Rome to suppress the Society of Jesus in 1773. The controversy antagonized Emperor Kangxi, who had initially been greatly disposed toward Western learning and preaching, and he issued an imperial edict in 1721 banning Christian mission to China. With the rapid expansion of commercial trading with the West during the nineteenth century, influential Protestant missionaries who gained access to China reiterated the opposition to ancestral veneration. At the First Conference of Protestant Missionaries in China held in Shanghai in 1877, against arguments from William Martin that ancestor rites contained few elements of idolatry, Hudson Taylor vigorously declared that the toleration of such rites would be treason against Christianity and won an overwhelming victory in his insistence that converts to Christianity must abandon ancestral veneration.[30]

Reflection on filial piety as an essential element in Confucian-based Chinese culture led the Catholic Church to reverse its position in 1939 with the declaration *Plane Compertum Est*, which permits Catholics to bow their heads and perform gestures of respect before ancestral tablets. The Catholic Church has since composed eucharistic liturgies incorporating elements of ancestral veneration for use during the Chinese festivals that feature ancestral veneration, like the Tomb-Sweeping Day and Chinese New Year, as well as festivals remembering the dead in the Western liturgical calendar, notably All Saints' Day and All Souls' Day.[31] Catholic teaching today generally recognizes Chinese rites of ancestral veneration as an appropriate fulfilment of Chinese filial piety and the fourth commandment, and as a gathering of prayers for the Church suffering (those in purgatory) and the Church triumphant (those in heaven) within the communion of saints. Elements of ancestral veneration which had once been dismissed as folk superstition have been adopted in church practice. For example, wooden ancestral tablets containing names of ancestors before which joss sticks are burned can now be included alongside invocations to ask the prayers of Our Lady and of angels. At Mass on days like the Lunar New Year, incense, flowers, fruit and wine can be offered while passages from the book of Sirach expressing honour to ancestors are read, prayers of intercession offered, and bowing as a sign of respect to ancestors are performed. By contrast, Protestant traditions – for the most part opposed to commemorative liturgies and offering prayers for the dead anyway – have remained generally reluctant to admit of any outward gestures such as incense burning, bowing and offerings of food which may have the appearance of idolatrous worship.

What concerns me here is not the compatibility of ancestral rites with Christian faith, or even how they can be useful to the indigenization or Sinicization of Christian practice, but how ethnic ancestors can fit into the genealogical mentality of Christian historicism. We recall Hervieu-Léger's argument that, in the face of crumbling collective memories, religious and ethnic identities actually share a common genealogical outlook and can fuse together and become inseparable, thereby reintegrating circles of memory which modernity has rendered distinct and renewing a lineage of belief for those who are bypassed in dominant histories. Chris White's research on the recent phenomenon of constructing distinctly Christian ancestral halls and homes in the coastal county of Huian in South Fujian offers practical insight into this argument. He notes that, as Protestant converts often influence family members to follow them in their faith, Christianity can begin to operate along the lines of a lineage organization. In south Fujian, it is not unusual to find Christians who can trace their religious heritage to ancestors five, six or more generations back: in their case, the construction of Christian ancestral halls and homes reflects not just devout belief but, more importantly, the assertion of a family line's Christian heritage.[32] In Huian, Christian ancestral halls are used for the whole range of the usual lineage activities (rituals for ancestor worship and funerals, and also more mundane activities such as family gatherings, and civic, business or philanthropic affairs) as well as for devotional meetings such as Bible studies and prayer meetings. They always feature the customary portraits of deceased ancestors and couplets for invoking blessings, but also clearly signal Christian identity via symbols like a cross or slogans like 'Christ is my Lord'. The most interesting expression of Christian faith is the presence of *dui lian* 對聯, or couplets, which decorate the pillars and doorways. In Chinese tradition, couplets serve an important function both as blessings to guarantee harmony and to bring good luck, and as totems to ward off evil and danger. They can also be used as slogans to convey both political dissent or political correctness and to promote moral and ethical messages. In the Christian ancestral halls studied by Chris White, Christian-inspired couplets are permanently etched on doorways or painted on pillars to convey the values and actions by which the family wishes to be characterized. Examples of these include:[33]

門第清華敬承先澤　堂家雍睦叩頌神恩
A family, pure and splendid, respectfully inherits ancestral blessings
A household, esteemed and harmonious, reverently praises God's grace

基督福音萬代傳　十架救恩千載頌
The gospel of Christ is proclaimed to all generations
The salvation of the cross is praised for a thousand years

救恩頌歌播五洲　福音鐘聲傳四海
Praise songs of salvation spread out to the five continents
The gospel's ringing bells sound throughout the four seas

百福千祥祈主佑　萬紫千紅感神恩
Pray for the Lord's blessings of immeasurable good fortune
Thank God's grace for innumerable gifts aglow with colour

基督聖德千秋頌　十架救恩萬年長
The sacred virtues of Christ are forever praised
The saving grace of the cross endures for all eternity

Christian couplets in ancestral halls and homes put faith and ancestry within the same frame, instructing descendants to understand their generational bonds as a lineage of belief. White concludes that for generational Christian families in South Fujian, their religious identity is not so much a matter of private faith as a family inheritance.

White's observations of what Hervieu-Léger would call an 'ethno-religion' assume a markedly pre-modern framework in which beliefs, memory, language and observances still operate within a coherent, family-based, ethnically homogenous paradigm. But can the fusion of ethnic ancestry with religious inheritance help 'the rootless oblivious individual to reposition him or herself' in the face of broken, fragmented or lost lineages?[34] And how can the fusion of ethnic and religious ancestry be a good thing if the terms of religious inheritance are predicated on Western history? Or if the reason that ethnic heritage and Christian heritage even have anything to do with each other at all is because of a prior relationship of power determined by colonialism? How does such a fusion enable the 'personal narrative [to be] bridged to the grand narrative' when between the ethnic and the religious lies an uneven relationship of power?[35]

The answer to this, in my view, lies in the 'ancestor effect' we discussed earlier and what invoking the memory of ancestors actually achieves. Fischer's study, we will recall, tested the hypothesis that, because our ancestors generally managed to overcome a multitude of personal and societal problems such as wars, bereavement and hardship, thinking about them conjures positive sentiments about their sacrifices, perseverance and success, and in turn induces increased levels of control, motivation and capacity for approaching problems. His team identified the positive psychological effects of 'ancestor salience' – thinking about both concrete and abstract ancestors – which they termed the 'ancestor effect'. Their study focused on identifying the 'ancestor effect', but what interests me equally is the hypothesis that had inspired it, the narrative of ancestors overcoming challenges and problems. Storytelling about the tribulations that our ancestors faced and overcame is precisely what appears to be at work in the fusion of ethnic and religious identity studied by White. He noticed that many ancestral halls in South Fujian have been given names such as Canaan 迦南 (*jia nan*), Bethel 伯特利 (*bo te li*), or Emmanuel (*yi ma nei li*). Often these are not just unthinking appropriations from biblical literature, but instead express a clan's collective memory. For example, the eldest surviving male descendant of a founding ancestor, a pastor in Huian, explains the choice of 'Canaan' as the name for an ancestral hall in a poem he wrote in traditional calligraphy, now displayed on the wall. The poem rehearses the difficult history and struggles of the previous generations who lived through the various revolutions in modern Chinese history, leading eventually to the construction of their 'promised land'.[36] In this fusion of family and Christian heritage, the narrative of ancestral faith in the face of adversity is the central message delivered to the descendant. The ancestor effect works, in other words, only if the descendant can appreciate the link between religious history, family history and the relevance of both to his or her own life.

Autobiography, as Eakin has stressed in his study, is 'the steady rhythm of the altercation' between 'two parallel streams of event, that of public history on the one hand and that of private life on the other'.[37] Eakin, quoting Wilhelm Dilthey, writes that we 'are historical beings first, before we are observers of history, and only because we are the former do we become the latter'.[38] Therefore, he continues, 'It is this radical stress on the individual as the site where history is experienced, transacted, and known that lies behind Dilthey's bold claim for autobiography as "the germinal cell of history".'[39] The fragmented, conflicted condition of postcolonial belatedness can therefore not be repaired so long as the 'personal' history of my family lineage exists as a separate domain from the 'religious' heritage of Western Christianity. The ethnic minority Christian must, following Eakin, investigate her relationship to Western Christian heritage via the 'active, conscious construction of the point of intersection between the individual's life and the larger movement of history of which it is a part'.[40] The methodological approach I take in the next three chapters is therefore to engage autobiographically with Britain's

Christian heritage, to encourage 'the imaginative perception of the link' which joins my life story to an external 'history of Western Christianity'. I resist the view, observed by Eakin, that 'history is to be encountered abroad, in Italy, in Armenia, in Czechoslovakia' – and for my purposes, I would add, in France with Charlemagne and his monasteries or in England with King James and his Bible, and so on – and 'that history is something distinct from us that we can get mixed up in or not, depending on our fates'. Rather, Eakin asserts, 'the lesson of the journey into the country of history ... is that history dwells in us'.[41] Thus the chapters that follow are an experiment in thinking about encounters with English church history with great *personal* interest, as if narrating the story of my life and my forebears. By doing this I am not attempting to propose a method or rule that can be generally and widely applied, nor am I writing a revisionist history. But, borrowing Watson's phrase, this is an effort to use autobiography in order to counteract the dominance of 'genealogical pedigrees', to 'destabilize the linear narrative with the complexity of self-experience'.[42] I hope to discover whether Western Christian heritage can be anything other than an impenetrable historical chain to which I shall be for ever late, and explore how the *subjectification* of church history – embedding my own narrative and my own self as the very site of these histories – might encourage 'the liberation of possible identities from past fixity'.[43] This, I believe, is a way to demonstrate practically the reintegration of fragmented pieces which Hervieu-Léger suggested is possible when the 'personal narrative is bridged to the grand narrative', when a group bypassed in dominant histories writes its own story into it. The experiment demands that I suspend (at least temporarily) the expectation to historicize with detachment and objectivity, principles to which I have signed up as a professional historian. It demands I stop viewing genealogy as a linear continuum in which predecessors take up a baton and pass it on to their descendants, and instead view genealogy as a relational and intergenerational story in which the line of descent is always the site of personal encounter. It demands that I replace a historicizing approach to Western Christian heritage with relationality. It demands resistance to the 'myth of monolithic power' so often accompanying Western Christian heritage, the assumption of its inherent superiority and the potential to master it as a subject – what Willie Jennings has called 'white self-sufficient masculinity'.[44] It demands I destabilize 'the presence of the tap root, the canon, the standard, the patented', and highlight instead the entangled web of personal relationships and experiences which have served to cement the tap root, canon, standard and patented in my life.[45] The aim is to disrupt the historicism that perpetually makes me a tourist of English heritage; to trouble established hierarchies that estrange me from things that happened in Europe before I arrived; to assume insider knowledge rather than outsider.[46] Ultimately, it means manoeuvring through my feelings of alienation by always and unwaveringly recalling the one thing from which I am lucky enough never to have felt alienated: family. So let me begin the next part of my book with this passage from the Prologue of Anita Diamont's *The Red Tent*:

Had I been asked to speak of it, I would have begun with the story of the generation that raised me, which is the only place to begin. If you want to understand any woman you must first ask about her mother and then listen carefully … The more a daughter knows the details of her mother's life – without flinching or whining – the stronger the daughter.[47]

Notes

1 He is more popularly known as the Duke of Zhou, which is the more widely used Mandarin pinyin translation of his name, but I am inclined, in this exploration of my genealogical history, to use instead the Cantonese transliteration 'Chow' for the character 周, my maiden surname which I share with him.

2 C. K. Yang, 1961, *Religion in Chinese Society*, Berkeley, CA: University of California Press; Francis L. K. Hsu, 1967, *Under the Ancestors' Shadow: Kinship, Personality, and Social Mobility in China*, 2nd rev. edn, New York: Columbia University Press; Hugh Baker, 1979, *Chinese Family and Kinship*, London: Macmillan; William Lakos, 2010, *Chinese Ancestor Worship: A Practice and Ritual Oriented Approach*

to *Understanding Chinese Culture*, Newcastle upon Tyne: Cambridge Scholars; Paulin Batairwa Kubuya, 2018, *Meaning and Controversy within Chinese Ancestor Religion*, London: Palgrave Macmillan.

3 Edward Shaughnessy, 1999, 'Chapter 5: Western Zhou History', in Michael Loewe and Edward L. Shaughnessy (eds), *The Cambridge History of Ancient China: From the Origins of Civilization to 221 BC*, Cambridge: Cambridge University Press, pp. 292–351; Edward L. Shaughnessy, 1992, *Sources of Western Zhou History: Inscribed Bronze Vessels*, Oakland, CA: University of California Press. For an overview of the archaeological remains at Zhouyuan, see Jessica Rawson, 1999, 'Chapter 6: Western Zhou Archaeology', in Loewe and Shaughnessy, *The Cambridge History of Ancient China*, pp. 352–449, and more recently, the Joint Excavation Team at Zhouyuan, 2017, 'The 2014–2015 Excavations of the Zhouyuan Site in Baoji, Shaanxi', *Chinese Archaeology* 17, pp. 32–43.

4 Ashley Barnwell, 2017, 'Locating an Intergenerational Self in Postcolonial Family Histories', *Life Writing* 14(4), pp. 485–93.

5 Barnwell, 'Locating an Intergenerational Self', p. 488, citing Robyn Fivush, Jennifer G. Bohanek and Marshall Duke, 'The Intergenerational Self: Subjective Perspective and Family History', in Fabio Sani (ed.), 2008, *Self Continuity: Individual and Collective Perspectives*, New York: Psychology Press, pp. 131–43 at 135.

6 Barnwell, 'Locating an Intergenerational Self', citing Karl Mannheim, 1972, 'The Problem of Generations', in Paul Kecskemeti (ed.), *Karl Mannheim: Essays*, London: Routledge, pp. 276–322, and Maurice Halbwachs, *On Collective Memory*, Chicago, IL: University of Chicago Press, 1992.

7 Barnwell, 'Locating an Intergenerational Self'.

8 Paul Ricoeur, 2004, *Parcours de la Reconnaissance*, trans. David Pellauer, 2005, *The Course of Recognition*, Cambridge, MA: Harvard University Press, p. 194.

9 H. Richard Niebuhr, 1941, *The Meaning of Revelation*, rev. edn, 1968, Louisville, KY: Westminster John Knox Press, p. 33.

10 Niebuhr, *The Meaning of Revelation*, p. 36, emphasis mine.

11 Niebuhr, *The Meaning of Revelation*, p. 36.

12 Niebuhr, *The Meaning of Revelation*, p. 38.

13 Arthur P. Bochner, 2016, 'Putting Meanings into Motion: Autoethnography's Existential Calling', in Stacy Holman Jones, Tony E. Adams and Carolyn Ellis (eds), 2016, *Handbook of Autoethnography*, Abingdon: Routledge, 2016, pp. 50–6 at 52.

14 Nathan Lents, 2018, 'The Meaning and Meaninglessness of Genealogy', *Psychology Today* [online]. Available at: www.psychologytoday.com/gb/blog/beastly-behavior/201801/the-meaning-and-meaninglessness-genealogy, (accessed 17.08.2021).

15 See David M. Goldenberg, 2003, *The Curse of Ham: Race and*

Slavery in Early Judaism, Christianity, and Islam, Princeton, NJ: Princeton University Press.

16 Alan J. Koman, 2010, *A Who's Who of Your Ancestral Saints*, Baltimore, MD: Genealogical Publishing Company.

17 Danièle Hervieu-Léger, 1993, *La religion pour mémoire*, Paris: Cerf, trans Simon Lee, 2000, *Religion as a Chain of Memory*, Cambridge: Polity, p. 125.

18 Hervieu-Léger, trans. Lee, *Religion as a Chain of Memory*, p. 127.

19 Hervieu-Léger, trans. Lee, *Religion as a Chain of Memory*, p. 130.

20 Hervieu-Léger, trans. Lee, *Religion as a Chain of Memory*, pp. 149ff.

21 Hervieu-Léger, trans. Lee, *Religion as a Chain of Memory*, p. 157, emphasis mine.

22 Hervieu-Léger, *Religion as a Chain of Memory*, p. 123.

23 Here I have used the translation by Brigitte Maréchal and Sami Zemni, 2013, 'Conclusion: Analyzing Contemporary Sunnite–Shiite Relationships', in Brigitte Maréchal and Sami Zemni (eds), *The Dynamics of Sunni–Shia Relationships: Doctrine, Transnationalism, Intellectuals and the Media*, London: Hurst and Company, pp. 215–42 at 240, of Hervieu-Léger, *La religion pour mémoire*, pp. 235–6.

24 Hervieu-Léger, trans. Lee, p. 81.

25 Hervieu-Léger, trans. Lee, p. 145.

26 Dominique MacNeill, 1998, 'Extending the Work of Halbwachs: Danièle Hervieu-Léger's Analysis of Contemporary Religion', *Durkheimian Studies*, 1998, New Series vol. 4, pp. 73–86 at 80, quoting Hervieu-Léger, 'Present-day Emotional Renewals: The End of Secularization or the End of Religion?', in W. H. Swatos (ed.), 1993, *A Future for Religion: New Paradigms for Social Analysis*, London: Sage, p. 146.

27 Hervieu-Léger, trans. Lee, *Religion as a Chain of Memory*, p. 157.

28 See Introduction, 'Are Ancestors a Problem?', in Paulin Batairwa Kubuya, 2018, *Meaning and Controversy within Chinese Ancestor Religion*, Basingstoke: Palgrave Macmillan. See also William Lakos, 2010, *Chinese Ancestor Worship: A Practice and Ritual Oriented Approach to Understanding Chinese Culture*, Newcastle-upon-Tyne: Cambridge Scholars Publishing.

29 Eugenio Menegon, 2009, *Ancestors, Virgins, and Friars: Christianity as a Local Religion in Late Imperial China*, Cambridge, MA: Harvard University Press.

30 H. K. Yeung, 2008, 'Ancestors: 1. Chinese Perspective', in William A. Dyrness and Veli-Matti Kärkkäinen (eds), *Global Dictionary of Theology: A Resource for the Worldwide Church*, Downers Grove, IL: Inter-Varsity Press Academic, pp. 28–31.

31 See for example the discussion about the Catholic Ancestor Memorial Liturgy for Church and Family Use issued by the Chinese Bishops Conference in Taipei in 1974 by Celia Chua, 2006, 'Mary,

Chinese Ancestor Veneration, and the Communion of Saints', unpublished Doctorate of Sacred Theology thesis, International Marian Research Institute, pp. 58ff.

32 Chris White, 2017, 'Sacred Dwellings: Protestant Ancestral Halls and Homes in Southern Fujian', in Yangwen Zheng (ed.), 2017, *Sinicizing Christianity*, Studies in Christian Mission 49, Leiden: Brill, 2017, pp. 233–60.

33 Couplets taken from White, 'Sacred Dwellings', p. 246; translations are my own.

34 MacNeill, 'Extending the Work of Halbwachs', p. 80.

35 MacNeill, 'Extending the Work of Halbwachs', quoting Danièle Hervieu-Léger, 1993, 'Present-day Emotional Renewals: The End of Secularization or the End of Religion?', in W. H. Swatos (ed.), *A Future for Religion: New Paradigms for Social Analysis*, London: Sage, pp. 129–48 at 146.

36 White, 'Sacred Dwellings', p. 248.

37 Paul John Eakin, 1992, *Touching the World: Reference in Autobiography*, Princeton, NJ: Princeton University Press, p. 143.

38 Eakin, *Touching the World*, p. 142, quoting Wilhelm Dilthey as quoted by David Carr, 1991, *Time, Narrative, and History*, Bloomington, IN: Indiana University Press, p. 4.

39 Eakin, *Touching the World*, p. 142.

40 Eakin, *Touching the World*, p. 143.

41 Eakin, *Touching the World*, p. 178.

42 Watson, Julia, 2017, 'Ordering the Family: Genealogy as Autobiographical Pedigree', in Sidonie Smith and Julia Watson (eds), 2017, *Life Writing in the Long Run: A Smith & Watson Autobiography Studies Reader*, Ann Arbor, MI: University of Michigan Library [online]. Available at: https://quod.lib.umich.edu/m/maize/mpub973 9969/1:11/--life-writing-in-the-long-run-a-smith-watson-autobiogra phy?rgn=div1;view=fulltext (accessed 17.08.21). Reference is made to Louis Renza, 1980, 'The Veto of the Imagination: A Theory of Autobiography', in James Olney (ed.), *Autobiography: Essays Theoretical and Critical*, Princeton, NJ: Princeton University Press, pp. 277–9.

43 See the contrasts drawn between 'autobiography' and 'genealogy' in Watson, 'Ordering the Family'.

44 Willie James Jennings, 2020, *After Whiteness: An Education in Belonging*, Grand Rapids, MI: Eerdmans, p. 6.

45 'Rhizome', in Bill Ashcroft, Gareth Griffiths and Helen Tiffin, 2007, *Post-Colonial Studies: The Key Concepts*, 2nd edn, London: Routledge, pp. 190–1.

46 See Jones et al., *Handbook of Autoethnography* on the 'Purposes of autoethnography', pp. 32ff.

47 'Prologue', in Anita Diamant, 2001, *The Red Tent*, London: Macmillan.

4

Ancestral Hardship and the Western Christian Canon

When drinking from a well, remember the source.

飲水思源

My mother was born into a well-off family living in the Western District where, over one hundred years earlier in 1841 on a site named Possession Point, Commodore Sir Gordon Bremer and Captain Sir Edward Belcher of the Royal Navy had raised the Union Jack to claim Hong Kong for Britain. Exceptionally among the Chinese in those days, my maternal grandfather was literate in English and ran a business importing foreign provisions. His business was so profitable that he could move his family into a flat in the prestigious area known as the Mid-Levels, favoured by expatriates including the Governor of Hong Kong. In a clear display of the family's sophistication, my mother called her parents 'Daddy' and 'Mummy' rather than the Chinese 'ah Ba' and 'ah Ma'. As children, my mother and her siblings would entertain themselves around the table after dinner by cutting out pictures from the boxes and tins of foreign goods their father brought home: canned sardines, Heinz baked beans, Danish butter cookies. The children were served by several maids, and my mother's mother was a lady of leisure, playing mah-jong by day and revelling in parties with other wealthy ladies by night.

But when my mother was ten, her father suffered a stroke which paralysed the right side of his body. Unable to work for over a year and facing the prospect of permanent disability, he watched helplessly as his business suffered and his wealth evaporated. Whenever his health allowed, he tried to recover the losses by manning shop stalls himself. Two years later, while managing the sale of goods at a park on a blustery cold day, he suffered a fatal aneurism. He had HK$50, equivalent to £5 today – it was all that he had left for his wife.

Overnight my grandmother took up a variety of jobs, which, for someone of her previous position, were considered truly humiliating: she worked as a nanny and became a cook for a wealthy family, she served drinks to businessmen in a night-club, and she even took up a job as a blackjack card dealer at a casino in Macau. My grandmother quickly realized that gambling was an easy way to pay off mounting debts. Success at the mah-jong table, at the Happy Valley Racetrack and at the casinos meant barbeque pork for dinner, her children learned; losses meant she'd lie to neighbours and relatives to borrow money. The family's ruin became undeniable when they were put under social welfare, with a 'Madame Choy' coming around regularly for monitoring visits and bringing used clothing for the children. From the nightly diversion of games and crafts they had once enjoyed, now the children per-formed manual labour, assembling plastic flower petals onto stalks and bringing them to artificial flower factories to earn a few dollars. Their home was divided up to house tenants, and six siblings crammed into one bedroom while my mother slept in the small kitchen at the back of the flat. The sound of loan sharks routinely shouting threats outside the window made my mother desperate to leave; only exhaustion prevented her from running away from home.

No wonder then that my mother tells me the story of her life firmly within the tradition of *Bildungsroman*, the Ger-man term referring to a story (*Roman*) about formation or development (*Bildung*), of the process of 'becoming'. The plot follows a conventional series of stages: the protagonist leaves home, encounters a dilemma, undergoes trial and testing but, thanks to friendship, wise counsel and moral virtue, ultimately reaches a pinnacle of growth and enjoys peace and success.[1] My mother's testing came in many forms. Apart from a diffi-cult home life, she felt the precariousness of the one thing that could rescue her from poverty – an education. In the days prior to free, compulsory education and as one of five girls in the family, her schooling was deemed less important than that of her two brothers. She was so happy to receive a government grant to attend school that she didn't mind the daily embarrassment of being seen in uniform at the market buying eggs and fish for the family dinner and carrying shopping bags – the job of servants, not schoolgirls. Despite consistently coming first in examinations and winning academic prizes, my mother was expected to leave school to take up full-time employment. But her success at a secondary school founded by the London Missionary Society had given her a different ambition: she desperately wanted to go to university. In the summer term as Form 6 drew to a close, my mother withdrew daily to the Hong Kong Zoological and Botanical Gardens and prayed the prayer of Gideon. One clear and sunny day, she asked God to bring a cloud if it was his will that she continue with her studies. A cloud appeared and home she went with an announcement to her family: she would enrol in university while fulfilling her duty by contributing HK$400 to the household each month, equivalent to her earnings if she had become employed after secondary school. When exam results were released, she obtained a place at the prestigious University of Hong Kong, which she took up along with multiple jobs, government loans and grants. She went on to graduate with honours, became a teacher herself, and was eventually promoted to school inspector. This surely is a *Bildungsroman* if ever there was one: looking back at the trials in her youth, she reflects, 'Out of this darkest moment I became who I am today. I think it's an amazing story, because the only way to get out of the poverty cycle in Hong Kong was through an education.'

Of course, a by-product of this development was her Anglicization. Judging from the books on her shelves, one could be forgiven for thinking that all theological writers must be an Anglophone with a two-syllable surname – Charles Spurgeon, Oswald Chambers, A. W. Tozer, Andrew Murray, C. S. Lewis – which is perfectly reasonable given that my mother's major religious influences were her British missionary teachers in secondary school and the British-educated professors involved with the Christian Association at the University of Hong Kong. But such writers are not important to my mother just because they represent the classics of Western evangelical spirituality. Rather, they are important because, in the solace of each night in the small kitchen where she slept, those books spoke about a good God, answered her doubts, schooled her in prayer. By this account, Harold Bloom would feel justified in his defence of the traditional Western canon against attack by the 'School of Resentment', whom he might call the 'School of Woke' today were he still alive: scholars of the New Historicism, post-structuralism, Marxist Studies, Feminist Studies, African-American Studies, and we can update his list to include now Critical Race Studies, War Studies, Postcolonial Studies, Queer Studies, Latinx Studies, and so on. Against them, Bloom protests that they have misunderstood the main authority of the Western canon, wherein its 'dignity' lies: contrary to popular assumption, although canons always do indirectly serve the social, political, and even spiritual concerns of the wealthier classes, yet 'The Western canon does not exist in order to augment preexisting societal elites'.[2] Rather, reading the canon has an essential 'solitary aspect':[3]

> The true use of Shakespeare or of Cervantes, of Homer or of Dante, of Chaucer or of Rabelais, is to augment one's own growing inner self ... All that the Western Canon can bring one is the proper use of one's own solitude, that solitude whose final form is one's confrontation with one's own mortality.[4]

The canon is impossible without 'the introspective consciousness, free to contemplate itself' – and, Bloom insists, 'to put it most bluntly, neither are we'.[5] So Bloom argues that the contemporary habit of taking greater interest in the political and social 'context' of a literary work rather than the 'text' itself reflects 'a generation made impatient with deep reading'.[6]

'Deep reading' my mother certainly has done, her character and vocation shaped deeply by English evangelical writings. But now let us turn to the prescient comments of Frantz Fanon:

> the native intellectual has thrown himself greedily upon western culture. Like adopted children who only stop investigating the new family framework at the moment when a minimum nucleus of security crystallises in their psyche, the native intellectual will try to make European culture his own. He will not be content to get to know Rabelais and Diderot, Shakespeare and Edgar Allen Poe; he will bind them to his intelligence as closely as possible.[7]

In her solitary reading of spiritual classics, her ingestion of the works of white Englishmen to feed her consciousness, nurture her formation and assure her mental survival amid adversity, the texts of Western Christian civilization have become inseparable from my mother's intellectual and spiritual life, the writers the people she calls her forefathers and mentors though she has never met them. This is the issue with which this chapter is concerned, perhaps most provocatively captured by the term 'colonial cringe', used by Australian academics to denote the deference shown by the colonized to the culture and institutions of the British metropole.[8] I would like to offer my reflections with reference to one of my mother's most treasured possessions. Over 50 years after her graduation from secondary school, my mother still cherishes the school hymn book containing the English hymns taught to pupils by teachers deployed to Hong Kong by the London Missionary Society. The classic hymns in the repertory of English church music, so integral to her Christian conversion, devotion and life, help me in this chapter to consider the question of colonial deference to the Western canon in light of familial experience. First, I will introduce the postcolonial dilemma via a discussion of No. 12 in my mother's hymn book, 'All Glory, Laud and Honour'. Then I will deploy 'ancestral feeling' to explore No. 43, 'Who Would True Valour See', contemplating what the hymn means in the light of my family history. I close the chapter with brief thoughts on No. 45 in my mother's hymn book, 'Lead, Kindly Light'.

In turning to No. 12 in their hymn books, 'All Glory, Laud and Honour', in the run-up to Palm Sunday every year, the 1,000 schoolgirls standing in the assembly hall wearing their Chinese 'cheongsam' dresses most likely did not know they were singing a medieval hymn with deep-seated imperial and martial overtones – that the triumph of which they were singing was not only the spiritual triumph of Christ riding into Jerusalem but also the regal triumph asserted by rulers in the Middle Ages. After existing for several centuries as a simple 'mobile act of worship' involving the waving of palms and shouts of 'hosanna', the Palm Sunday ritual in the Western Church underwent a major dramatization in the eighth century when it became associated with royal processions following military victories.[9] Returning from military victories against the Lombards in 774, an entourage of nobles, clerics and armed forces rode into Rome with the king of the Franks, Charlemagne, at the head, received by Pope Hadrian I, ceremonial guard, young boys carrying palm and olive branches, and clergy and monks singing 'Blessed is he who comes in the name of the Lord'. The ritual rendered religious and imperial triumph indistinct, drawing on the tradition of the *laudes regiae* (royal acclamations) chanted by crowds to greet Roman leaders returning from victorious battles and Christianized into the liturgical acclamation 'Christus vincit! Christus regnat! Christus imperat!' ('Christ conquers! Christ reigns! Christ commands!'). It was in this tradition of rulers' triumphal entries that eighth- and ninth-century churchmen composed processional hymns and antiphons, most famously the hymn 'Gloria Laus et Honor' for Palm Sunday by the bishop Theodulf of Orléans around the year 820.[10] During the Middle Ages, the Palm Sunday procession often represented an occasion for showcasing what Lionel Adey has called 'that spirit of martial triumph', and one such demonstration of this was the ostentatious display by Pope Julius II on 28 March 1507.[11] Following a victorious military campaign to restore Bologna to papal control, Pope Julius II ordered an extravagant

Palm Sunday procession featuring a triumphal float pulled by four white horses and him riding through the city under eight triumphal arches and past temporary altars set up for the occasion, presided over by clergy waving palm branches.[12]

When, in England, the Palm Sunday procession was suspended following the Reformation, 'Gloria Laus et Honor' lay largely buried until, in the nineteenth century, Anglo-Catholic churchmen looked to the Middle Ages to restore many elements of traditional belief, practice and ritual.[13] Towering among them was John Mason Neale, who while a student at Cambridge had co-founded the Cambridge Camden Society (later the Ecclesiological Society), promoting the study of medieval ecclesiastical art and architecture. Resulting from his painstaking research of medieval liturgical manuscripts, Neale's greatest legacy is his English translations of medieval sequences, chants, carols and hymns. Neale translated 'Gloria Laus et Honor' into English in 1851 for his *Medieval Hymns and Sequences*, and set it to a tune which the seventeenth-century Polish-German Melchior Teschner had composed for the hymn 'Valet will ich dir geben', used later by J. S. Bach in *St John Passion*. Another proponent of High Anglicanism, the composer William Henry Monk, composed the harmonization for the hymn in 1861. In 1861, 'All Glory, Laud and Honour' was published in the highly influential hymnal of which Monk was the music editor, *Hymns Ancient and Modern*, and it was through this that the ninth-century hymn of Theodulf came into popular use not only in England but around the world in English colonies.

The exporting of English hymns of medieval Latin provenance around the globe was a consequence of developments in nineteenth-century hymnography coinciding with the period of British expansionism. The successes of *Hymns Ancient and Modern* and other Anglican hymnals prompted a surge in hymnody production from Nonconformist churches.[14] By the 1860s, most denominations had their own authorized hymn books which were then exported to the colonial mission field. Many hymns transported to the colonies via Anglican and Nonconformist hymnals invoked 'imperial' imagery (e.g.

'Praise to the Lord, the Almighty, the King of Creation'; 'O Worship the King, All Glorious Above'; 'Praise, my Soul, the King of Heaven'), but this, in my view, is more suggestive of biblicism than overt imperialistic propaganda.[15] Indeed, nineteenth-century hymnography was a 'democratic and popular movement' which was supposed to transcend class: as Ian Bradley observes, 'the same verses were being sung to the same tunes in Eton College Chapel and Westminster Abbey as at the Rusholme Street Congregational Church'.[16] Nevertheless the transportation of hymns to the colonies asserted a clear sense of English superiority: the nineteenth-century High Churchmen responsible for many of the best-known hymns and tunes still sung today not only sought to recover ancient Latin hymns but believed English to be their best contemporary carrier. Noting the metrical similarities between English and Latin, Neale believed that ancient and medieval hymns 'have a depth and a fulness of meaning which cannot be expected in other hymns'. To sing a Latin hymn, for instance by Ambrose or Fulbert or Theodulf, was to invoke a reliable past and venerable tradition, one that his contemporaries sought to revive in everything from poetry to buildings to craftsmanship.[17] One High Churchman extolling Neale's medieval hymn translations was Percy Dearmer, best remembered for his influential guide on church ceremonial, *The Parson's Handbook*, first published in 1899 and decried by some as 'British Museum Religion'.[18] Like Neale, Dearmer singled out depth and fullness of meaning as the characteristics of ancient hymnody, now in his day best expressed by the 'English use' of medieval Latin rites and prayers.[19] This is the context in which we must understand his notorious statement that 'The white man has still many faults; but he has moved, while other races have stood still: even the cleverest nations of the East can only advance by learning from him.'[20] Dearmer believed that advancement came from Christianity, and it was the white man who had been formed by Christianity first. Pre-Reformation hymns, prayers and rites showed Christianity to be a religion of both 'body and soul', and medieval ceremonial, far from mere pedantry, would actually serve such socialist principles as 'brotherhood, justice (including for all races), honesty, purity, peaceableness, self-education, cleanliness, care of health and the Christian call to public duty'.[21] Neale and Dearmer exemplify nineteenth-century English medievalism, which associated the racial and national superiority of the English with the aesthetic superiority of the Middle Ages.[22] In Dearmer's vision, the 'nations of the East' advance by adopting the Christian ceremonial of the 'white man' with its powerful combination of ancient words and splendid drama, such as the Palm Sunday ritual comprising procession with the Blessed Sacrament, blessing of the palms, a procession inside and outside the church as all sing 'All Glory Laud and Honour', and an unveiling of the altar-cross. These are components still adhered to by many churches in England and around the world today.[23]

The power dynamics operating in the Palm Sunday rite easily lend themselves to postcolonial critique, like the one made by Chimamanda Ngozi Adichie in *Purple Hibiscus*. The novel opens with the protagonist, 15-year-old Nigerian Kambili Achike, describing events on Palm Sunday:

> Things started to fall apart at home when my brother, Jaja, did not go to communion and Papa flung his heavy missal across the room and broke the figures on the étagère. We had just returned from church. Mama placed the fresh palm fronds, which were wet with holy water, on the dining table and then went upstairs to change.[24]

Like Chinua Achebe's *Things Fall Apart* referenced in the first line of this quotation, *Purple Hibiscus* uses Palm Sunday to show the social implosion caused by the coming of missionaries and colonialism to Nigeria, and to explore the theme of conflicting loyalties, honour and shame as the protagonist's father, obsessed with displaying devout Christian faith in public, engages in violent aggression inside the home. The many references to palm, palm oil and palm oil products throughout the novel clearly alludes to the history of trade between Europe and West Africa and the role these commodities played in fuelling the European annexation of West Africa in the nineteenth century. The trauma that unfolds in this family on 'Palm Sunday' is thus depicted as a consequence of both the economic exploitation of Nigeria and the ideological hold of Christianity which perpetuates Western dominance.[25]

What palm was to Nigeria, tea was to China. Great Britain had an insatiable thirst for Chinese tea, which the British paid for in silver. But as an ever-greater percentage of the world's silver supply was funnelled into China, Britain began to face the real prospect of a trade deficit and currency crisis. This monetary imbalance set the stage for the Opium War. British merchants had discovered that opium, as a highly addictive drug, was a commodity for which there was incessant and growing demand from the Chinese market despite its contraband status. While 3,000 to 5,000 chests of opium were being imported annually between 1800 and 1820, by 1838 British suppliers were shipping 40,000 chests annually to China, almost all of it entering through the Pearl River Delta and Guangzhou, the land of my ancestors since the tenth century.[26] As addiction rates soared, causing major social problems, and as the trade in opium completely reversed China's position in the global silver market, the Chinese government reacted by forcing foreign merchants to sign agreements not to trade opium in exchange for the right to trade in China at all. Merchants specializing in the opium trade faced financial ruin. When in 1839 Commissioner Lin Zexu ordered the destruction of 20,000 chests of opium and forced the British out of Guangzhou, the major opium trading firm Jardine, Matheson and Company lobbied Parliament for war, and even offered to loan the government ships and navigators to secure by force the right to trade the drug. The First Anglo-Chinese War (otherwise known as the Opium War) resulted in the 1842 Treaty of Nanking, the first of China's humiliations under a series of 'Unequal Treaties' with Western powers, by which Britain extracted from China an indemnity of 21 million silver dollars to cover the value of destroyed merchandise, obtained access to another five seaports and formally gained possession of Hong Kong, a strategic point from which British merchants could carry out a hugely profitable trade.[27] Though formally prohibited in 1943, opium smoking had hardly been wiped out by the time my mother was growing up. She recalls watching puffs of smoke rise in a small dimly lit room as her mother's aunt reclined on a wooden bed, head on a hard pillow, using a smoking pipe and opium lamp to feed her addiction. Hong Kong was a colony forged by this history: the British government understood its actions as a defence of free trade rather than in moral terms, but for the sake of economic gain and financial profit, the health of generations was destroyed.

Back on British soil, the mid-nineteenth century saw the publication of Neale's 'All Glory, Laud and Honour'. The hymn was transported to British Hong Kong via missionaries, appearing in churches of various denominations – Anglican, Baptist, the Church of Christ in China, and so on. It was eventually learnt by my mother and embraced with great affection, symbolic to her of the gift of education and of her spiritual communion with the Lord who had answered her prayers for this gift. Thinking about the chain of events leading from the Opium War and the British possession of Hong Kong to the publication of the girls school hymn book, how is it possible to read the following quotation from 1892 without a knot in the stomach?

> The fact is, that the best hymns of Watts, Doddridge, Cowper, Newton, Wesley, Heber, Lyte, Keble, Bonar, Miss Steele, Miss Havergal, and other English authors, – the best German hymns, – the best hymns of American composition, – are now sung in China and South Africa, in Japan and Syria, among the peoples of India, and in the isles of the Pacific Ocean, – indeed in almost every place where Protestant missionaries have uplifted the Gospel banner and gathered Christian churches.[28]

I find myself asking: is this not a perverse state of affairs? Shall we not deal with this corrupt inheritance by discarding the hymn – and the hymn book – altogether?

Hymn No. 12 has illustrated the postcolonial predicament. The thorny question of 'canon de-formation' and its potential to redress imbalances of power has long been contemplated by feminist critics like Griselda Pollock.[29] Yet, to the question, 'Is feminism to intervene to create a maternal genealogy to compete with the paternal lineage and to invoke the voice of the Mother to counter the text of the Father enshrined by existing canons?', she answers a definitive no.[30] For to do so is to risk ending up in a position

> where insiders – representatives of Western masculine European canons – gird themselves to defend truth and beauty and its traditions against what Harold Bloom dismisses as the School of Resentment, while former outsiders remain outsiders, 'the voices of the Other', by developing 'other' subdisciplinary formations – African American or Black Studies, Latino Studies, Women's Studies, Lesbian and Gay Studies, Cultural Studies, and so forth.[31]

Instead, influential critics like Henry Louis Gates Jr have called for us to resist mere imitation through the production of alternatives, and instead to challenge the monopoly over what a canonical 'voice' should sound like in the first place – what he has described as 'a revoicing of the master's discourse in the cadences and timbres of the Black Mother's voice'. He explains this point via a personal story, which has now become itself canonical, about the time as a small boy that he was required to perform a religious recitation in church but forgot the words:

> After standing there I don't know how long, struck dumb and captivated by all of those staring eyes, I heard a voice from near the back of the church proclaim, 'Jesus was a boy like me, and like Him I want to be'. And my mother, having arisen to find my voice, smoothed her dress and sat down again. The congregation's applause lasted as long as its laughter as I crawled back to my seat. What this moment crystallizes for me is how much of my scholarly and critical work has been an attempt to learn how to speak in the strong, compelling cadences of my mother's voice.[32]

The incident reinforces his appeal that the work of decolonization be about 'learning to speak in the voice of the black female', here representing all marginalized 'others'. But can it be possible to hear the 'strong, compelling cadences of my mother's voice' if what she sings are the words and tunes of white men in the Western musical canon? To contemplate this question, let us turn to No. 43 in our hymn book, 'Who Would True Valour See', also known more commonly as 'To Be a Pilgrim'.

Owing to its role in the funerals of Clement Attlee, Winston Churchill and Margaret Thatcher, this hymn, much like 'I Vow to Thee, My Country' and 'Jerusalem', has become synonymous with patriotic duty and service. The hymn exemplifies British influence around the globe, together with the text from which it is lifted, John Bunyan's *The Pilgrim's Progress*, often the first work in British colonies to be translated after the Bible. Usually we assume that it was thanks to the status of *The Pilgrim's Progress* as an English canonical work that it was successfully exported to the colonies at peak of empire, where it then became 'international'. As the nineteenth-century editor of John Bunyan's writings, George Offor, wrote about the Bedford County Gaol where Bunyan, imprisoned for his Nonconformist beliefs, began to write *The Pilgrim's Progress*:

> Thus, by an irresistible impulse from heaven upon the mind of a prisoner for Christ's sake, did a light shine forth from the dungeon on Bedford bridge which has largely contributed to enlighten the habitable globe ... Even the Caffrarian and Hottentot, the enlightened Greek and Hindoo, the remnant of the Hebrew race, the savage Malay, and the voluptuous Chinese – all have the wondrous narrative in their own languages.[33]

As Brown notes, 'Offor's image of a heavenly beam emanating from homely Bedford, searching into and lighting up the dark heathen corners of the world, is a colonialist image of the civilizing power of English "enlightenment" over the "habitable globe"', with 'habitable' meaning 'ours for the inhabiting'.[34]

But this portrayal of Bunyan's influence is the wrong way around, Hofmeyr argues. Bunyan was writing at a time when, in fact, Nonconformity was maligned by the Anglican establishment. But in the colonies, *The Pilgrim's Progress* with its plot and imagery was an accessible model of the believer's conversion and spiritual journey.[35] Nonconformists used the huge success of *The Pilgrim's Progress* in the colonies and reports of how it was catalysing 'heartwork' around the world to strengthen their identity in England; at the same time, they chose to emphasize Bunyan's 'Englishness' so that he would be perceived as a literary hero of national importance rather than as a writer associated with non-white, colonized peoples.[36]

In the nineteenth century, Percy Dearmer extensively modified the poem featured in the encounter with Valiant in Part Two of Bunyan's *The Pilgrim's Progress*, and included it in *The English Hymnal* of 1906 under the title 'He Who Would Valiant Be'. It employed a new tune by Ralph Vaughan Williams, based on a traditional folk song ('Our Captain Cried All Hands'), which he had encountered in a West Sussex hamlet called Monk's Gate, the name by which the hymn's melody is today referred in hymn books. The canonical status of all these titles (*The Pilgrim's Progress*, 'Who Would True Valour See', 'He Who Would Valiant Be' and Monk's Gate) benefited from the earnest reading and singing of people like my mother in the colonies, from their 'conversion of the heart'.[37] But our tendency to consider these works as quintessentially English results from our amnesia about the role their faith played in establishing the importance of these compositions.

Understanding this background helps me understand that it's my mother's voice that I want to – and should – hear in this hymn, not only the sound of English nationalism as I have been so accustomed. When I throw postcolonial theories at her and suggest that her hymn book symbolizes the unjust and lasting legacies of empire, she retorts by telling me the story of the former headmistress at her school who had compiled it. During the Japanese occupation of Hong Kong, as British citizens were being evacuated to England, she refused to leave and insisted on staying behind with her pupils. As a result, she was held in a Japanese internment camp for over three years. This, says my mother, has governed how she understands the presence and influence of missionary teachers upon her life: they helped her understand life's toil and hardship, and recourse to faith, themes that made *The Pilgrim's Progress* and 'Who Would True Valour See' deeply poignant. The Slough of Despond, Difficulty Hill, the Valley of Humiliation, Doubting Castle – these were not abstract ideas but concrete realities in my mother's youth, connoting her father's death and her family's sorrow, her mother's debts, anxiety over the results and finances required for school, doubt that her dreams would be fulfilled. Thus references in 'Who Would True Valour See' to the struggle with wind and weather, lions and giants, hob-goblin and fiend referred to real events and obstacles. And the lines 'There's no discouragement shall make him once relent his first avowed intent to be a pilgrim', or, 'he'll labour night and day to be a pilgrim', meant the practical actions of believing, resisting temptation, being disciplined in prayer and reading of Scripture, abiding by virtue.

But I return to the problem concerning the words and melodies by which the colonized express their trials and hopes – in this case, an allegorical novel written in the seventeenth century by a man from Bedford, a folk tune from a hamlet in West Sussex, a textual rendition written by a nineteenth-century graduate of Oxford, and a melody composed by a national figure who at his death was interred in Westminster Abbey. There are two ways to think about this situation, commonly described as 'the postcolonial condition'.[38] The first is to address what makes it possible for a person in Hong Kong to adopt these English compositions personally and intimately in the first place. In *Truth and Method*, Gadamer discusses Protestant hermen-eutics as they developed during the seventeenth century, when the movement of *applicatio* became central to the interpre-tation of Scripture: correct interpretation of the word was accomplished not only by understanding (*intelligentia*) or by exposition (*explicatio*), but also by applying the word to one's own life (*applicatio*). Gadamer argues that Protestant hermeneutics made this true of every encounter with a text and every experience of interpretation, not just of Scripture, by prioritizing above all else the goal of self-formation (*Bildung*).[39] The reader consciously identifies an experience, situation or problem which presents an opportunity for the self to be augmented, edified, discipled. Gadamer calls the crucial process that serves this self-formation the 'fusion of horizons', whereby the reader applies and fuses a text with his or her own situation ('horizon') in order to gain insight and develop as a person. Gadamer's theory of applied hermeneutics helps us understand why a text foreign to one's native culture can be received with intimate familiarity. Yet, second, and by complete contrast, in the view of Indian philosopher Jarava Lal Mehta, this fusion of horizons, far from augmenting and supplementing the self as Gadamer assumes, disrupts it, leading to irretrievable loss and devastation.[40] Opposing the presumption that the self is enriched by the hermeneutic encounter with the other, Mehta points instead to the resultant destruction. Gadamer's 'fusion of horizons' is edifying and supplementary only for the white person, like an Englishman learning to speak Chinese. But in reverse, the participation requires not a peripheral supplementation but an '*an appropriation of the substance itself*'.[41] This is the difference, in Mehta's rendering, between the Hero and the Pilgrim. For the Hero (read: colonizer), the other is a supplement, an edifying expansion of the Hero's being. Like Ulysses, 'who through all his peregrinations is only on the way to his native island', the colonizer is never ultimately displaced by his adventures.[42] The Pilgrim (read: colonized), on the other hand, returns home displaced at his core, for *Bildung* requires his complete reconstruction, the absorption of his total being. The pilgrim's journey involves the destruction of his own native idols, symbols and philosophy. Indeed, for Mehta, the pilgrim's anguish is that homecoming – the outcome of education, formation, *Bildung* – is a ruinous destination in which tradition is irreparably broken. This is why Mehta refers to the 'death of the pilgrim'. For Mehta, the 'fusion of horizons' at the service of *Bildung* means the very destruction of self.[43]

If, as Mehta argues, the postcolonial hermeneutic – the postcolonial fusion of horizons – is characterized by rupture and loss rather than enrichment and gain, then the 'revoicing of the master's discourse in the cadences and timbres of the Black Mother's voice' must require compensating for this loss by allowing my mother's fusion with the text to change the way it is heard, and who is imagined singing it: not just members of the British establishment such as those invited to the funerals of Atlee, Churchill, Thatcher, but my mother and countless Hong Kong schoolchildren, and generations of African, Asian and Latin American Christians and *their* children, who have voiced their experiences of moral pursuit, suffering, faith and aspiration through the words and tune of this hymn. I think this is what James Baldwin meant when he resolved his bitter resentment towards Shakespeare (Shakespeare acting here as a proxy for the entire Western canon) by realizing that Shakespeare understood, 'as I think we must, that the people who produce the poet are not responsible to him: he is responsible to them'. By this, Baldwin meant that Shakespeare understood that poetry is found not in the appreciation of excellent words but 'in the lives of people', and that Shakespeare could achieve great poetry 'only through love – by knowing, which is not the same thing as understanding, that whatever was happening to anyone was happening to him'.[44] Personally, one of my most powerful experiences of Shakespeare was not a performance by professional actors but by the Primary Shakespeare Company. The charity collaborates with inner-city London schools, usually with high proportions of ethnic minority students, pupils on free school meals and pupils with special educational needs, to produce a Shakespeare play. During a performance of *A Midsummer Night's Dream*, I thought about what I was witnessing as the children, using the words of Puck, belted out their final song about being naughty, making amends and being friends: the canonical figure most associated with Englishness was, by his poetry and storytelling, amplifying the life and energies of children with some of the highest indices of deprivation in the country. Might we understand Bunyan as working from the same compulsion identified by Baldwin? That he recognized something of his reader's lives, their toil and doubt and temptation to stray from the path of faith, and *knew* them, and wrote out of love? That his text resonates with those whose desire for personal sanctification is so great that they adopt his 'ethic of suffering' even if the weaknesses of their flesh are near the point of collapsing under the weight of trial and pain?[45] The challenge is to understand why the marginalized believe that his words about spiritual victory are personally relevant, recognizable and valuable. Owing to the power and influence that the Western canon has had over the colonized, it is important that the thing we listen for in its performance or reading is the 'the voice of the Other/Mother' telling us about their experiences, dilemmas and hopes.[46]

Perceiving the ongoing influence of the Western canon in terms of a genealogical transfer of knowledge, like an English hymnal transferred by missionaries to my mother and then from her to me, cannot get us past the problem of white European hegemony. But, argues Tim Ingold, let us discard 'tree-diagrams of taxonomy' and instead look to the example of the Chewong of Malaysia who navigate their jungle environment by attend-ing to a fruit tree planted by an ancestor.[47] Ingold observes that

> his (the ancestor's) contribution to successors was not to hand anything down by way of substance or memory ... it was rather to play a small part ... in creating the environ-ment in which people now live, and from which they draw their sense of being. Passing by the fruit tree, contemporary Chewong may be reminded of the ancestor's erstwhile pres-ence and deeds, but it is in such acts of remembrance, not in any transmitted endowment carried in their bodies and minds, that he lives on.[48]

The connection between ancestors and living people cannot therefore justifiably be described in terms of geometric points and lines of transmission.[49] Instead, ancestors establish a 'sphere of nurture' by their presence and their activity.[50] Lived experi-ence comprises what Chakrabarty has called 'time-knots', the intersections of plural lines of histories that exist together and operate within the present, the traces and fragments of the multiple pasts that converge in a moment. Modernism has conditioned us to constantly force these multiple, disjunctive experiences into linear histories: although we all live in 'time-knots', historicism is the exercise of wrongly straightening out these knots into a proper 'chronology'.[51] *This* is the genealogy that renders us the perpetual latecomers, this arborescent chain from the Europe of Theodulf and John Mason Neale and the London Missionary Society to my mother in the East. But the ancestral relationship between the English composers in the hymn book and my mother lies in a time-knot involving a story of death, debt, poverty and faith, and an encounter with the Western religious canon. The time-knot renders people like my mother not only the deferential students of English hymnography but also as much an authority as liturgists, musicians and historians. The marginalized can often read and sing a work of Christian devotion better than anyone else.

Canonical hymns of the English musical repertoire will continue to present postcolonial dilemmas about Western origins and colonial descent, and nowhere is this more acute than in the conventions for naming hymn tunes. 'Peruse the names of tunes in the *English Hymnal*', Roger Scruton writes patriotically, 'and you find yourself taken on a journey through rural England, knowing the spirit of each place from the melody that arose from it, and understanding, in another way, the inseparable connection between our Church and our country.'[52] When at Compline I sing John Henry Newman's 'Lead, Kindly Light', Hymn 45 in my mother's school hymn book, I admit feeling envious of Roger Scruton. For he can sing this hymn as part of his native heritage while I must approach it as a foreigner to England, a student of English who must use a map to locate 'Sandon', the village in Essex giving the hymn tune its name. Yet at the closing lines, my thoughts turn to my family:

> So long Thy power hath blest me, sure it still
> Will lead me on.
> O'er moor and fen, o'er crag and torrent, till
> The night is gone,
> And with the morn those angel faces smile,
> Which I have loved long since, and lost awhile!

As was the case with the other 'great figures' of the Western Christian canon I have already discussed, it was a time-knot of multiple, discordant events – the Opium War, the founding of a missionary school, the death of my grandfather, sudden poverty, the threat of a discontinued education, a school hymn book – which conspired to make Newman and his hymn personally relevant to my life and to render him a spiritual ancestor of sorts. Whether it be a sign of my 'enrichment' or 'loss' that I think nightly of my biological ancestors through the words of this nineteenth-century Englishman, I dare not say. But I know that it was my mother who first taught me about virtue, faith and prayer in the face of sorrow, fear, disappointment and doubt – and this mostly through the words and tunes of English writers and composers. Consequently, the association between the famed forebears of the Western Christian tradition and my mother constitutes an ancestral sphere of nurture. This incontrovertible legacy of empire means that I ought, when drinking from the well of Western spirituality, to remember that its source is found not only in the renowned progenitors of the Western Christian canon but also in my predecessors who, in the trials and hopes of their daily lives, showed that this well was beneficial to drink from.

Notes

1 Sarah Graham (ed.), 2019, *A History of the Bildungsroman*, Cambridge: Cambridge University Press.

2 Harold Bloom, 1994, *The Western Canon: The Books and School of the Ages*, revd edn, 1996, London: Papermac, pp. 32–3, 36.

3 Bloom, *The Western Canon*, p. 36.

4 Bloom, *The Western Canon*, p. 30.

5 Bloom, *The Western Canon*, p. 73.

6 Bloom, *The Western Canon*, p. 65.

7 Frantz Fanon, 1961, *Les damnés de la terre*, Paris: Maspero, trans. *Wretched of the Earth*, 'On National Culture', in Lee Morrissey (ed.), 2005, *Debating the Canon: A Reader from Addison to Nafisi*, Basingstoke: Macmillan, pp. 65–70, at 69.

8 Gerhard Leitner, 2004, *Australia's Many Voices: Australian English – The National Language*, Berlin: Mouton de Gruyter.

9 What follows is from Max Harris, 2017, 'The Processional

Theatre of Palm Sunday', in Pamela King (ed.), *The Routledge Research Companion to Early Drama and Performance*, Abingdon: Routledge [electronic version accessed 08.06.2021 at the British Library], 1212.0/ 1335-1275.6/1335. See also Max Harris, 2019, *Christ on a Donkey: Palm Sunday, Triumphal Entries, and Blasphemous Pageants*, Leeds: Arc Humanities Press.

10 Colin Morris, 2007, *The Sepulchre of Christ and the Medieval West: From the Beginning to 1600*, Oxford: Oxford University Press, p. 109.

11 Lionel Adey, 1986, *Hymns and the Christian 'Myth'*, Vancouver: University of British Columbia Press, p. 63.

12 Harris, 'The Processional Theatre of Palm Sunday', p. 318.

13 The use of palms and foliage in Palm Sunday processions was at first permitted by Henry VIII but forbidden by Edward VI, then mandated by Mary, before finally being forbidden again by Elizabeth I along with all other processions apart from Rogation Day. Harris, 'The Processional Theatre of Palm Sunday', p. 324.

14 Other Anglican hymn books: Monsell's *The Parish Hymnal*, Thring's *The Church of England Hymn Book*. Followed by the *Baptist Hymnal* in 1879, the *Congregational Church Hymnal* in 1887, *Wesley's Hymns* in 1876, the *Primitive Methodist Hymnal* in 1886, the *United Methodist Church Hymnal* in 1889, etc. See J. R. Watson, 2004, *The English Hymn: A Critical and Historical Study*, Oxford, Clarendon Press.

15 Jeffrey Richards, 2001, *Imperialism and Music: Britain, 1876– 1953*, Manchester: Manchester University Press, p. 375.

16 Ian Bradley, 1997, *Abide With Me: The World of Victorian Hymns*, London: SCM Press, pp. 45–6, quoted in Richards, *Imperialism and Music*, p. 368.

17 See Watson, *The English Hymn*.

18 See Donald Gray, 2000, *Percy Dearmer: A Parson's Pilgrimage*, Norwich: Canterbury Press. Gray notes that Dearmer's friend James Adderley had in fact first used the phrase 'British Museum religion' as a compliment rather than a derision. Gray, *Percy Dearmer*, p. 2. Percy Dearmer, 1899, *The Parson's Handbook containing practical directions both for parsons and others as to the management of the parish church and service according to the English use as set forth in the Book of Common Prayer*, London: Grant Richards.

19 Watson, *The English Hymn*, p. 379.

20 Percy Dearmer, 1909, *Body and Soul. An enquiry into the effects of religion upon health, with a description of Christian works of healing from the New Testament to the present day*, London: Sir Isaac Pitman & Sons.

21 B. D. Spinks, 2020, 'The Intersection of "English Use" Liturgy and Social Justice: Snapshots of Augustus Pugin, Percy Dearmer,

Conrad Noel and William Palmer Ladd', *Journal of Anglican Studies* 18(2), pp. 1–16 at 8, quoting Percy Dearmer, 1910, *The Church and Social Questions*, London: A. R. Mowbray & Co., p. 20.

22 See generally Joanne Parker and Corinna Wagner (eds), 2020, *The Oxford Handbook of Victorian Medievalism*, Oxford: Oxford University Press. On race, see Amy S. Kaufman, 2004, 'Purity', in *Medievalism: Key Critical·Terms*, Cambridge: D S Brewer. For a discussion about the relationship of medievalism to racism and white supremacy in contemporary events, see for example 'Medieval Scholars Joust with White Nationalists. And One Another', *New York Times*, 5 May 2005 [online]. Available at: www.nytimes.com/2019/05/05/arts/the-battle-for-medieval-studies-white-supremacy.html.

23 The Alcuin Club, 1930, *A Directory of Ceremonial: Part II*, London: A. R. Mowbray & Co., pp. 18–19.

24 Chimamanda Ngozi Adichie, 2003, *Purple Hibiscus*, New York: Anchor, p. 3.

25 Julie Mullaney, 2010, *Postcolonial Literatures in Context*, London: Continuum, pp. 49–58, especially the section on 'The Politics of "Palm Sunday" – Colonialism, Capitalism and Christianity' at pp. 51ff.

26 Carl Trocki, 1999, *Opium, Empire and the Global Political Economy: A Study of the Asian Opium Trade, 1750–1950*, London: Routledge.

27 Steve Tsang, 1997, *A Modern History of Hong Kong, 1841–1997*, London: I. B. Tauris.

28 Becca Whitla, 2019, 'Hymnody in Missionary Lands: A Decolonial Critique', in Mark Lamport et al., *Hymns and Hymnody: Historical and Theological Introductions, Volume 2: From Catholic Europe to Protestant Europe*, Eugene, OR: Cascade, pp. 285–302, at 293.

29 On the relationship between postcolonial theology and feminism, see Pui-lan Kwok, *Postcolonial Imagination and Feminist Theology*, London: SCM Press, 2004.

30 Griselda Pollock, 1999, *Differencing the Canon: Feminist Desire and the Writing of Art's Histories*, London: Routledge, pp. 5–6.

31 Pollock, *Differencing the Canon*.

32 Henry Louis Gates Jr, 1992, 'The Master's Pieces: On Canon Formation and the African-American Tradition', *Loose Canons: Notes on the Culture Wars*, in Morrissey, *Debating the Canon*, pp. 193–8, at 198.

33 George Offor (ed.), 1861, *The Pilgrim's Progress: A New Edition, with a Memoir and Notes*, London: Warne, & Routledge, p. xxv, quoted in Sylvia Brown, 2018, 'Bunyan and Empire', in Michael Davies and W. R. Owens (eds), *The Oxford Handbook of John Bunyan*, Oxford: Oxford University Press, pp. 665–81, at 667.

34 Brown, 'Bunyan and Empire', p. 667.

35 Isabel Hofmeyr, 2018, *The Portable Bunyan: A Transnational*

History of The Pilgrim's Progress, Princeton, NJ: Princeton University Press, p. 59.

36 Hofmeyr, *The Portable Bunyan*.

37 The Interpreter's words to Christian: 'This fire is the work of grace that is wrought in the heart … This is Christ, who continually with the oil of his grace, maintains the work already begun in the heart; by the means of which, notwithstanding what the Devil can do, the souls of his people prove gracious still. And in that thou sawest, that the man stood behind the man to maintain the fire; this is to teach thee, that it is hard for the tempted to see how this work of grace is maintained in the soul.' John Bunyan, 1678, *The Pilgrim's Progress: from this world, to that which is to come*, Roger Pooley (ed.), 2008, London: Penguin, p. 35.

38 For an overview, see Sandra Mezzadra and Federico Rahola, 2015, 'The Postcolonial Condition: A Few Notes on the Quality of Historical Time in the Global Present', in Pavan Kumar Malreddy and Diana Brydon (eds), *Reworking Postcolonialism: Globalization, Labour and Rights*, Basingstoke: Palgrave Macmillan, pp. 36–54.

39 This and what follows from Gadamer, Hans-Georg, 1960, *Wahrheit und Methode*, trans. Joel Weinsheimer and Donald G. Marshall Truth, 2004, *Truth and Method*, 2nd rev. edn, London: Continuum, *passim*, but especially pp. 307–62.

40 Thomas B. Ellis, 2013, *On the Death of the Pilgrim: The Postcolonial Hermeneutics of Jarava Lal Mehta*, Dordrecht: Springer.

41 Ellis, *On the Death of the Pilgrim*, p. 189, quoting Jarava Lal Mehta, 1986, 'Modernity and Tradition', in *Philosophy and Religion: Essays in Interpretation*, New Delhi: Indian Council of Philosophical Research, p. 230.

42 Thomas B. Ellis, 2009, 'On the Death of the Pilgrim: The Postcolonial Hermeneutics of Jarava Lal Mehta', in Purushottama Bilimoria and Andrew B. Irvine (eds), *Postcolonial Philosophy of Religion*, Dordrecht: Springer, pp. 105–19, at 109, by way of Emmanuel Levinas, 1986, 'The Trace of the Other', in M. C. Taylor, *Deconstruction in Context: Literature and Philosophy*, Chicago, IL: University of Chicago Press, pp. 345–9.

43 Ellis, *On the Death of the Pilgrim*, pp. 108–9, with various references to Mehta. See also the important footnote 34 on p. 108 on Gananath Obeyesekere's call to *resist* the fusion of horizons.

44 James Baldwin, 19 April 1964, 'Why I Stopped Hating Shakespeare', *The Observer*, repr. in Randall Kenan (ed.), 2010, *The Cross of Redemption: Uncollected Writings*, New York: Vintage.

45 Arlette Zinck, 2018, 'Piety and Radicalism: Bunyan's Writings of the 1680s', in Michael Davies and W. R. Owens (eds), *The Oxford Handbook of John Bunyan*, Oxford: Oxford University Press, pp. 290–306, at 291, quoting Richard Greaves, 1992, *John Bunyan and English*

Nonconformity, London: Hambledon Press, 'Amid the Holy War: Bunyan and the Ethic of Suffering', pp. 169–83.

46 Pollock, *Differencing the Canon*, p. 8.

47 Tim Ingold, 2000, chapter on 'Ancestry, generation, substance, memory, land', in *The Perception of the Environment: Essays on Livelihood, Dwelling and Skill*, London: Routledge, p. 138.

48 Ingold, *The Perception of the Environment*, p. 140.

49 Ingold, *The Perception of the Environment*, p. 142.

50 Ingold, *The Perception of the Environment*, p. 144.

51 Dipesh Chakrabarty, 2000, *Provincializing Europe: Postcolonial Thought and Historical Difference*, Princeton, NJ: Princeton University Press, p. 112.

52 Roger Scruton, 2012, *Our Church: A Personal History of the Church of England*, London: Atlantic Books, p. 124.

5

Ancestral Nostalgia and
Ecclesiastical Heritage Sites

The moon is brightest at the Mid-Autumn Festival,
and the feeling of homesickness is strongest then.

月到中秋分外明，每逢佳節倍思親

Located some 30km across the coast of Guangzhou, the island
of Hong Kong, the New Territories, and the Kowloon Peninsula
boast a population of 7.5 million, making for a density ratio
of 6,930 persons per square kilometre and one of the world's
most crowded cities.[1] Hong Kong's development since 1841,
when the first census recorded a population of only around
7,000, has frequently been described as 'frantic', for Hong
Kong people have always lived under the threat of expiration.
Modern history has made the city a bargaining chip in negotiations, its fate decided by state powers setting out new expiry
dates in each successive treaty. Britain first occupied Hong
Kong Island in 1841 and, in 1860, having won the Second
Opium War, further gained the Kowloon Peninsula. In 1898,
in the wake of China's greatly weakened position following
the First Sino-Japanese War, another convention was signed
between China and the UK. Claude MacDonald, wanting to
expand British control but not wanting to be perceived as causing the break-up of China, negotiated a 99-year rent-free lease
on the northern portion of the Kowloon Peninsula, later named
the New Territories. Under the presumption that China would
never be in a strong enough position to enforce the termination
of the lease, the British believed it to be a permanent cession
in disguise.[2] And so within five decades Britain's occupation of
the 'barren island' encompassed all of Hong Kong Island, the

Kowloon Peninsula and the New Territories – the former two in perpetuity, but the latter with an expiration date of 1997. China called this the 'century of humiliation'. In 1982, as the 1997 deadline loomed and it became increasingly clear that China would not accept anything less than the return of all three parts together, formal negotiations began. The Sino-British Joint Declaration of 1984 was reached by Deng Xiaoping and Margaret Thatcher, with Britain reluctantly conceding that when the lease on the New Territories in 1997 expired, the whole of Hong Kong Island and the Kowloon Peninsula would also revert to China. China agreed to allow the region to maintain, for a period of 50 years, a degree of autonomy not permitted on the mainland, such as the right to free speech, a free press and a free market economy. Expirations have therefore shaped Hong Kong's psyche in fundamental ways: the first, the deadline of midnight 30 June 1997 when Britain's possession would expire and Hong Kong would return to Chinese rule, and the second, the deadline of 2047 when the 50-year 'One Country, Two Systems' transition period would expire. Hence the popular description of Hong Kong as the city that survives 'on borrowed time in a borrowed place'. Han Suyin quoted this phrase, which she had heard from a Hong Kong businessman, in her 1959 *Life* magazine article titled 'Hong Kong's Ten-Year Miracle': the city was prosperous but precarious, its frenetic energy owing to the fact that its fate depended on contentions for power between mighty states.[3] The pragmatic people of Hong Kong have learned to retain a sort of insurance policy, prepared to stay or leave (or leave and then return) depending on the outlook for business and success. Today it is estimated that approximately 400,000 native-born Hong Kongers currently resident in the city hold a foreign passport, ready to leave quickly if things get out of hand. In the light of recent upheavals in Hong Kong, the Home Office expects that, via its new 'British National (Overseas) Visa' route, between 258,000 and 322,400 Hong Kongers and their dependants will immigrate to the UK between 2021 and 2026.[4]

My father was born in Hong Kong at the start of the 1950s,

a time when the city's economic growth was occurring at a rate in excess of 7 per cent a year, rendering it one of the world's most remarkable economic achievements. While mainland China isolated itself from the West, Hong Kong engaged in a beneficial exchange with the global economy and, it is said, came of age during this period. My paternal grandparents, peasant emigrés from their rural village of Luopo on the mainland, must have felt both the exhilaration of new opportunity and disorientation at the speed of change. It was during this period that my grandfather began to replace his traditional Chinese clothing with Western-style shirts, jackets and trousers. Technological developments punctuated my father's early childhood: modern toilets, a new refrigerator, double-decker bus rides to the cinema with his sisters. Yet the 'expiration date' of 1997 loomed so large in the Hong Kong mentality that it produced a peculiar perception of time: a frenzied obsession with seizing the small window to make a profit before everything changed, in tandem with what Stephen Teo has called 'a certain syndrome of fear and insecurity causing citizens to drift and wander'.[5] The famous Kai-Tak Airport, with an approach to the runway jutting 8,000 feet into the water and requiring a 90-degree turn over the high-rise condominiums of Kowloon, so spectacular and dangerous that one reporter compared it to crossing the Andes, was a symbol of the restlessness of Hong Kong in the face of an unknown future.[6] The airport was the site of many departures and farewells that resulted from Hong Kong people's anxiety as they counted down to the 1997 handover, and epitomized the dislocations and discontinuities created by this state of limbo. It was from this airport that my father, like so many of his generation who wanted to gain a university qualification abroad as a sort of insurance policy for post-1997 Hong Kong, boarded a flight to Canada from whence he would not return for nearly four years. Long-distance telephone calls were so unaffordable in those days that my father only made one call home during the entire period of his study. Instead, he maintained contact with my grandparents by posting aerograms once a month. With business correspondence, my illiterate grandfather would supply only a general indication of content and leave it to my aunt to write the letter, but when it came to letters for my dad, he would require her to compose multiple versions from which he would select the best version. For Chinese festivals, he and my grandmother would ship parcels of food all the way to Canada at great expense. Many more separations followed. Between 1981, when it became clear that Hong Kong would revert to China, and 1996, six months before the handover, 503,800 Hong Kong people emigrated abroad, of which 61 per cent left for Canada.[7] Among them were five out of my grandparents' seven children. My father says that this was one of only a few subjects about which my grandfather expressed his opinion and emotions verbally: 'If you didn't emigrate then, that would have been good.' There were good economic reasons for wanting his sons nearby: my grandfather had rental properties and now had hardly any sons or daughters left to help him read the contracts. The emigrations of his children from Hong Kong forced him to sell, to his great regret, those properties that he could not manage on his own. My father recalls that my otherwise cool and unflappable grandfather expressed regret on only this matter. Reflecting in his twilight years on his hard-earned success in business, he once joked with wry exaggeration what a great pity it was that so many of his children moved overseas at just the moment when he had finally gathered enough capital to purchase an entire street for them and their families all to live together on.

Nostalgia for Hong Kong between the 1950s and 1997 points to the existential crises marking the transitional period in the run-up to the handover. 'The whole experience of this community is like a dream, it is lost and gone', laments the famous Hong Kong film-maker Wong Kar-Wai, reflecting on the themes of homesickness, temporal dislocation and evocation of the past so persistent in his filmography.[8] The people of Hong Kong feel like 'an endangered community': this was true in the run-up to 1997 and is certainly truer now than ever.[9] Loss triggers nostalgia, and Hong Kong is a prime site for this. The Hong Kong of my father's youth is considered by many to be the golden era of the city, a suspended time, a flash of momentary stability before the dislocations and fragmentations arising from, first, Hong Kong's handover to Beijing in 1997, and now more recently the implementation of the National Security Law, and then inevitably the next deadline of 2047. To this day, many objects arouse nostalgia for the 舊香港 (*gauh heung gong*, Old Hong Kong) of my father's youth. One such object was my grandfather's favourite possession, two Ming-style vases which every Chinese New Year would be filled with giant pink peonies, bright red dahlias and tall, fuzzy pussy willows I loved to touch. Even now the sight of Ming vases reminds me of my grandmother and aunts gathered noisily around the round mahogany table to make dumplings for Chinese New Year, a real occasion of *gou hing* (高興, festive merriment). Another nostalgic object from my family is now displayed in the Museum of Hong Kong History. The exhibition about life in Hong Kong after World War Two features a photograph of a vintage mooncake box sold in one of my grandfather's restaurants ahead of the Mid-Autumn Festival. This important festival in Chinese tradition, also known as the Lantern Festival, dates back 3,000 years to when China's emperors worshipped the moon for bountiful harvest, and is celebrated on the fifteenth day of the eighth moon. On this day, the moon is believed to be at its brightest and fullest size, coinciding with harvest time in the middle of Autumn. For the festival, bakeries and restaurants supply mooncakes, rich multi-sided pastries densely filled with lotus and sesame seed paste, offered as gifts to friends and family. The festival evokes fond memories from my childhood of large family gatherings, of playing with colourful paper lanterns each containing a thin candle inside, and especially of eating mooncake from my grandfather's teahouse, the photo of the square tin container now displayed in Hong Kong's museum. I think the last time I celebrated the Mid-Autumn Festival with extended family was 1986; after that, our family dispersed throughout Canada and the USA.

I commit here what Chakrabarty has called 'the sin of all sins'[10] – indulging in nostalgia, even in a mooncake box that's now been 'museified' to evoke a longing for a more innocent past. Nostalgia, that 'highly complex emotional response that combines feelings of sadness and painful longing with joy and human warmth', can often be mocked or dismissed as simple-minded, shallow, useless sentimentality.[11] The term was coined by a Swiss medical doctor, Johannes Hofer, in the seventeenth century to define a medical condition caused by severe homesickness, whereby Swiss mercenaries working abroad suffered from fatigue, lack of appetite, pallor, muscle weakness and palpitations. The 'treatable' illness was initially associated only with the longing for home and the familiar, for the landscape and customs of one's birth, but in the eighteenth century it became possible, as Kant did, to define 'nostalgia' in temporal terms also – as a remembrance of childhood, a longing for the carefree existence and pleasures of youth. For the Romantics, nostalgia came to denote innocence, a lost paradise. 'Nostalgia' was painful because it was not possible to return to one's childhood or youth, and also because modernization and industrialization destroyed our innocence by breaking our tie to nature. Thus, the term 'nostalgia', once describing a disease, came to denote an emotional state, of pining for the past. Whether this past had actually existed or not is beside the point; the longing for the irretrievable need not be based on fact. Memories of the past are frequently constructed, sometimes even imagined, but they exist as an important antidote to despair caused by a transient, uncontrollable, unpredictable present. Many psychologists today consider nostalgia to be a healthy feeling which ought even to be cultivated as a response to our anxieties about contemporary situations.[12]

Undeniably, nostalgia plays a fundamental role in the heritage industry. Nostalgia for the past is what encourages the conservation and exhibition of everything from old jars and toys to bridges, trains and stately homes. Heritage sites capitalizing on nostalgia also include many buildings for sacred uses: cathedrals and abbeys come immediately to mind. English Heritage calls the over 50 monasteries it conserves an 'unmatchable array' and 'the pride of our collection'.[13] In this chapter I want to address the predicament of diasporic groups when they enjoy a personal identification with ecclesiastical sites that are classified as 'national heritage'. I shall be using the term 'English Heritage' to refer both to the charity founded in 1983 that manages over 400 historic monuments, buildings and places including a great many ecclesiastical sites, and to the vision of the national past that is constructed by designating these sites as both 'English' and 'heritage'.

We are accustomed to viewing heritage sites such as monastic ruins through the nostalgic eyes of nineteenth-century Romantics, who promoted a certain view of ancient ecclesiastical sites like cathedrals, parish churches and monasteries to justify England's claim to antiquity and therefore its exceptionalism.[14] The nation-state required national heritage, and, as Graham, Ashworth and Tunbridge argue, the 'origins of what we now term heritage lie in the modernist nexus of European state formation and Romanticism, which is defined in political terms by nationalism'.[15] Labadi's study shows that the vast majority of applications for UNESCO World Heritage Site status still today rely on arguments about how a site upholds centuries of tradition, is a foundational pillar of the nation and defines national identity. She argues, 'Conveying these notions of continuity and tradition are essential for the construction and justification of the nation.'[16] Graham, Ashworth and Tunbridge observe, for example, that the popular association of the Netherlands with a maritime Golden Age and the art of Rembrandt and Vermeer reflects the economic interests and tastes of the nineteenth-century capitalist, Protestant bourgeoisie more than the seventeenth century itself.[17] Similarly, the 'picturesque ruins' of English abbeys dissolved under Henry VIII caught the imaginations of eighteenth- and nineteenth-century English poets, as the image of ivy prettily climbing over stonework tied English artistic and cultural achievements permanently to the nation's soil and landscape, constituting England's 'soul'.[18] Today, English Heritage acts as custodian of the majority of monastic ruins in this country, its purpose captured by the tagline inviting us to 'Step into England's story'. Thus heritage functions as the validation and legitimation of an English identity.

Undergirding the relationship between heritage sites and

national identity is a dominant approach to heritage management commonly referred to as the 'Authorized Heritage Discourse'.[19] This established and normative discourse privileges expert values and knowledge about the past and its material manifestations, in order to regulate conservation, management and presentation of heritage assets. Professionals assess and explain the importance of a site, object or monument based on qualities such as aesthetic merit, authenticity and importance to a national story.[20] The approach takes historic sites to possess fixed meanings which must be correctly uncovered, carefully conserved and expertly explained by professionals for the populace's learning and appreciation.[21]

However, scholars and practitioners have argued that approaching a heritage site as a text of the 'dead past' ignores contemporary social issues and the current contexts of individuals attracted to a site. Resisting the Authorized Heritage Discourse, many curators, collection managers and museum educators have begun to adopt a 'Living Heritage' approach, which prioritizes the meaning of sites and objects to living people, acknowledging how they engage emotionally with their material world.[22] Pioneered in Australia, the United States and Africa, this intentionally inclusive perspective attempts to acknowledge and explore conflicts of meaning around indigenous heritage, and is a practical response to the criticism that Authorized Heritage Discourse is complicit in the displacement and silencing of indigenous peoples and their histories. Living Heritage emphasizes an interactive, community-based approach to heritage management: it wishes to hear and legitimize a diverse range of voices, and prioritizes empathy, contemporary beliefs and views, and local voices in decision-making about heritage assets. Thus, rather than relying on the professional expert, Living Heritage seeks input from the community emerging from oral traditions, myths, rituals, local memory, in order to appreciate both the site's influence and the tensions embedded in it. It recognizes that heritage is not objective but affective, involving a range of emotions (pride, awe, joy, pain, fear, etc.) which are the product of configurations of power.[23]

As a cardinal principle, the Living Heritage approach considers heritage to be something emerging in the present, renewable and limitless rather than finite and passively received.[24] Thus it sheds light on the problem I am trying to raise concerning what Tunbridge and Ashworth have termed 'dissonant heritage'.[25] Dissonance ensues when heritage attractions present 'someone's heritage and therefore logically not someone else's'.[26] As Graham, Ashworth and Tunbridge write, 'The creation of any heritage actively or potentially disinherits or excludes those who do not subscribe to, or are embraced within, the terms of meaning defining that heritage.'[27] This might not be a problem if the people being 'excluded' from a definition of heritage don't mind, but in a postcolonial era, dissonance occurs between, on the one hand, hybrid expectations forged in a decolonized, globalized world of migrations and, on the other, antiquated notions of heritage as a nostalgic harking back to a homogeneous nation-state (whether real or imagined). In fact, the colonized can – whether naively, absurdly, perversely or subversively – identify personally with the national heritage of the metropole. Thus dissonance occurs when tourism economies unhelpfully perpetuate *metropolitan heritages* but fail to realize that visitors from former *colonial* countries actually recognize their own identities therein.[28]

Dissonance therefore also occurs when the authorized presentation about a site's historic and national significance neglects the personal meanings about the site held by a wide range of people, describing why the site is important to certain people in a way that implies 'inclusion and exclusion – who qualifies and who does not'.[29] As Smith has pointed out, heritage tourists are in fact purposeful, questioning agents who are actively engaged in acts of meaning-making and self-making when they visit heritage places.[30] The experience of visiting a heritage site is a complex interaction between the site, the 'authoritative' interpretations provided and, crucially, *'the background and biographies of visitors themselves'*.[31] Recognizing this is essential because, as Emerick notes, places have a 'social biography': the meaning of a place does not stem only from rationalist knowledge (that is, 'this site is important because such and such happened here'), but also from the visitor's own back-ground, persuasions and sense of identity.[32] Thus in making conclusions about the value and significance of a particular his-toric site, we should not balk at personal sources of knowledge, for an individual's story about a place can in fact illuminate a social and community theme that is more important than the history.[33] Poria argues therefore that the distinction commonly drawn between 'world heritage', 'national heritage' and 'local heritage', with only the latter taking into account 'personal' sentiments, is unhelpful. For 'heritage is ultimately a personal affair'.[34] Individuals assemble their own sense of heritage from their background, experiences, memories and values, and it would therefore be absurd to associate a particular set of feelings with different types of sites – for example, that world heritage invokes awe, national heritage patriotism, and local heritage personal attachment.[35] In fact, private and emotional connections operate at every site to produce a wide range of possible feelings. To this effect, the Faro Convention adopted by the Council of Europe rightly prefers the term heritage *community* to heritage *site*, emphasizing the commonality of people who feel affiliation to the site for whatever reason, be it patriotic or autobiographical.[36]

For the Christian, religious faith and background mean that – regardless of nationality – he or she possesses an intimate rela-tionship with ecclesiastical heritage sites, and Christians ought therefore to be considered part of the 'heritage *community*'. I have been arguing that the personal connections that the colonized feel to the heritage of Western Christianity were forged by the fact of imperialism, and therefore this identifi-cation is by no means naturally and effortlessly experienced, especially when Christian heritage is still largely conceived in nationalistic terms. I therefore want to reflect on the Christian subaltern's sense of belonging at English heritage sites. A diasporic Christian visitor can ascribe a meaning to that attrac-tion in myriad ways to suit his or her own religious needs, self-understanding and aspirations, and a heritage attraction can either disregard these meanings in favour of an authorita-tive historical interpretation or, alternatively, take an interest in how successive generations and changing social contexts give the site new value. To explore these contrasting approaches, I want to compare my visitor experiences at two monastic ruins.

I turn first to Beaulieu Abbey in the New Forest, Hampshire, which together with the National Motor Museum forms the Beaulieu Estate, home of the Montagu family, where my husband, three young children and I enjoyed a fantastic outing during the summer holidays. Our day here began in a queue to show our admission ticket and to collect my official Beaulieu guidebook. The guidebook employs a chronological structure, narrating how the estate was passed down through various descendants. It opens with this suggestive statement by Ralph Douglas-Scott-Montagu, 4th Baron Montagu of Beaulieu:

> The ownership of a country estate and a stately home was once an expression of wealth, power and status; now it's about the custodianship of the nation's heritage. The motivation to accept these responsibilities comes from a deep-rooted attachment to the place, and the knowledge that I am but one in a line of descendants who have owned the estate since 1538.

Though I noted the reference to 'custodianship', I wasn't sure whether to be impressed or repelled by so honest and unapologetic an admission about the dependence of 'the nation's heritage' on 'ownership' of estate. Indeed the guidebook appears unabashedly to adopt 'ownership' as an organizing theme. On the first page, I am told that King John had owned the land and gifted it in 1204 to a group of Cistercian monks to atone for a past sin, thereby founding Beaulieu Abbey. During the Dissolution of the Monasteries, the then-abbot Thomas Stevens formally surrendered the abbey to the Crown in 1538, and the Abbey Church, Cloister and Chapter House were demolished. Ownership of the land, woods, river and remaining monastic buildings of the Beaulieu estate were transferred into the hands of a secular owner, Thomas Wriothesley, of whom the current Baron Montagu of Beaulieu is a direct descendant. My visit to the former abbey gatehouse, which Wriothesley had converted into a family dwelling, began in the Portrait Gallery. Here I surveyed portrait after portrait of illustrious Montagu ancestors, including Charles II, Ralph the 1st Duke of Montagu and ambassador to France at the Court of Versailles, Henry the 3rd Earl of Southampton and patron of William Shakespeare, and the 5th Duke of Buccleuch who was called the 'Uncrowned King of Scotland' because it was said he could walk the 60-odd miles from the Cheviots to Edinburgh without once stepping off his own land. I quickly realized that my preoccupation with evaluating my 'sense of belonging' in such a place as this was absurd and foolish. Nevertheless, I found it insightful to note how 'ownership' of heritage – in this case, a literal ownership – affects the curation of history, here at Beaulieu standing firmly in the tradition of the Authorized Heritage Discourse. In point of fact, the Montagu family are not only literally *owners*, but also literally *authorities* in the heritage industry: in addition to their private hobbies in collecting, Lord Montagu was the first chairman of English Heritage from 1984 to 1994, his son is Head of Heritage at the *Radio Times*, and both have contributed in countless ways to conserving and widening access to England's historic environment. Their presentation of Beaulieu's historic abbey was deliberately and meticulously curated. My family and I spent much time in the fifteenth-century 'Domus Conversum' of the abbey, used as the living quarters of the lay brothers and one of the few abbey buildings to survive intact, now functioning as the abbey museum. Here we studied the various displays: a scale model of the abbey ground plan and buildings, a scene featuring figures of medieval monks to illustrate Cistercian farming methods, copies of illuminated manuscripts and an impressive film explaining the history of the Cistercians and the monastic life of prayer and devotion at Beaulieu. Outside, the ruins at Beaulieu Abbey are set in idyllic surroundings and typically picturesque, with the requisite foliage growing over the patinaed stone. The lawns are manicured, perfectly preserving the outlines of the monastic plan. We followed the paved paths tracing the contours of the choir monks' dormitory, the warming house, lavatorium, refectory, chapter house and church. We inspected the remains of the day stairs and the spot where bookcases would have stood, signs of the everyday activities of the monks. We remarked on the skill of medieval builders. We toured the precincts in delicate and orderly fashion, anxious not to behave like ill-mannered guests squandering the hospitality (hefty entrance fee aside) of the estate's owners. My children probably learnt more spending an hour at Beaulieu Abbey than they ever would have sitting in my lectures for a whole term.

During the same summer, we spent time at Lesnes Abbey, which like Beaulieu had been founded as an act of penance. Formerly known as the Augustinian Abbey of St Thomas the Martyr, it was founded by Richard de Lucy, Chief Justiciar of England in 1178, probably to atone for his role in the murder of Thomas Becket. Also like Beaulieu, the abbey achieved prominence in the Middle Ages, attracting a great number of visitors drawn to the chapel of the Virgin by reports of miracles.[37] And again like Beaulieu, after the Dissolution of Monasteries most of the monastic buildings of Lesnes were demolished and the site transferred to private ownership. The abbot, William Tysehurst, surrendered the abbey in 1525 to Cardinal Wolsey's agent, and it became the property of Cardinal College, Oxford. After the fall of Wolsey, the abbey became the property of the King until it was granted in 1534 to Sir William Brereton, whereupon ownership changed hands through a succession of landowners until it was bequeathed to Christ's Hospital, London, in 1633. London County Council purchased the grounds in 1930 and, following excavations and restoration, opened it as a public park in 1931, before ultimately handing the site to the London Borough of Bexley in 1986, under whose guardianship it remains to this day.

Here the similarities seem to end: with regard to visitor experience, Beaulieu and Lesnes could not be more different. Now a part of a public park which comprises a nature reserve and a designated fossil bed, the ruins are left as open land, free to enjoy. Visitors walk through the ruins and picnic there, dogs roam freely, and large groups congregate on the grass, blasting music on sunny days. Its location near Woolwich means it attracts ethnically and socio-economically diverse visitors, quite different from the predominantly white middle-class fee-paying demographic of the New Forest. The site exposes the wide range of possible activities that can occur at a heritage site beyond learning from displays, guidebooks and video presentations. Play is one such activity, as Light describes:

> Many heritage sites – particularly ruins – lend themselves to various forms of play, and yet these sorts of ways of appropriating (or performing) heritage sites have been largely overlooked. For example, at one ruin a group of children were enthusiastically dashing around enacting a scene from Dr Who while their parents sat chatting on the grass nearby. At another site, two children were having a competition for who could climb highest on a part of the ruin.[38]

These sorts of behaviour illustrate that there is much more going on during a visit to a heritage place than might be expected; a visit to a heritage site is as much an imaginative and emotional event as it is a cognitive or intellectual one.

Play at Lesnes my children have certainly done, probably to the utter dismay of this individual writing to the *Oxford Mail*: 'I am writing concerning the article "Father calls for action after son falls from ruins" on October 6. I was sorry to hear a boy had been injured. Ruins are not playgrounds, they are our heritage.'[39] The opposition imposed here between 'play' and 'heritage' bears noticing and is as noteworthy as the alliance between 'ownership' and 'heritage' at Beaulieu. Clearly this writer wants 'ruins' to be subsumed under an Authorised Heritage Discourse, and visitors to submit to the monumentality of ruins; play is not an appropriate activity for places that must be kept intact as 'our heritage'. To put clearly on record, my children have never scaled the ruins at Lesnes nor defaced and damaged them, but because the ruins are not blocked off and therefore invite tactile exploration, they have certainly treated the ruins as a 'playground', which I think is a good thing. After all, where we find children playing, that is where we can see children displaying a healthy sense of security. If ruins are our heritage, should they not be the best of playgrounds, where memories are forged, where all can ramble and run carefree, where we feel happy and at ease with ourselves, and most importantly where one possesses a sense of total belonging?

Indeed, the example of children's play is fascinating because, as I think all adults know, children tend not to care very much for hierarchies of power, their approach to life instinctively mischievous and inclined to test limits. To illuminate the way children play at heritage sites, Jones' work on children's geographies is instructive, especially in the distinction he borrows from Deleuze and Guattari between 'striated' and 'smooth' spaces. Striated spaces are 'sedentary, over-determined, Euclidean, hierarchical, orientated (metrically divisible) and multiple work space', while smooth spaces are 'nomadic, folded, non-hierarchical, unorientatable, "nonmetric" free-action space'.[40] Jones argues that while adult geographies present strongly striated spaces and are constrained to strict social order, children's geographies are anarchistic, for children are 'dedicatedly unstable, systematically subversive and uncontained and all of these manifestations are managed, barely, under the rubric of creativity, self-expression, primitiveness, simplicity or even ignorance'.[41] How children use space shows their ability to negotiate and subvert 'adult-ordered striated' spaces: to our great irritation, they often find short-cuts and 'incorrect', 'inappropriate' routes. Children, as we know, are much less aware of – or care much less about – the significance of sharply defined boundaries of ownership and private property. Jones argues that adult striated spaces become smooth through the physical and imaginary geographies of childhood.[42]

At Lesnes Abbey one sunny afternoon, I watch my children play hide-and-seek, explorer and (for reasons I don't understand) pretend fishing. I observe that the spatial organization of monastic architecture structures their play, but the play in turn gives the space an entirely new meaning. The historic religious function of the site does not control how they explore the site today: they're not playing 'pretend monk', and they're certainly not busy singing psalms or reading the Bible or praying in the remains of the church nave. Yet, somehow, they know the space is different, that their fun is occurring against the backdrop of something profound. As my daughter says, 'You know what you're standing on, it's not like you're just standing on a piece of wood or that sort of thing ... You know it's not just made for children. Monks actually lived here. And I know people used to consider this place holy ... Also [pointing to her little brothers playing inside a small recess in the stonework] they are in a toilet, a historic toilet. Which is kind of gross.' My son says, 'This is a place for an adventure. I like being adventurous, and "old stones adventurous" is different from "forest adventurous" or "playground adventurous" or "haunted house adventurous".' My youngest, only five, says to me, 'There was a snail. It was on a fireplace. But it's not a fireplace any more. Bad guys broke it' (translation: a snail was climbing what used to be the caldarium, or the warming house, which now exists as ruins because after the Dissolution the building was demolished and the stone pillaged for building material). These sentiments tell me that although they are treating the ruins as a playground, it is a playground like no other: here in the ruins, they are aware of deep historical time. Yet it is not an experience of history as cognitive learning to obtain facts about the Cistercians or Augustinians, but a form of embodied learning, which is now widely considered essential to the development of children's learning in the curricular areas of history and geography.[43] Crucially, through play my children are forging a relationship *with* a historical site as participants, rather than merely acknowledging the relationship between the site and chronological history. I rely here on Ingold's ideas, applied by Elizabeth Curtis in her discussion about how children experience, understand and create their own histories in relation to the places they inhabit.[44] Ingold notes two ways of experiencing time: the first, the experience of time in a place, and the second, the experience of time in relation to chronology and in terms of historicity.[45] Ingold argues that temporality (*dwelling* time in a historical place) should not be opposed to historicity (understanding events as dated chronologically), but 'rather merge in the experience of those who, in their activities, carry forward the process

[of] social life'.[46] Thus, as Curtis argues, when it comes to children's experience of an archaeological place, they should be made to feel that it matters that *they* have been there, that their activities imbue it with historical meaning; they should not be made to feel that they are only the recipients of a 'ready-made, event-driven account of life in the past'.[47] In fact, one could argue that it's their play which gives the best meaning to heritage sites: the most vulnerable members of a society take the venerable symbols of a nation's antiquity and make their mark simply by playing there.

I do not simply conclude from this discussion that heritage attractions need to be more 'child-friendly' – that is, more sensory, hands-on, providing more opportunities for object-handling or soft play, and so on. What interests me instead is the *kind* of memory which is formed at a historic site, and its counter-hegemonic potential. From interviewing children about their experience at heritage attractions, Quinn and Roché observed that the degree of activity associated with particular visits emerged as a strong factor shaping their memories, in a similar way that the social dimension of holidays is more important to children than to adults.[48] Their observation emphasizes the manner in which heritage sites are generally associated with the broader experience of being out on a special trip with family: indeed, abbey ruins are frequently listed in websites for 'Best Places for a Family Day Out' or 'Top 10 Family Days Out', and 'taking the children' is the most frequently cited reason chosen by survey respondents for visiting museums and other heritage sites.[49] Not the educational benefit, but more crucially, the *memory-making potential* of heritage sites is their biggest draw. Furthermore, the power of a heritage site, though heightened by the knowledge of its historic or cultural significance as declared by experts, lies in its potential to engender and effect attachments between place, time and people. Watching my children play at Lesnes Abbey, it is simply impossible to isolate the various factors at work in memory-making: the twelfth-century monastic space, the opportunity for mischief and adventure, being with family ... This, I believe, is part of what Chakrabarty must mean when he speaks of the ways we '"world the earth" in order to live within our different senses of ontic belonging'.[50] The 'time-knots' discussed in the previous chapter 'always modify and interrupt the totalizing thrusts' of a chronological view of time such as an Authorised Heritage Discourse. Rather than experiencing ruins strictly as an 'event' taking place on the timeline of Western civilization, what I see as my children run and play in them are new attachments being forged, a multiplicity of activities imbuing the site with a living memory.

What we are really speaking about here is the role nostalgia plays at a heritage site and, more specifically, how a heritage site can induce a 'nostalgic reverie' in which 'the mind is "peopled"'.[51] The 'peopling' of the mind is crucial because it becomes a 'counter-memory': it replaces the authoritative discourse about what a place is *supposed* to mean and to whom it belongs, and replaces it with a new, often counterhegemonic identity.[52] Understood in this way, nostalgia 'becomes a symptom of the rebellion against the modern reconfiguration of temporality ... a reaction against the linear notions of history as progress and the accelerated time of modernization'.[53] Heritage sites such as ruins are, after all, evocative not only because they point to a time irrevocably lost, but also because they suggest a lost future, an alternative universe where what has been lost might still have existed. The nostalgia – what Galli has called 'objectified melancholy' – that heritage sites induce is often for the past's 'hidden, non-realized potentials', provoking a yearning to go back in time to relive or change a moment.[54] Ruins are where we truly feel the 'visceral experience of the irreversibility of time', wrote Svetlana Boym; heightened existentialism 'lingers on ruins, the patinas of time and history, in the dreams of another place and another time'.[55]

By way of a personal illustration, I want to show how nostalgia, with its inducement to partake in 'mental time travel' to another place and another time, rebels against the imperializing hegemony of linear historicism.[56] On the outskirts of Canterbury is a small but important parish church, St Martin's Church in Canterbury, which, along with Canterbury Cathedral and St Augustine's Abbey, is a UNESCO World Heritage Site. It is considered 'the oldest church in the English-speaking world'. A claim such as this is undoubtedly par for the course in any application submitted for heritage protection status. Such superlatives ('oldest', 'first', 'earliest', 'largest', 'longest in continuous use', etc.) justify claims to both primacy and precedence, and provide the basis for arguments about the significance of a site.[57] As Labadi notes, claims to superiority can sometimes be so extravagant that they border on fallaciousness or contradiction: Aachen and Speyer cathedrals both claimed, for example, in their 1978 and 1980 bids for UNESCO World Heritage status, to be the world's first major vaulted building.[58] The claim that St Martin's Canterbury is 'the oldest church in the English-speaking world' is, even if accurate, an audacious one. It demonstrates with precision Chakrabarty's observation about the imperialism of European historicism: 'first in Europe, then elsewhere'.[59] Apparently the claim to be the oldest church in England is not sufficient: the church must also lay claim to the rest of the world! I admit bewilderment that the claim is still so confidently splashed in large letters on the church's signboard, showing an apparent unawareness that the phrase 'English-speaking world' recalls not only empire and colonization but also, potentially, Anglo-Saxonism, understood by some to be a supremacist ideology.[60] The phrase pre-dates the set of books Churchill wrote in the 1950s about 'the fraternal association of the English-speaking peoples'.[61] In 1896, speaking about 'the future of the English-speaking peoples', Sir Walter Besant wrote:

> There remains, however, that in a hundred years the English-speaking race has leaped up from twenty millions to a hundred and twenty millions, and has extended its possessions by something like a fifth part of the habitable globe. It would be impossible to find any other example in history of an increase so rapid, and an extension of territory so vast. This, then, is the present position of our race; we possess the finest and most desirable parts of the earth; we are more wealthy than the rest of the world put together; we are connected together by a common ancestry; by a common history up to

a certain point; by the same laws which we have inherited from our common ancestors, by the same speech; by the same religion, not speaking of sects; by the same literature; by the same customs, with minute differences ... It would be difficult to find stronger bonds: they are such as nothing in the world can cut asunder. No fighting between ourselves, not centuries of warfare, not rivers of blood, can destroy these bonds.[62]

Like Milton exhorting, 'Let not England forget her precedence of teaching nations how to live', so George Beer in 1918 wrote of the resulting gift of the 'common mind' which is now, thanks to England, the 'inalienable heritage *of* all English-speaking people, whatever be their physical race *or* geographical origin'.[63] Four years later, the American President-elect Warren Harding declared, 'Destiny has made it a historical fact that the English-speaking peoples have been the instrument through which civilization has been flung to the far corners of the globe'.[64]

Clearly, therefore, the claim is rhetorically and politically laden; the phrase 'oldest church in the English-speaking world' is by no means a neutral statement. Nevertheless, I admit, the phrase has personal resonance for me, for I not only consider myself to belong to the English-speaking world but, further-more, am a churchgoer in the English-speaking world. The fact is that I recognize my own identity in this church and its claim. But this ancient sixth-century church is not personally rele-vant to me owing to reasons of birth, race and nationality, but rather, to manifold connections over time and space, between England and Hong Kong and Canada, the temporal-spatial lineage of my family history. Perhaps the phrase 'oldest church in the English-speaking world' ought to make me think of gun-boats off the coast of Hong Kong about to add the small island to the 'English-speaking world'. But intuitively and unthink-ingly, the phrase instead conjures up the memory of my family dispersed across the world: my grandparents in British Hong Kong, my father's migration to Canada, aunts and uncles and family friends in the lead-up to 1997 spreading out across the USA, Australia, New Zealand, Malaysia, Singapore – the

English-speaking world. Does the title 'oldest church in the English-speaking world' trigger patriotism? No, not for me. I do not feel the pride of the English. For me, instead, the phrase triggers nostalgia and homesickness.

And this is the sort of homesickness that the oldest church in the English-speaking world triggers as I step inside. Things so familiar to me – the architectural form, the pulpit, the pews, the hymn board, the Bibles, the altar – bring to my mind places so very, very far away. For the 'English-speaking world' was not constructed in the abstract, impersonally, as if constructing a palace, but was forged from the partings, separations, and farewells between my grandparents and their sons and daughters. So this short, seemingly innocuous phrase opens up the floodgates of homesickness and prompts a dream-like nostalgia for a lost time and an unrealized future. Then certain images flash before my mind which cause what we in Cantonese call 思親心痛 (*si chan sam tung*), a remembrance of parents or relatives which causes heartache. Like the image of my grandparents, for many years until their old age and infirmity would permit no longer, insisting on making the long journey to the airport to greet my father on his visits home. Like my grandparents saying to my father, 'We understand why after every visit back home you must leave again; we know you work hard.' Like my grandmother shipping dried scallops and tinned abalone to her sons, separated by an ocean. Like my parents receiving me at the airport after each year away, welcoming me home with a multi-course feast and herbal soups, and then seeing me off at the airport again a few short days later. Like my mother spending far too much in shipping costs to send our favourite honey and weird Chinese medicines to the UK. Like my father sending me money to buy my children new shoes and toys for Chinese New Year on his behalf.

English heritage sites will never evoke for me the sort of nostalgia that many white British people say they feel when they visit vintage motor shows and seaside fairgrounds. The sort of nostalgia I feel is for the family unit which, owing to the uneven distribution of geopolitical power that represents one legacy of imperialism, was pulled to different ends of the globe.

So, 'The post-colonial is about the diasporic consciousness,' observes Friedman.[65] Nicholas Tapp, President of the Hong Kong Anthropological Association in the lead-up to the 1997 handover, described Hong Kong in this manner:

> Husbands are constantly being parted from their wives, children from their parents and each other, every day, and in their absences we create imaginary images and representations of those who have left us or whom we have left which are continually confirmed, or challenged, by their returns or failures to return. *This* is what community is about; *not* 'face-to-face' communications, for there never was much of that – but absence, parting, separation, and death. This is the real meaning, and importance, of community; that somehow we form abstract bonds of representation of those from whom we are regularly parted and who regularly return or are returned to us.[66]

As Ien Ang notes, diasporic cultures embody the 'lived tension ... of separation and entanglement, of living here and remembering/desiring there'.[67] The tensions which come from a diasporic existence mean that I doubt my children will ever feel a total, unconflicted sense of belonging at any national heritage site. After all, diaspora 'unsettles the tendency to locate heritage value in the longstanding ties and attachments to place'.[68] Forcing a sense of belonging onto a heritage site is a meaningless endeavour, but perhaps in our memory-making (or rather, a counter-memory which opposes the 'authorized' memory of the dominant culture), we can 'world' a heritage site with the attachments formed by being there, by 'peopling' the site in our mind. For me, every return to Hong Kong is an increasingly conflicted experience: on each visit back, I find that more and more of the things for which I feel nostalgic have evaporated. For one thing my grandparents have passed away; my uncles and aunts look unrecognizably aged. The places associated with my father's childhood have long gone: the 1920s building block where he grew up has been demolished to make way for high-rise condominiums, and my children will never know the thrill of the dramatic approach to the runway at Kai-Tak Airport, the airport having closed long ago and been replaced by the massive Hong Kong International Airport at Chek Lap Kok. Gone even is my grandfather's teahouse with its ubiquitous spittoons, where my father enjoyed many a bowl of sliced beef noodle soup with his siblings at weekends. Today the site of the teahouse is occupied by a supermarket, and the photograph of the mooncake container now displayed in a museum is all that remains of this place. And so in England I realize that I must not make heritage sites do more than they're meant to here either. If not even my 'ancestral home' – ever changing in the face of the unstoppable march of time – can give me an unimpeded sense of belonging for ever, surely for a diasporic people neither can a 'national' heritage site. For at the very heart of the nostalgia that a heritage site evokes is a sense of loss, the transitoriness of time, the fleeting moment, a reminder that nothing lasts for ever. But what a heritage site can do, if we take the time to ask the varied people who feel a tie to it, is show itself to be a repository of memories spanning ages, continents, backgrounds and meanings. In this way, what counts as relevant 'memories' in a heritage site should not be subjected to an authoritative and interpretive monopoly by any one famous person, wealthy family, endowed organization or, indeed, powerful nation. Heritage sites too often induce recollections of family and ancestral feeling to be contained in this way.

Notes

1 Hong Kong government website [online]. Available at: www.gov. hk/en/about/abouthk/facts.htm (accessed 19.08.2021).

2 Steve Tsang, 1997, *A Modern History of Hong Kong 1841–1997*, London: I. B. Tauris, pp. 39–40.

3 Ming K. Chan and John D. Young, 1994, *Precarious Balance: Hong Kong between China and Britain, 1842–1992*, London: M. E. Sharpe. And a review of this book by Derek Davies, 1995, 'Precarious Balance: Hong Kong between China and Britain, 1942–1992 (Review)', *China Review International* 2(2), pp. 406–11, for correct attribution of the famous phrase.

4 UK Home Office, 29 January 2021, 'Media factsheet: Hong Kong BN(O) Visa route' [online]. Available at: https://homeofficemedia.blog.gov.uk/2021/01/29/media-factsheet-hong-kong-bnos/ (accessed 19.08.2021).

5 Stephen Teo, 2005, *Wong Kar-Wai: Auteur of Time*, London: British Film Institute, p. 142.

6 NPR Throughline, 'A Borrowed Time', 17 October 2019 [transcript online]. Available at: www.npr.org/transcripts/770699746 (accessed 19.08.2021).

7 Bruce Bain and Agnes Yinling Yu, 2003, 'The Hong Kong Immigrant Ethos on the Eve of the Handover in 1997', Leonore Loeb Adler and Uwe Peter Gielen (eds), 2003, *Migration: Immigration and Emigration in International Perspective*, London: Praeger, pp. 51–72, at 62ff.

8 Wong Kar-Wai, *In the Mood for Love*, special feature interview, quoted in Viktoriia Protsenko, 2018, 'The Emotional Cinema of Wong Kar-Wai', unpublished PhD thesis, Universitat Pompeu Fabra Barcelona (unpaginated).

9 Lewis Loud, quoted in 'Hong Kong Students See Independence as the Only Way Out for Future of Hong Kong Following Beijing's Disavowal of Sino-British Joint Declaration', Hong Kong Local Press, 8 July 2017 [online]. Available at: www.localpresshk.com/2017/07/hong-kongstudents-see-independence-as-the-only-way-outfor-future-of-hong-kong-following-beijings-disavowal-of-sino-british-joint-declaration.html (accessed 13.05.2021).

10 Dipesh Chakrabarty, 2000, *Provincializing Europe: Postcolonial Thought and Historical Difference*, Princeton, NJ: Princeton University Press, p. 27.

11 Silke Arnold-de Simine, 2013, *Mediating Memory in the Museum: Trauma, Empathy, Nostalgia*, Basingstoke: Palgrave Macmillan, p. 54.

12 See chapter and references in 'Nostalgia and Post-nostalgia in Heritage Sites', in Arnold-de Simine, *Mediating Memory*, pp. 54–67.

13 English Heritage [online]. Available at: www.english-heritage.org.uk/about-us/our-places/ecclesiastical-sites/ (accessed 18.08.2021).

14 Laurence Goldstein, 1977, *Ruins and Empire: The Evolution of a Theme in Augustan and Romantic Literature*, Pittsburgh, PA: University of Pittsburgh Press.

15 Brian Graham, Greg Ashworth and John Tunbridge, 2016, *A Geography of Heritage: Power, Culture and Economy*, London: Routledge, pp. 12, 55.

16 Sophia Labadi, 2013, *UNESCO, Cultural Heritage, and Outstanding Universal Value: Value-based Analyses of the World Heritage and Intangible Cultural Heritage Conventions*, Lanham, MD: AltaMira Press, p. 63.

17 Graham et al., *A Geography of Heritage*, p. 57.

18 Anne Janowitz, 1990, *England's Ruins: Poetic Purpose and the National Landscape*, Oxford: Blackwell.

19 Laurajane Smith, 2006, *Uses of Heritage*, London: Routledge, p. 4.

20 Keith Emerick, 2014, *Conserving and Managing Ancient Monuments: Heritage, Democracy, and Inclusion*, Woodbridge: Boydell & Brewer, pp. 1–5.

21 Emerick, *Conserving and Managing Ancient Monuments*, p. 6.

22 What follows relies on Roberta Gilchrist, 2020, *Sacred Heritage: Monastic Archaeology, Identities, Beliefs*, Cambridge: Cambridge University Press, pp. 2–3, with citations.

23 Divya Tolia-Kelly, Emma Waterton and Steve Watson (eds), 2017, 'Introduction', in *Heritage, Affect and Emotion: Politics, Practices and Infrastructures*, Abingdon: Routledge, pp. 1–11, at 4.

24 Emerick, *Conserving and Managing Ancient Monuments*, p. 7.

25 J. E. Tunbridge and G. J. Ashworth, 1996, *Dissonant Heritage: The Management of the Past as a Resource in Conflict*, Chichester: Wiley.

26 Tunbridge and Ashworth, *Dissonant Heritage*, p. 21.

27 Graham et al., *A Geography of Heritage*, p. 24.

28 My reversal of Graham et al.'s statement: 'the principal dissonance is between new national identities based upon revised and unifying heritage values, and tourism economies, which perpetuate colonial heritages in order to sell them to visitors from former metropolitan countries who recognize their own identities therein.' Graham et al., *A Geography of Heritage*, p. 94.

29 Graham et al., *A Geography of Heritage*, p. 18.

30 Smith, *Uses of Heritage*, p. 152.

31 Duncan Light, 'Heritage and Tourism', in Emma Waterton and Steve Watson (eds), 2015, *The Palgrave Handbook of Contemporary Heritage Research*, Basingstoke: Palgrave Macmillan, pp. 144–58, at 152, citing Adrian Franklin, 2003, *Tourism: An Introduction*, London: Sage.

32 Emerick, *Conserving and Managing Ancient Monuments*, pp. 208–9 and *passim*.

33 Emerick, *Conserving and Managing Ancient Monuments*, p. 220.

34 Tunbridge and Ashworth, *Dissonant Heritage*, p. 70, quoted in Yaniv Poria, Avital Biran and Arie Reichel, 2006, 'Tourist Perceptions: Personal vs. Non-Personal', *Journal of Heritage Tourism* 1(2), pp. 121–32, at 129.

35 See discussion in Poria et al., 'Tourist Perceptions' with reference to D. J. Timothy, 1997, 'Tourism and the Personal Heritage Experience', *Annals of Tourism Research* 34, pp. 751–4.

36 Council of Europe Framework Convention on the Value of Cultural Heritage for Society, Faro, 27 October 2005 [online]. Available at: www.coe.int/en/web/conventions/full-list/-/conventions/rms/090000 1680083746?module=treaty-detail&treatynum=199 (accessed 19.08.

2021). Article 2b: 'a heritage community consists of people who value specific aspects of cultural heritage which they wish, within the framework of public action, to sustain and transmit to future generations.'

37 Diana Webb, 2000, *Pilgrimage in Medieval England*, London: Hambledon and London, p. 105.

38 Light, 'Heritage and Tourism', p. 155.

39 *Oxford Mail*, Letters, 8 October 2014 [online]. Available at: www.oxfordmail.co.uk/news/11519952.ruins-not-play-heritage/ (accessed 13.05.2021).

40 Owain Jones, 2000, 'Melting Geography: Purity, Disorder, Childhood and Space', in S. Holloway and G. Valentine (eds), *Children's Geographies: Playing, Living, Learning*, Abingdon: Routledge, pp. 28–47, at 44 and n. 1.

41 Jones, 'Melting Geography', p. 29, with reference to Jenks I. Frönes, I. C. Rizzini and S. Stephens, 1997, 'Childhood and Social Theory' (Editorial Introduction), *Childhood* 4(3), pp. 259–63.

42 Jones, 'Melting Geography', p. 36.

43 Mitchell J. Nathan, 2021, *Foundations of Embodied Learning: A Paradigm for Education*, Abingdon: Routledge.

44 Elizabeth Curtis, 2015, 'The Place of Time in Children's Being', in Abigail Hackett, Lisa Procter and Julie Seymour (eds), *Children's Spatialities: Embodiment, Emotion and Agency*, Basingstoke: Palgrave Macmillan, pp. 39–53.

45 Tim Ingold, 2000, *The Perception of the Environment: Essays on Livelihood, Dwelling and Skill*, London: Routledge, p. 190.

46 Ingold, *Perception of the Environment*, p. 194.

47 Curtis, 'The Place of Time in Children's Being', p. 42.

48 D. Roche and B. Quinn, 2016, 'Heritage Sites and Schoolchildren: Insights from the Battle of the Boyne', *Journal of Heritage Tourism* [online June 2016]. Available at: doi:10.1080/1743873X.2016.1201086 (accessed 19.08.2021). Citing H. Schanzel, I. Yeoman and E. Backer (eds), 2012, *Family Tourism: Multidisciplinary Perspectives*, Bristol: Channel View Publications.

49 Laurajane Smith, 2013, 'Taking the Children: Children, Childhood and Heritage Making', in Kate Darian-Smith and Carla Pascoe (eds), *Children, Childhood and Cultural Heritage*, Abingdon: Routledge, pp. 107–25.

50 Chakrabarty, *Provincializing Europe*, p. 254.

51 D. G. Hertz, 1990, 'Trauma and Nostalgia: New Aspects on the Coping of Aging Holocaust Survivors', *Israel Journal of Psychiatry and Related Sciences* 27, pp. 189–98, at 195, quoted in Constantine Sedikides and Tim Whildschut, 2016, 'Nostalgia: A Bittersweet Emotion that Confers Psychological Health Benefits', in Alex M. Wood and Judith Johnson (eds), *The Wiley Handbook of Positive Clinical Psychology*, Oxford: Blackwell, pp. 125–36, at 128.

52 Stephen Legg, 2005, 'Contesting and Surviving Memory: Space, Nation, and Nostalgia in Les Lieux de Mémoire', *Environment and Planning D: Society and Space* 23(4), pp. 481–504, at 500.

53 Arnold-de-Simine, *Mediating Memory*, p. 56.

54 Giovanni Galli, 2013, 'Nostalgia, Architecture, Ruins, and their Preservation', *Change Over Time* 3(1), pp. 12–26, at 15; Slavoj Žižek, 2008, *In Defence of Lost Causes*, London: Verso, p. 141, quoted in Arnold-de-Simine, *Mediating Memory*, p. 56.

55 Svetlana Boym, 2001, *The Future of Nostalgia*, New York: Basic Books, p. 41.

56 On 'mental time travel', see Clay Routledge, 2015, *Nostalgia: A Psychological Resource*, Abingdon: Routledge.

57 Labadi, *UNESCO, Cultural Heritage, and Outstanding Universal Value*, p. 71, citing D. Lowenthal, 1998, *The Heritage Crusade and the Spoils of History*, Cambridge: Cambridge University Press, p. 174.

58 Labadi, *UNESCO, Cultural Heritage, and Outstanding Universal Value*, p. 71.

59 Chakrabarty, *Provincializing Europe*, pp. 7–8.

60 See Peter Clarke, 2011, 'The English-Speaking Peoples Before Churchill', *Britain and the World* 4(2), pp. 199–231, and Peter Clarke, 2013, *Mr Churchill's Profession: Statesman, Orator, Writer*, London: Bloomsbury.

61 Winston Churchill, 1956–58, *A History of the English-Speaking Peoples*, 4 vols, London: Cassell & Co. Quotation from 'The Sinews of Peace', speech given on 5 March 1946 at Westminster College, Fulton, Missouri [online]. Available at: www.nato.int/docu/speech/1946/s460305a_e.htm (accessed 19.08.2021).

62 Sir Walter Besant, 1896, 'The Future of the Anglo-Saxon Race', *The North American Review* 163(477), pp. 129–43, at 136.

63 John Milton, 1644, *Areopagitica*; George Louis Beer, *The English-Speaking Peoples: Their Future Relations and Joint International Relations*, New York: Macmillan, 1917, p. x. See Clarke, *Mr Churchill's Profession*, p. 107.

64 Clarke, *Mr Churchill's Profession*, p. 113.

65 J. Friedman, 1999, 'The Hybridization of Roots and the Abhorrence of the Bush', in M. Featherstone and S. Lash (eds), *Spaces of Culture: City, Nation, World*, pp. 230–256, quoted in Nicholas Tapp, 1999–2000, 'Post-Colonial Anthropology: Local Identities and Virtual Nationality in the Hong Kong-China Region', *Journal of the Hong Kong Branch of the Royal Asiatic Society* 39, pp. 165–93, at 169.

66 Friedman, 'Hybridization', p. 180, author's emphasis.

67 Ien Ang, 2011, 'Unsettling the National: Heritage and Diaspora', in H. Anheier and Y. R. Isar (eds), *Heritage, Memory and Identity*, London: Sage, pp. 82–94, at 86.

68 Ang, 'Unsettling the National', p. 87.

6

Ancestral Migration and Christian Cultural Capital

Just as the rear waves of the Yangtze River
drive on the waves ahead,
so each new generation surpasses the previous.

長江後浪推前浪, 一代新人勝舊人

Hong Kong is a city built on diaspora, the majority of its 7.5 million population the descendants of people who had fled China during decades of turmoil. China at the turn of the twentieth century was beset by a host of problems of which the threat of foreign invasion was only one. With a population of over 400 million in 1900, representing a quarter of the world's population, rural poverty spiralled out of control due to land shortages, drought and famine, made worse by heavy taxation, inflation and the corruption of local officials.[1] It was into this situation that my paternal grandfather was born in 1908, during the twilight years of the Qing Dynasty, the third child of peasants in Dongpo Village (東鄱村) in Foshan (佛山), Guangdong Province. So extreme was the poverty of his family that his younger brother was sold off. It fell to a great grand-aunt to find my grandfather a wife among the young women planting rice: she pointed to my grandmother across the paddy field and counselled, 'It's that one.' After marriage, to remain in poverty was a man's shame and dishonour, so like his uncles had all done, and with some basic instruction from them on the art of making dim sum, my grandfather moved to Guangzhou to work in a restaurant while his young wife stayed in Foshan, even after the birth of their first child.

In the late 1930s, my paternal grandfather was part of the

enormous wave of mostly Cantonese-speaking migrants from Guangdong province who, driven by famine and political instability on the mainland, flooded into Hong Kong. He came to Hong Kong alone, finding his first job pouring tea to customers at a teahouse in Sheung Wang, and then moving up the ranks to make dim sum at a teahouse in Sai Ying Pun disctrict. My grandfather's business acumen and reliability impressed the owner, and he was soon made manager. Having now become more established, he brought his wife and child to Hong Kong, and their second child, my aunt, was born soon afterwards. But 1941 saw the outbreak of war and the brutal Japanese occupation of Hong Kong. The stories my grandfather told about this episode in Hong Kong's history terrified me as a child. He told me of commands made at gunpoint to salute Japanese soldiers on the street, of seeing old men and young women beaten, tortured and mutilated. With a gravely inadequate food supply, the Japanese rationed necessities including rice, oil, flour, salt and sugar. My grandfather saw a man so desperate with hunger that he ate dog vomit. Under martial law and heavily restricted movement, my grandmother would sneak into my grandfather's restaurant to obtain extra food, hiding with my uncle and aunt in a cupboard as the Japanese passed by in case the cries of her 4-year-old child or newborn baby disclosed her infraction. The Japanese did not prevent, and in some cases even forced, Hong Kong residents to return to the mainland, and between 1941 and 1945, a million people migrated back to China, including my grandfather and his family.[2] His third child, my second uncle, was born just as the war ended. With another mouth to feed, poverty rife in Foshan, and no means of earning an income, my grandfather decided to return to Hong Kong with only his eldest son. He told me how he boarded a coal train and turned around to see the shrinking figures of my grandmother holding my aunt's hand and carrying her newborn son on her back, not knowing when he would see them again. Separations like this were not unusual. When my grandmother left Foshan for a second time, she left behind, again, her mother (her father's first wife) and her half-sisters from her father's second wife.

My grandparents never believed their migration to Hong Kong would be permanent: they were like many people of their generation who had initially only seen Hong Kong as a place of short-term transit, but, having found success, abandoned their expectations of returning to their ancestral villages in China. I do not know very much about my ancestors in Foshan: though the *juhk póu* (genealogy record) gives me some names, I have no photographs, no stories. Even my great-grandfather's name is not recorded in the genealogy. My aunts tell me this is because the members of my grandfather's branch were 'just poor rice farmers', and though his surname may have been illustrious, our direct lineage was not. In our particular family we do not talk about the 'Chow clan' very much. Yet there is one clan activity that sees my uncles and aunts swell with pride, and this is the donation to a school in his ancestral village which my grandfather made in 2001, over 60 years from the date he had first moved to Hong Kong. While I am more interested in the black-and-white photos from my grandfather's childhood, the photo which his eldest son wants to talk about instead is the one from 2001 showing my grandfather and his sons in front of this school. Among the men of Guangzhou of my grandfather's generation who had left their ancestral villages to pursue business and profit in South and South East Asia – Hong Kong, Singapore, Malaysia, Macau, etc. – this represented a common trope: the refugee from the mainland who had not forgotten his origins after finding success abroad. Schools were common beneficiaries of donations from émigrés, signalling at once a recollection of one's own childhood and care for future generations of children.

'Rags to riches' stories about migrants have become so commonplace that the cliché threatens to diminish my grandfather's extraordinary achievement: having started out life so poor that he did not even have the one item required for attending school in his village in 1915, a stool to sit on, he died at the age of 103, the shareholder and director of no less than 15 restaurants in Hong Kong, with a significant real estate portfolio. The cliché also masks the powerful ways in which the narrative works in my family's collective memory. My grandfather's 'rags to riches' story is not circulated in my family simply as a morality tale about the rewards of hard work: it differs radically from the 'American Dream', an individual's pursuit of happiness and opportunity. Rather, the meaning inscribed onto my grandfather's life lies in a resolutely Confucian tradition in which the pursuit of individual goals is always subjugated to the larger obligation to family. My grandfather's success, transferred onto his descendants in the form of both financial provision and a work ethic, produced an unspoken but unequivocally understood rule within our family, that the tie that binds generations together is diligence and mutual sacrifice: elder generations work hard to provide for younger generations, and by the same hard work younger generations honour the memory of their elders. Shame is conceived in terms of dishonouring both future and past generations, the former by failing to provide for them, the latter by squandering their sacrifices. Thus among family-oriented societies, the upward mobility which is sought is specifically *intergenerational* mobility. Whether it be the satisfaction of basic human needs (food, safety, security) or economic opportunity, ensuring progress from one generation to the next is an ancestral obligation, an expression both of gratitude to elders and duty of care for the young.

The stereotypical Chinese 'tiger parent' – controlling, authoritarian, pushy, competitive and unreasonably ambitious – is the easy target of vitriol in Western societies, but attacks usually overlook the fundamental impulse that drives the effort and desire to produce high-performing, top-attaining, overachieving children. This is the belief held by many Chinese families that children must recall the sacrifices and hardships of our ancestors, be on the alert for complacency and never feel entitled to a life of security and ease. 'Tiger-style' parenting is largely a response to the fear that the traits which make an immigrant generation successful – hardworking, motivated, aspirational, sacrificial – do not automatically get passed down to successive generations who, born into comfort and never having known hardship, tend towards laziness.[3] Therefore every generation has a duty to remember the virtues associated with ancestral immigrants, those of thrift, modesty, selflessness, perseverance and diligence. After explaining her great fear of 'generational decline', Amy Chua recounts why she insisted her daughters learn classical music:

> I knew that I couldn't artificially make them feel like poor immigrant kids. There was no getting around the fact that we lived in a large old house, owned two decent cars, and stayed in nice hotels when we vacationed. But I *could* make sure that Sophia and Lulu were deeper and more cultivated than my parents and I were. Classical music was the opposite of decline, the opposite of laziness, vulgarity, and spoiledness.[4]

With its presupposition that classical music represents progress, this quote gets to the heart of the matter. For perhaps the most biting accusation levelled against 'tiger parents' is that they produce 'model minorities' in Western nations, people who choose to be racially ignorant, to overlook or even forgive racial prejudices, deliberately acculturating to white society for the sake of upward mobility. Chinese immigrants win approval by playing classical music rather than engaging in protest and resistance against racism. In a word, it has been said, we are sell-outs: white-washed, white apologists.

The charge of being a racial traitor – insert relevant epithet here (banana, gorilla, Oreo, Uncle Tom) – is particularly astringent when it comes to Christian heritage. The seriousness of the problem becomes apparent when we note that the first black person usually to appear in textbooks and syllabi on modern church history, and who is proudly held up as a symbol of the globalization of Christianity and democratization of Anglicanism, receives this verdict from Wole Soyinka:

> There is nothing to choose ultimately between the colonial mentality of an (Samuel) Ajayi Crowther, West Africa's first black bishop, who groveled [sic] before his white missionary superiors in a plea for patience and understanding of his 'backward, heathen, brutish', brother ... and the new black ideologues who are embarrassed by statements of self-apprehension by the new 'ideologically backward' African.[5]

When it comes to Chinese Christians, this 'groveling' – the adoption of the terms and references of the dominant, ruling class – often occurs as a result of the pressure to achieve inter-generational social mobility. Academic ambition and aspiration for success, so closely tied to the obligation to honour ancestors in the Chinese world view, necessitates the adoption of many features of whiteness – including the mastery of European Christian heritage. In mainland China this is especially true of the generation of intellectuals who flourished during the Chinese Communist Party's policy of reform and opening in the 1970s, which not only permitted but embraced the study of Western Christianity – its philosophy and history in particular – as a topic of academic intellectual interest (*sichao* 思潮). The trend in scholarship attracted the label 'religion fever' (*zongjiao re* 宗教熱) and 'Christianity fever' (*jidujiao re* 基督教熱). Highly educated and well-established intellectuals contributed to the phenomenon in China known as 'cultural Christianity'.[6] Among them are He Guanghu, Zhuo Xinping, Zhao Dunhua and Gu Weimin and, most influentially, Liu Xiaofeng 劉小楓 (b. 1956), often considered the most representative 'cultural Christian' who had found his way to Christian thought through Western philosophy, Russian literature and German theology. Today as then, interest in Christianity as a system of thought and culture reflective of Western civilization can lead to conversion, but often intellectuals refrain from Christian practices, rites and participation in congregational life. Thus conservative evangelicals, mostly from Hong Kong, have disparaged these intellectuals, branding them 'China's Apollos' (Acts 18.24–28) and 'China's Nicodemus' (John 3.1–10) or, worse, 'anonymous Christians'. They have accused 'cultural Christians' of being modern-day 'rice Christians', the Chinese poor who lived in the growing list of treaty ports during China's 'century of humiliation' and, seeking food, shelter and employment, saw conversion to Christianity as a way to achieve social mobility. Protestant missionaries helped converts acquire language, education and foreign connections, which translated into social status and material benefits, bestowing on them what Lian Xi has called the 'prestige of the

West'.[7] A similar dynamic, some have argued, operates today to promote Chinese interest in Christianity – not hunger for rice, but for intellectual and cultural sophistication. Liu Xiaobo, political dissident and Nobel Peace Prize winner, for example, asks whether or not the 'divine value in Christianity' will 'become a real spiritual resource, or will instead be reduced to a "spiritual white collar" of the *cultural nouveau riche*'.[8] Hong Kong scholar of theology Leung Ka-lun derides the perceived snobbery and presumptuousness of 'cultural Christians':

> Can a person who never goes to church nor accept [sic] any of the ideas and patterns of behaviour handed down by the traditions of Christian faith call himself a 'Christian' just because he is attracted to one single quote of Augustine?[9]

This chapter is an attempt to disentangle the complex dynamics between ancestral obligation, intergenerational mobility and Western Christian heritage, particularly as they relate to the vexed issue of racial betrayal. I begin with the correlation between ethnicity, class and acculturation – or, to put it crassly, the correlation between ethnic success and 'acting white'.[10] This contemporary dilemma has undoubtedly historic origins which lie in the 'grooming' of colonized 'mimics' into a colonizing social élite. It is no secret that nineteenth-century English imperialists, for reasons of tact, generally preferred imperialism by delegation ('indirect rule') to direct legislation. This informal but widespread policy meant that in every colony over which the British ruled, the primary objective was to raise a class of indigenous leaders. What is meant by 'indigenous leaders' has been the subject of much discussion. The classic work of anti-colonialism, Frantz Fanon's *Wretched of the Earth* began with the following preface by Jean-Paul Sartre:

> The European élite undertook to manufacture a native élite. They picked out promising adolescents; they branded them, as with a red-hot iron, with the principles of western culture, they stuffed their mouths full with high-sounding phrases, grand glutinous words that stuck to the teeth. After a short

stay in the mother country they were sent home, white-washed. These walking lies had nothing left to say to their brothers; they only echoed.[11]

Thus, in Blauner's schematization, the mechanism by which colonial oppression worked was not just the forced entry of a foreign group into a territory for the purposes of exploiting it (first phase), nor simply the imposition of the colonizer's culture upon indigenous culture (second phase). But the colonizer's most sinister move is to ensure that his truth and standards become everyone's truth, by transmitting his world view to native élites so they then defend the interests of the colonizing powers. Thus the third phase of colonization is in place when a distinction is drawn between the wild/savage/uncivilized and the cultured/civilized. Finally, established institutions (for example, churches, schools) reward those who assimilate to the colonizer's ways (fourth phase). The colonizer's view is thereby passed on to an indigenous élite, who reproduce colonial ideology through their 'internalized colonialism'.[12] These are the 'mimic men' in V. S. Naipaul's 1967 novel, and those envisaged by Lord Thomas Babington Macaulay in 1835 as 'a class of persons Indian in blood and colour, but English in tastes, in opinions, in morals and in intellect'.[13]

At the height of British imperialism, Thomas Arnold, father of Matthew Arnold and the headmaster of Rugby from 1827 to 1842, articulated his educational aims in terms of producing 'Christian gentlemen' capable of governing the country and empire, thereby establishing the long-lasting alliance between Christian culture, status, influence and British élite schooling. Public schools like Harrow, Westminster and Eton are a legacy of empire, having trained pupils for roles in colonial offices and imperial service overseas.[14] The school chapel nurtured awareness of Christian morality; at the same time, the public school inculcated gentry-class tastes, style and manners.[15] The younger Arnold's oft-quoted definition of culture as 'the best which has been thought and said in the world' stemmed from his hope that *culture* could unify society and carry forward Christian ideals without the divisiveness of religion. Because cultural legacies like philosophy, art and literature share the same aim as Judaeo-Christian religion, man's perfection, and because the 'very language which they both of them [*sic*] use in schooling us to reach this aim is often identical', England's Christian character ought to be transposed from religion to culture, and thereby achieve a more expedient universalism.[16] The link articulated here between religion and English culture persists many decades after the formal end of British imperialism. Ingrid Storm's 2011 analysis found that the association of Christianity with national traditions or ethnic heritage rather than private faith is very much prevalent within the UK.[17] Christianity remains stubbornly tied to English cultural symbols.

Our discussion here of course recalls Bourdieu's notion of cultural capital – an idea reliant on Weber's model of uneven distribution. 'Capital' is valued because it is perceived as scarce and finite, and individuals and groups compete for it as part of their quest for power and legitimation. 'Capital' in this sense extends beyond economics to varied forms of distinctive tastes, skills, knowledge and practices which are embodied in cultural objects and credentials. There is nothing objective about these cultural preferences; they serve merely to produce cultural standards which in turn generate social distinctions – and thus the title of Bourdieu's book *Distinction: A Social Critique of the Judgement of Taste*.[18] Cultural capital helps us distinguish between the refined and vulgar, the sophisticated and common, the educated and the uneducated, the ruling classes and the working classes, the respectable and the delinquent. Economic theorists argue that religious behaviour is one very important kind of cultural capital: religion produces cultural traits which can be acquired, accumulated, used to generate value and secure competitive advantage over others.[19] There are many ways in which religious factors constitute cultural capital, but the aspect I'd like to focus on is how 'Christian heritage' elevates certain cultural forms ('highbrow culture') to produce distinctions in social class. McKinnon has explored one such example, the selection of diocesan bishops, an overwhelming number of whom come from professional families, attended a public (independent) school and Oxford or Cambridge.[20] McKinnon argues that their upper-middle-class background influenced not only career choices but also dispositions, ways of carrying oneself, tastes, manners of speaking and ambitions, which gave them a competitive advantage. His observations suggest that, in the UK, the sort of Christianity more generally useful for improving social status has less to do with spiritual, confessional – evangelical – religiosity than 'cultural capital' in the Bourdieusian sense.[21]

Crucially, this means that the aspect of Christianity that is much more amenable to social mobility is the *historical* rather than the dogmatic or confessional. For example, the art decorating the Houses of Parliament serves to remind MPs and Lords of the historic legacies of Christianity in the country they govern: the central image above the monarch's throne in the House of Lords is a painting of the baptism of King Æthelberht of Kent in 597, St Stephen's Hall features George Clausen's *The English People Reading Wycliffe's Bible*, the floor of the Central Lobby is inscribed with the Latin Vulgate rendering of Psalm 127.1, the clockface of the Elizabeth Tower contains a prayer in Latin for Queen Victoria. Some choose to interpret these features merely as heritage symbols tied to the historic legacy of Western Christendom rather than signs of 'real Christianity'. For example, Matthew Engelke quotes the Bible Society's Parliamentary Officer as saying, regarding the Christian references in the Houses of Parliament, 'What we were looking at and where we were standing was, in an important sense, the stuff of museums. Britain carried the mantle of Christendom, but such fineries and trappings were ultimately inconsequential.'[22]

Yet the reality is that these cultural references are not 'inconsequential' at all. In an oft-cited study about 'religious effects' among American adolescents, Christian Smith points out just how potent 'Christian heritage' as cultural capital remains today. Attempting to articulate a systematic theory about religion's positive, constructive influence on American youth, Smith argued that youth who are biblically literate 'better understand the Western historical context'. For one thing, they acquire 'substantial musical education' through participation in choirs and exposure to 'rich traditions of sacred music, learning to sing four-part harmonies for hymns'. Religious education means American youth are more knowledgeable about 'world civilizations and empires' (the Babylonians, Egyptians, the Roman Empire, etc.), Western history (the Middle Ages, the Reformation, etc.), major religious traditions (Jewish, Protestant, Catholic, etc.), and also important theological and philosophical categories. His conclusion is strikingly blunt:

> [S]imply because familiarity with the Jewish and Christian (and Greek) traditions is a precondition for truly understanding Western history, civilization, and culture[,] acquiring through religion the knowledge and appreciation of matters such as those described above also tremendously advantage youth who accumulate this cultural capital. *The adolescent who soaked up the various kinds of cultural capital available through involvement in his or her religion may have gained a relative edge over the one who has not* ... The young person will likely converse more comfortably with a broader array of social contacts, perform better in humanities and social science classes, be more impressive in the lunch and dinner conversations of job interviews, and more. All this tends to work positive, constructive attitudinal and behavioral outcomes.[23]

Smith is here trying to make a case for why religion continues to be relevant and socially beneficial. But for me the real power of this study is what it suggests about the sort of capital society continues to value, the relationship which persists between Christianity, Western civilization and 'high culture', even in liberal secular societies, and, crucially therefore, how attractive Christianity remains to aspirational immigrant groups. Historic dimensions of Western Christianity – those tied to philosophy, music, art, literature – stubbornly retain their status as 'capital', representing cultural resources and assets available for acquisition and transmission that bring competitive advantage to those who possesses them.

So strong is the pull of the cultural capital represented by 'Western Christian heritage' that it has more or less recovered from its violent purge during China's Cultural Revolution of the 1960s, when anyone inclined towards 'bourgeois elements' including Western learning and ideas was brutally expunged as a counter-revolutionary. Today, Chinese foreign students make up 44 per cent of the total 28,910 pupils at British independent schools, and this statistic doesn't even include Chinese nationals living here. Chinese pupils bring in about £220 million annually to British boarding schools and are by far the largest and still fastest growing group of foreign students.[24] The influence of this education extends even further: many exclusive British public schools have now opened branches in China, so that one can be a student at Chengdu Westminster School, Charterhouse School Shenzhen, Wellington College International Tianjin, Harrow International School Shanghai, Dulwich College Shanghai. Parents pay hefty fees for their children to be conferred the symbolic capital of a British élite school even when the physical site is in mainland China: the promise of credentials, manners, tastes and hobbies associated with the prestige of English gentry holds significant appeal to the Chinese market. Without a doubt, the Arnoldian image of the 'Christian gentleman' fit for ruling is alive and well in the twenty-first century.[25]

The dilemma, of course, is that for the ethnic minority, the process of capital acquisition depends on 'mimicry'. In order to illustrate the nature of this problem, allow me a personal anecdote. When my first cohort of students approached their graduations, they sent me flowers. I happened to place the flowers next to photos of my grandparents, and when I stood back, the story of intergenerational mobility told by these objects on my windowsill suddenly dawned on me. I tried to express my thoughts in a note of thanks to my students:

Growing up, I heard my parents and grandparents say many times, 'In Hong Kong, we respected the British a lot, but we never felt the respect was mutual. We were always the students, never the teachers.' When I came to St Mellitus, the situation was different. Would it be acceptable if I were now the 'teacher', and in the metropole itself, no less? I worried whether my first cohort of Anglican ordinands would accept me. Now, at the end of your time at St Mellitus, I can conclude you have embraced me with affection, respect, gratitude. As I look at the photographs of my grandparents next to these flowers from you, I think they would feel really happy knowing that the relationship of respect and affection is no longer unidirectional.

To some this may sound a note of triumph, of social progress. But equally some may well accuse me of becoming a 'mimic man', having adequately imitated Western learning and manners to the extent that I am permitted to teach a Western subject in a Western institution to Western students. As the term suggests, 'mimicry' is indeed the colonized's successful adoption of the colonizer's cultural habits and values. But, as Homi Bhabha has influentially argued, mimicry can never be an exact reproduction; rather it is a 'partial presence', an incomplete imitation. Bhabha believes mimicry possesses subversive potential, that it can expose cracks in colonial dominance, writing, 'The menace of mimicry is its double vision which in disclosing the ambivalence of colonial discourse also disrupts its authority.' 'Ambivalence' occurs because the colonized is not an exact replica of the colonizer: he is 'almost but not quite', 'almost but not white'. As a result, this partial imitation introduces a 'double vision': the colonized mirrors the colonizer, but the reflection is 'inappropriate', a disturbing image and even a parody, because its incomplete imitation reveals cultural and racial differences that threaten the total hold and authority of colonizing powers. Mimicry is therefore 'at once resemblance and menace', the threat coming not from the colonized's overt resistance but from his capacity to work within the paradigms of the colonizer while managing to escape its full disciplinary power. The mimicry of the colonized person is therefore always a destabilizing force because it reveals that imperial dominance can never be total.[26]

Bhabha's theorization about mimicry helpfully complicates the 'sell-out' narrative that presumes a binary choice between racial betrayal and shameless mimicry. For in the case of many

Chinese parents, the appropriation of the colonizer's culture – far from being a straightforward attempt at imitation – can often reflect a striving for intergenerational mobility which is in itself an act of filial piety, a show of respect towards one's ancestors. The appropriation of Western heritage cannot therefore be attributed *exclusively* and *solely* to the sheer force of an imperial power, but rather also stems from an intergenerational consciousness that attaches progress to migration. To expose how this operates, let me suggest that a white British person does not usually feel a great deal of discomfort with the concept of England's 'Christian heritage', even if history isn't his or her cup of tea. Most will know the Lord's Prayer, some basic idioms from the Bible, some famous pieces of Christian art and sculpture, some hymns and carols from the Christian tradition, what a church service generally looks and sounds like ... It is simply taken for granted that this is 'heritage'. For ethnic minorities, however, understanding this heritage represents an act of learning, of acquisition, and therefore, crucially, of *progress*. And so it becomes clear why, in the story that circulates in my family about our history, the very nature of 'progress' is geographical, migratory and cross-cultural. For in order to acquire the cultural capital that would allow each generation to transcend the previous (to be better educated, to be more respected, to have a higher status), like a wave pushing on a wave, crossing a sea was *literally* required.

Cartography is central to the narrative of intergenerational success engendered by migration; conceived in terms of progress resulting from movement across lands and oceans, 'ancestral feeling' inspires graphic representation and spatial imagination. But our cartographic imaginations do us a disservice when they promote unidirectional thinking, visualizing the flow of people from one side of the ocean to another, either benevolently bearing gifts or desperately pursuing them.[27] Yet this is precisely how many of us have learned to visualize the transmission of our religious heritage, with the arrow as the graphic representation of choice in maps. Tim Dowley's *Atlas of Christian History* introduces us to Christian geography with a map of the 'Mission of the Twelve', 16 red arrows each representing the apostles and their associated traditions emanating from a single red dot in Jerusalem outwards in 360 degrees, reaching India, Ethiopia, Egypt, Persia, Armenia, Syria, Greece, Italy, Spain and even Britain. Many subsequent maps follow this approach: coloured arrows trace the 'Medieval Missions to the Mongol Empire and the East' of thirteenth- and fourteenth-century Franciscans and Dominicans from France, Italy and Germany eastward through North Africa, the Middle East and Asia; 'Protestant Settlers in North America' originating from Europe; the influence of George Whitefield from England and the Pietists from Germany via England on the 'Great Awakening in North America'. Maps of Asia, Latin America and Africa in the nineteenth and twentieth centuries are dominated by incoming arrows to symbolize the establishment of mission stations by societies originating in Europe or the Anglosphere, or the movement of missionaries into the interior of a land.[28] Granted this graphical technique is highly effective at achieving the purported aim of Dowley's atlas – 'to examine the origins, beginnings, growth, and worldwide spread and development of Christianity' – but it also carries an ideological message, particularly when prefaced with the rather audacious quotation from Oliver Cromwell included in the inside cover: 'What are all histories but God manifesting himself?'[29]

This general manner of charting the migration of movement and ideas has drawn much critique, not least because it represents a mode of constructing truth which, when applied to people, can be particularly dangerous.[30] In the creation of modern European states, it was the map that emerged as the crucial tool for establishing and maintaining geopolitical power over commerce, population movement and military activity. Houtum directs his critique at maps that use red arrows to represent the movement of migrants into Europe and the USA: a 'map of a state border and migration as a unidirectional ... arrow crossing that state border', he argues, takes into account neither the heterogeneity of those who move, nor the complexity and multidimensionality of borders and migration.[31] Winther similarly castigates the arrow, lambasting what he has termed 'arrowized assumptions' which over-simplify a subject matter 'by abstracting away and averaging out differences among individual people, objects, or processes' in a 'Euclidean, GIS space' of linear, continuous, isotropic time.[32]

Particularly problematic is the way that arrowized maps visualizing unidirectional flows present a 'statist narration' which features 'a chosen set of historically materialized social relations'.[33] When it comes to Christian heritage and its relationship with migration, of what this 'chosen set of historically materialized social relations' comprises is quite clear, as evident from the maps I have mentioned above. The expansion of Christianity, the processes of denominational development, the proliferation of Christian culture – these are all processes that originate in the West. Similarly, I have long relied on a map to visualize the process by which my parents in Hong Kong became Baptists, a map admittedly reliant on all the irksome indicators of linear historicism: it overlays 'decisive turning points' in church history onto geographic sites and shows the movement of time and ideas via arrows. My map begins in England with the Reformation during the reigns of Henry VIII, Edward VI, Mary Tudor and Elizabeth I. With Separatists from the Church of England arguing that the English Reformation did not go far enough, we go into exile to the Netherlands in 1609 with John Smyth, Thomas Helwys and their Baptist communities, escaping religious persecution during the reign of James I. In 1612 we travel with Helwys back to London, where he establishes the first Baptist church in England. Then we trace the journey of Roger Williams across the ocean to Rhode Island, where in 1639 he establishes what is widely considered the oldest Baptist congregation in North America. With the founding of the American Baptist Home Mission Society in 1832, we travel with Jehu Lewis Shuck and Henrietta Hall Shuck to Macau in 1836. Upon the British possession of Hong Kong, we then follow the Shucks and their colleagues William Dean and Issachar J. Roberts as they become some of the first missionaries to reside in the new colony, establishing the first Baptist congregation on Queen's Road. William Dean then organizes a separate Chiu Chow-speaking congregation composed of three members meeting on rented premises, which benefits greatly in

1896 from a visit by a wealthy American woman called Mrs Vanderpool who offers a donation to purchase a building. Five years later in 1901, a new building on Peel Street opens as the Hong Kong Baptist Self-Governing Chinese Christian Church with 38 members.[34] This is the congregation that becomes the Hong Kong Baptist Church on Caine Road – and by this line of descent, we finally get to my parents, introduced to the youth fellowship at this church by their classmates and my aunt.

Visualizing my Baptist roots in this manner, it's easy to see the subaltern's problem of belatedness. It locks my parents into a 'a peculiar diasporic itinerary informed by the historical connections established by European colonialism', including settler colonialism in America.[35] It relies on a conventional way of conceiving the transfer of culture (religious or otherwise) from the West to the rest, like the *translatio studii* (transfer of learning) described by Kwame Anthony Appiah: 'from the late Middle Ages until now, people have thought of the best in the culture of Greece and Rome as a civilizational inheritance, passed on like a precious golden nugget.'[36] Appiah urges us to abandon the concept of Western civilization altogether as though it were something we can inherit, possess, pass on. His argument is liberating in so far as he assures us 'Western Christian heritage' should not be perceived as an 'asset' which some possess by right of birth or nationality or skin colour and others have literally to cross oceans in order to obtain. Responding to Appiah, however, the journalist Josh Glancy observes that even if we abandon the concept of Western civilization, the stories and narratives we tell about ourselves are incredibly powerful, 'so what do we replace it with?', he asks.[37] The question is an exceedingly good one, for 'Western civilization', even if not actually a 'golden nugget' transferable from generation to generation, nevertheless still exists as such in many a migrant's aspirations and imaginations. It is the thing that one crosses an ocean to pursue and, at least in many Chinese families, this not for the sake of individual gain, but so that one may observe filial piety through service to family. For example, migration fulfils obligations to previous generations when one earns money that can be sent home to elderly parents and extended family in the form of remittances; migration also fulfils obligations to future generations when a child is sent to a foreign boarding school so that he or she has better life outcomes. These are the stories and narratives that migrants commonly tell, and they are insistently intergenerational. The challenge facing critical geography, therefore, is to find an appropriate spatial representation of these multidimensional, multi-layered relationships which move beyond the simple linear arrow. As Houtum argues, maps today should make every effort to 'visualize the human rhizomatic becomings, zigzag connections, traces, tracks and linkages, and the movements and (e)motions that cannot be universally rationalized, yet are felt, sensed and believed'.[38] Maps 'should be as dynamic as the human beings who make and give meaning to territory. The tempo, rhythm and (e)motions of people in space and not the fixity or the settling down should be central.'[39]

The concept of 'tidalectics' developed by the poet and philosopher Kamau Brathwaite will help us here.[40] Characterized by DeLoughrey as a 'geopoetic model of history', 'tidalectics' is inspired by the rhythms and flow of the ocean in relation to the land.[41] Wanting to emancipate us from our dependence on terrestrial conceptions, on land-based modes of thinking and an obsession with solidity and fixity (that is, identarian and essentialist), Brathwaite would instead have us attend to fluctuations and fluidity: tidal dynamics are waves surging forward, hitting shores, staying but for a moment, retreating to the sea, only to repeat this process again and again. This is a metaphor designed specifically to reject the Hegelian notion of historical progress: tidalectics (as opposed to dialectics) allow a fluid and complex relationship between time and space, preferring 'alter/native' (that is, alternative, or native) historiography to linear models of source, origin, transmission, progress and destination.[42] Relying on the metaphor of fluid lines flowing back and forth across the surface of the ocean, this mode of thinking aims to move us beyond restrictive national, colonial and regional frameworks and to foreground shared histories, particularly as they are shaped by geography.[43] The primary aim is to produce better histories of diasporic people: to emancipate 'routed' (diasporic) peoples from the tyranny of 'rooted' identities grounded on notions of 'a sacred past, a national filiation, a physical territory, and a colonial project'.[44] Thus, tidalectics emphasizes what Glissant has called a 'poetics of relation' which highlights process, crossings and interchange, rejecting the attempt to retrace a pure lineage of descent.

The implications for how we 'map' history are profound. As DeLoughrey observes by quoting the poet Derek Walcott, our obsession with maps to show territories and boundaries is precisely how 'the mind was halved by a horizon'. Walcott's poem highlights that 'the stick to trace our names on the sand' is just a temporary, provisional tool, because ultimately the sea will 'erase' all human uses for cartography.[45] The map I visualize to explain my Baptist roots betrays such a restricted horizon, and the problem is shared by any denominational history that recounts a 'genealogy' focused on Anglo and Anglo-American origins. In fact, as Johnson argues in his *Global Introduction to Baptist Churches*, Baptists cannot point to a single individual or group as the source of their faith tradition. Although numerous histories identify the Anglican priest John Smyth (mentioned above) as the first Baptist, in reality his influence was limited. Several of his followers organized his community into English General Baptist denominations, while other Baptist groups developed without any contact with his ideas, especially in the Anglo-American, Anglo-Canadian, Native, African and African American cultural bases. So Johnson argues, 'the movement cannot be conceived as originating out of a single core from which subsequent schisms produced division', and apprehending the development of Baptist churches with reference to their origins in 'Anglo identity' obscures the influences from other independently derived sources.[46]

Taking into view even just a few more dimensions, the map I visualize, described above, no longer makes any sense. The strands that explain my religious lineage are a complex web which, even when simplified for the sake of explanatory ease, are a bewildering mess resisting partitioning along clear lines and strands. How could I possibly select which of the following stories of religious ancestry to tell?

I have already traced the movement of Separatists and their missionary descendants from England via America to Hong Kong: John Smyth, Thomas Helwys, Roger Williams, Jehu Lewis and Henrietta Shuck, William Dean. But in fact, Hong Kong only became a centre of vital Baptist expansionist activity when many Chinese people and foreign missionaries escaped the mainland during the civil war between the Kuomintang and the Communist Party, and during the Chinese Communist Revolution. Therefore we must acknowledge the 'pre-history' of the Shucks and the Deans in mainland China, a strand that explains the conversion to Christianity of my husband's great-grandparents. The Shucks and Deans had been sent to Hong Kong but, at this point in 1842, Hong Kong was perceived as merely the entry point and headquarters for missionary activity inland. Shortly after establishing the first Baptist congregation in Hong Kong, the American Baptist Mission in Hong Kong was closed and its work transferred to the newly opened port of Shantou.[47] The new base for missions in Shantou attracted the attention of the itinerant minister John Sung, who achieved fame when, having earned multiple degrees from American universities, including a PhD in Chemistry, he threw his diplomas overboard during his sea voyage back to China in a vow to commit his life to preaching. Back in Shantou, the story intersects with my husband's family history. My husband's paternal great-grandfather was a successful businessman but addicted to opium. During one of John Sung's evangelistic revival meetings, he underwent a dramatic conversion experience and repented of his opium addiction. Believing in the gospel preached by John Sung and in healing by faith, he abruptly quit smoking opium, oblivious to the danger of severe withdrawal. Diarrhoea and dehydration led to cardiovascular collapse, sending him into a coma. Thinking that he had died, his family dressed him in burial gowns and placed him in the salon for relatives to pay their respects. It was said that he suddenly awoke, delivered a few words of comfort, then passed away peacefully. Inspired by her husband's strength in the face of unbearable physical suffering, his wife vowed to pass the faith on to her children.

Or shall we tell of the religious inheritance that comes to my family through the 'big names' of missions to China, individuals with no direct connection to the churches in Hong Kong but who have attained legendary status in Chinese Christian history? Names like Hudson Taylor, Pearl S. Buck, Robert Morrison and Lottie Moon populate memoirs, charities and buildings, and all are considered the spiritual forebears of Chinese Protestant Christians.

Or shall we turn to the genealogy of Christian publishers who first provided vital reading material to converts? We should mention the Baptist Press, which claims a lineage via Chen Jinsheng, a Chinese living in New York in the 1880s who became a Christian after reading a gospel tract. Visiting a Baptist bookshop during a trip to Philadelphia, he was stirred by a vision that such a place should also exist in China. Upon returning to Guangzhou where he became a pastor, he prayed to the Lord every morning for the opening of a Christian bookshop and press. He died without seeing his prayer granted, but in 1895 a missionary from the Southern Baptist Convention, R. E. Chambers, was sent to Guangzhou and there opened in 1899 the Meihua ('America-China') Baptist Publication Society. The publishing ministry flourished and moved to larger premises in 1932, an eight-storey building in Shanghai, where it was renamed the 'China Baptist Publication Society', supplying the nation with their Christian literary needs. When the Communist Party was established in 1949, missionaries moved their operations to Hong Kong, from where they printed gospel leaflets for use throughout Asia. In 1955, a new building in Kowloon was purchased as the base for the publication ministry in Asia. Renamed the Baptist Press in 1980, the organization has steadily produced Chinese-language devotional, evangelistic and Sunday school materials, such that many of Asia's Christians, including my parents, ascribe their religious formation to this ministry.[48]

Or shall we turn to the Student Christian Movement, which propelled Christian campus ministry, the womb that nurtured my parents' faith in locations as far apart as Hong Kong, Edmonton and Winnipeg? To this day Chinese diasporic communities still model their student ministries on the secondary school and university student unions of the early-to-mid-1900s, by which 'fellowship counsellors' mentored generations of young Christians to lead Bible studies and prayer meetings, engage in preaching and mission, and hold one another to expected standards of morality. My parents' experience with student fellowship is owing to the large influx of Christian university students fleeing to Hong Kong from China following the Communist victory. Having experienced persecution for their faith, they sparked a huge revival on Hong Kong campuses. Tracing this lineage further back, we can name Calvin Chao, David Adeney and the China Inter-Varsity Christian Fellowship in the mainland. And then further back still, we can speak of the Student Volunteer Movement and household names in evangelical circles like John Mott. Prior to this, we could pursue any number of strands, like the evangelist D. L. Moody who led a summer conference for Christian university students in Mount Hermon in 1886. Many trace the lineage further still to John and Charles Wesley's Holy Clubs at Oxford in the eighteenth century, which focused on Bible study, prayer, fasting and the pursuit of holiness.

But we cannot overlook the influence of 'white' churches in university towns who warmly embraced so many foreign students like my father as he spent years far from home. Church members 'adopted' students into their homes, hosted them at Thanksgiving and Christmas, and even attended their weddings. How do you represent in an arrow the missionaries and professors who, drawn by the vast numbers of foreign students, chose to move or retire to university towns specifically to nurture the faith of the student generation? And then how do we describe – let alone spatially depict – the fact that many of these same graduates returned to Asia to lead the churches and Christian ministries there? Ask many of them and they will tell you that they consider Canada and the USA their 'spiritual homeland' because of how their faith was nurtured on the university campus.

And then, given my parents' eventual emigration to Canada, there is the Canadian Baptist ancestry that also needs to be traced. The Baptist community in Canada began as an ad hoc colonial outpost in the early 1800s with pioneering pastors from Scotland and the United States gradually organizing themselves into associations of churches in Upper Canada. The Toronto Association of Baptist Churches was founded on 26 June 1874 in the vestry of the Second Markham Baptist Church in Port Perry. Of the Toronto churches, the Baptist church on Bond Street is of particular interest to me. Initially renting a room in a Masonic lodge in 1827, the fledgling congregation grew until it finally relocated to a 2,000-seat church on Jarvis Street in 1886. From here, the Jarvis Street Baptist Church established an outreach congregation, the Beverley Street Baptist Church. In 1967, three families began meeting in the church's basement, and within five years had grown into such a large congregation that they were able to buy the building and rename it the Toronto Chinese Baptist Church. In the 1980s, recognizing the large influx of immigrants from Hong Kong, the Toronto Chinese Baptist Church led an expansion into the suburb of Scarborough, and in 1986 Scarborough Chinese Baptist Church was inaugurated. Today, the church has 1,842 members and an average Sunday attendance of 1,675, and reaches an audience of over 1,850 on its weekly livestream. It is the church that my parents called their home in the year of their immigration to Canada in 1987, and the church in which I was baptized.

Behind every arrow in the map I had previously visualized hides a hundred relationships, a thousand stories, ten thousand influences, prayer meetings, discipleship meetings, church committee meetings ... For every one strand pursued here, there are dozens missed. I have not, for example, even touched on the Baptist involvement in civil rights protests during the 1960s, which paved the way for me to grow up in Canada with fair access to housing, healthcare and education. How could everything discussed here possibly be flattened out into an arrow from England to America to Hong Kong to Canada?

Thus in attending to the many influences that have fed into our spiritual heritage, it becomes clear how relationships complicate the Hegelian narrative upon which the arrowized maps are based. At the risk of stating the obvious, imagining the people and the stories behind the arrows makes a difference. It was, in fact, the act of watching an old peasant woman in Jamaica, imagining it was his grandmother, that inspired Brathwaite's concept of tidalectics. As he watched the impoverished woman sweeping sand away from her front door, he finds himself asking why she bothers to do this, and discovers the answer to his question:

> It seems as if her feet, which all along I thought were walking on the sand ... were really ... walking on the water ... and she was travelling across the middle passage, constantly coming from where she had come from – in her case Africa – to this spot in North Coast Jamaica where she now lives.[49]

The realization leads him to ask:

> Why is our psychology not dialectical – successfully dialectical in the way that Western philosophy has assumed people's lives should be, but tidalectic, like our grandmother's – our nana's – action, like the movement of the ocean she's walking on, coming from one continent/continuum, touching another, and then receding ('reading') from the island(s) into the perhaps creative chaos of the(ir) future.[50]

Brathwaite's revelation, writes DeLoughrey, leads her to resist conflating territory with ancestry, to reject the unidirectional narration of movement from 'origin' to 'destination', and allows her to 'reposition [her] own genealogy in the complex intersection of multiple colonial histories'.[51]

So we are now in a better position to address the complex dynamics between ancestral obligation, intergenerational mobility and Western Christian heritage, and to acknowledge how the many possible genealogical strands of Christianization complicate simplistic, linear cartographical representations of origin and destinations from the West to the rest. Seen through the tidalectics of religious ancestry, the acquisition of Western Christian heritage as cultural capital by people with upwardly social aspirations should no longer be dismissed as simple 'racial betrayal'. I would like to discuss this argument by returning to the idea of 'ancestral duty'. In the context of Chinese family lineages, the centrepiece of written documentation is the collection of family rules which are the possession of every prominent clan. 家訓 (*jiaxun*) are instructions passed down by elders to provide advice for younger members of their family, especially sons, to regulate one's own family. Traditionally, lineages played a crucial role in conflict resolution and jurisdiction, so this genre of literature is well established, with precedents going back to Zhou dynasty speeches in the eleventh century BC. An important example of *jiaxun* is the sixth-century *Family Instructions for the Yan Clan* by Yan Zhitui (531–91), and from the sixteenth century onwards, clan genealogies consistently include family rules.[52] Though suppressed in the 1950s during the Cultural Revolution along with other ancestral customs, the economic reforms of the 1980s recognized the productive value of clan-related activities, and clan rules made a resurgence. Today they are being intensively restored and promoted, endorsed even by Xi Jinping himself. The Chow clan prescribes various rules, such as: 'promote ancestral virtues and respect ancestors', 'pray for ancestral protection so every generation will prosper', 'keep upright spousal relations', 'maintain harmony with village neighbours', 'esteem clan members', 'maintain ancestral tombs', 'respect teachers', 'choose friends carefully', 'be diligent at work', 'be frugal', 'choose entertainment carefully', 'obey the country's laws', 'build schools and magnify ancestral accomplishments'.[53]

The emphasis on regulations, rites and respect that the family must uphold serves the Confucian ideal of social harmony and public service. Family and ancestors are to be honoured in business, education and all other areas of work and living. Filial piety and ancestral consciousness are thus linked to success, which ought to be manifest in acts of philanthropy and munificence. For we are but a small link in the lineage: receiving the gift of life from our parents and the endowments with which our ancestors have blessed us, we contribute something to pass on to the next generation. Marina Tan Harper has described this philanthropic orientation in terms of 'ancestral actualization' as opposed to self-actualization (as is common, she says, in the Western value system): deeds of benevolence and service are a way of showing not only allegiance and honour to ancestors, but also keeping the memory of ancestors alive. Success in education, business and hobbies all 'actualize' our ancestors and honour one's family and village.[54] Migrants from China to all regions of the globe from the late eighteenth century onwards did not only view the West as an opportunity to make a quick fortune for themselves, but resolved that if they found success they should direct it towards philanthropy back to their home village – invest in paddy fields or shares in local firms and shops, or endow and build schools or family temples or public works improvements.[55] And so, of all my grandfather's achievements, it is his donation to establish a school back in his home village that is most highly praised in my family.

There are today a range of views about Western Christianity as 'cultural heritage', and I find that 'nominal Christians' provoke highly negative reactions from some quarters: 'They're the worst,' says the Parliamentary Officer for the Bible Society mentioned earlier.[56] The opposition is often made between 'real Christianity', which requires sacrifice, self-denial, poverty, even persecution, and a nominal, cultural Christianity which is disingenuous, insincere, self-deceiving and self-serving.[57] Growing up I had instinctively assumed that the world of white Anglicanism, with its base in the wealthiest area of Toronto, the world of Sung Eucharists and Evensong and Carol Services, a world inhabited by families with memberships to exclusive athletic and social clubs, had practically nothing to do with my weekends spent at Scarborough Chinese Baptist Church attending youth group and Bible studies and prayer meetings and all manner of committee meetings. But I now realize that this is a dangerous opposition to make. To declare that 'cultural Christianity' is intrinsically different from 'real Christianity' is to carve out exclusionary spaces, one belonging to ethnic evangelicalism, and standing in fundamental contrast with the world of Victorian chapels and Choral Evensong: guitars for black and Asian Christians, organs for white Christians. What is frequently labelled a more 'fervent Christianity' easily becomes a code word for a Christianity that does not possess the economic and social power of the latter type. In England, the nation's top roles in government have been occupied not necessarily by those with more 'fervent' and 'devout' forms of Christianity, but by those who have been taught since infancy to recognize the references littered throughout the art and literature of its historic Christian heritage. That is why 'cultural capital' is such a highly sought-after commodity. Therefore, as far as aspirations for upward mobility are concerned, this binary does nothing to address the fact that, in order to gain fluency in the language of power, to gain a seat at the table of government, one needs to adopt and master 'cultural Christianity' – a fact that applies equally to 'real Christians', 'cultural Christians' and 'non-Christians'.

There is a funny perception today that, in a stark role reversal, Western Europe has become the 'new mission field', and yesterday's converts have become the missionaries of today. This sort of thinking depends, once again, on a unidirectional arrowized spatialization, as illustrated in this statement by Dana Roberts. Here, reflecting on the use of Andrew Murray's writings by Watchman Nee, she employs a cartographic imaginary:

> And so the circle was complete. [Andrew] Murray's spiritual writings in English contributed to major missionary revivals in England from the 1890s through the 1910s. From England, a pietistic missionary named Margaret Barber took them to China, where she introduced them to an intense young Chinese Christian named Watchman Nee. And now, in the twenty-first century, the works of Watchman Nee were awakening the spiritual lives of Murray's own ethnic group of white South Africans.[58]

This 'reverse mission' narrative – and particularly the use of the 'coming full circle' image – can really fire missionary zeal. But I find it puzzling. Though it might make for a good film, upon reflection it is condescending both towards Watchman Nee and towards the South Africans who are reading Nee's writings. For the 'real Christianity' of the ethnic evangelists exists always against the backdrop of a more historic Christianity in England which, by mere fact of chronology, is reserved for the white ruling classes. Established forms of cultural Christianity in the metropole might now be considered something that is collecting dust in a museum and in need of revival from ethnic evangelists, but it will always retain a greater authority and higher status over and above forms of Christianity coming from the provinces. The ethnic Christian may, having adopted an evangelical Christianity once transported from England to the periphery, now return to the metropole to preach a hard gospel, but he can never penetrate the ruling class accustomed to the language of Christianity as a language of power, capital and governance. This is the reason why 'reverse mission' from China to England is a delusion, and the idea of 'coming full circle' a platitude. To illustrate the problem, it is sufficient to mention a personal experience – variations of which have occurred so many more times since that it has ceased to surprise me. I was in a famous art gallery in London inspecting a painting of the Virgin and Child, when a well-meaning elderly woman came over and, clearly assuming on the basis of my ethnicity that I needed help understanding English medieval art, proceeded to 'whitesplain' to me who Mary the mother of God was, and who the Christ-child was, and the symbolism of the lily and the colour of Mary's clothing. I wanted neither to cause embarrassment to her nor to me by asserting that I am a professing Christian with great personal devotion to the Lord and Our Lady, in addition also to being a historian of Christianity. In this European art gallery abounding in Christian devotional art, what mattered most was not the sincerity of my belief but my ethnicity.

Thus my problem with the binary between cultural Christianity and real Christianity, and the language of 'reverse mission' which insists on making an opposition between the two. The binary perpetuates the politics of respectability, foisting upon ethnic minorities the impossible choice between an activist, fervent, evangelical Christianity, often connected to revivals in the provinces, and a historically white, ruling-class Christianity at home in museums, art galleries, palaces and royal chapels. Choosing the former, the ethnic Christian remains for ever at the margins; choosing the latter, he or she is accused of being a racial sell-out. But this is a false binary. The deception and danger lurking behind the idea of 'Christian heritage' as a golden nugget transmitted across territories, like an arrow from one point on a map to another, is that it erases the complexities in the stories across generations that occupy the oceans, fluctuating, surging and retreating like waves rather than staying stationery within bounded lands. The arrow hides from Brathwaite the image of his grandmother walking on the ocean, for ever looking forwards and backwards to the land on both sides. Successive generations within my family have transcended their previous generations, and each wave of migration has produced improved educational attainment and economic security. But the story of upward mobility in my family is not just the story of a trans-Atlantic pursuit of Western cultural capital, but is instead complicated by an infinite number of entangled strands coalescing in my family story. It is as the American film-maker Tyler Perry, who grew up in poverty, explained: when asked by Al Sharpton to what he attributed his success, he spoke of his praying mother, grandmother and great-grandmother, and the community of church elders who kept watch over him.[59] Like Perry, upward social mobility and success in my family story is associated with Christianity, and it would not be right to call this racial betrayal, for our Christianization is tied to the countless configurations and tangled strands recounted earlier. Because the genealogical lineages are so complex, our adoption of a 'Western Christian heritage' – and the fact that I feel at ease with the symbolic capital of cultural Christianity – likewise defies a simplistic story of cultural capital accumulation, mimicry and racial betrayal. The unavoidable legacy of imperialism is the pinning of social mobility in colonized groups to the currency of Western Christian heritage: it is an association too strong to ever realistically be rejected or supplanted by racial protest. But the saving grace is that social mobility in the Chinese world view is predicated upon a consciousness of past and future generations: it is by nature altruistic and collectivist. And thus is 'Christian heritage', ironically, de-territorialized and de-nationalized when it merges into my own family history of progress between generations.

Clearly we are no longer in the position we were at in the early twentieth century when the saying was frequently heard in China, 'one more Christian, one less Chinese'. The dismissal of Christianity as a 'foreign religion' or a 'Western religion' holds less and less weight due to the successful inculturation of the religion into indigenous systems. But the final barrier to break down – the one that needs our full resistance and protest – is the barrier that reserves 'high culture' for Western Christendom and a fervent, private, sincere Christianity for ethnic minorities. Thus as Liu Xiaofeng argues, the relationship between Chinese culture and Western Christian heritage must no longer exist as a negotiation or a dialogue between cultures, but as an existential transformation:

> The development of Chinese Christendom, from a form influenced from the outside to a form of its own, does not only ... change the traditional relationship between Chinese culture and Christendom, but also the direction of the future development of Chinese culture itself.[60]

The relationship of Western Christian culture to Chinese culture must not be conceived in terms of inculturation and assimilation but as a full-on 'cultural rearrangement'.[61] For too long the realm of 'Christian heritage' – Christian literature, music, art, philosophy – has been neglected by ethnic minority Christians, while at the same time the 'cultural Christians' who have perceived their main task as enriching this culture are accused of betrayal of the ideals of Christianity. But today there appears a new force, gaining its energy not so much from inside the walls of a church but above all from a new generation of scientists, philosophers, writers, poets, artists and scholars who take serious interest in the history of Western

Christianity for reasons that perhaps could best be described as 'citizenship': they exhibit a strong sense of cultural awareness, a proud cosmopolitanism, intellectual curiosity and a tendency towards an inclusive humanism. What we should be expending our energy protesting here is not that the cultural Christians aren't 'Christian enough' or that they have sold out to whiteness; rather, what we ought to be protesting against is the association of the culture of Western history with ethnic whiteness. In the same way that Chinese pianists have now become authoritative interpreters of Beethoven and Chopin, changing the way we experience Western cultural heritage, so it can be with Augustine and Aquinas. Reflecting on my grandfather's donation for building a school, I can't help but think this represents one important way in which the rear waves of the tides drive on the waves ahead, each new generation surpassing the previous.

Notes

1 William T. Rowe, 2009, *China's Last Empire: The Great Qing*, Cambridge, MA: Belknap of Harvard University Press.

2 Steve Tsang, 2017, 'Modern Hong Kong', *Oxford Research Encyclopedia of Asian History* [online]. Available at: https://eprints.soas.ac.uk/25230/1/Modern%20HK%20in%20Oxford%20Research%20Encyclopedia%20of%20Asian%20History.pdf (accessed 25.08.2021).

3 Amy Chua, 2011, *Battle Hymn of the Tiger Mother*, London: Bloomsbury, pp. 21–2.

4 Chua, *Battle Hymn*, p. 22.

5 Wole Soyinka, 1976, *Myth, Literature and the African World*, Cambridge: Cambridge University Press, p. xii.

6 Influentially studied by Fredrik Fällman: see ISCS (Institute of Sino-Christian Studies), 1997, *Cultural Christians: Phenomenon and Argument*, Hong Kong: Institute of Sino-Christian Studies; Fredrik Fällman, 2008, *Salvation and Modernity: Intellectuals and Faith in Contemporary China*, Lanham, MD: University Press of America; Fredrik Fällman, 2012, 'Calvin, Culture and Christ? Development of Faith among Chinese Intellectuals', in Francis Lim (ed.), *Christianity in Contemporary China*, London: Routledge, pp. 153–68. See also Lian Xi, 2010, *Redeemed by Fire: The Rise of Popular Christianity in Modern China*, New Haven, CT: Yale University Press; Yangwen Zheng, 2015, 'Conversion in Post-Mao China: From "Rice Christians" to "Cultural

Christians"', in Bryan S. Turner and Oscar Salemink (eds), *Routledge Handbook of Religions in Asia*, London: Routledge, pp. 174–90; Gerda Wielander, 2013, *Christian Values in Communist China*, New York: Routledge.

7 Xi, *Redeemed by Fire*, p. 231, quoted in Yangwen Zheng (ed.), 2017, *Sinicizing Christianity*, Studies in Christian Mission 49, Leiden: Brill, p. 26.

8 Liu Xiaobo, 2003, Preface, 'Zai richang shenghuo zhong jujue shuohuan [Reject Lies in Daily Life]', to Yu Jie, *Jiujue Huanyan [Reject Lies]*, Hong Kong: Kaifang chubanshe, pp. 8–9, quoted in Fuk-tsang Ying, 'Liu Xiaobo and the Metaphor of Cross: An Intellectual Journey of a Post-Tiananmen Dissident', in Paulos Z. Huang (ed.), 2017, *Yearbook of Chinese Theology 2017*, Leiden: Brill, pp. 51–74, at 65, emphasis mine.

9 Leung Ka-lun, 1996, 'A Discussion with Zhang Xianyong on Issues Relating [to] "Cultural Christians" (Part II)', *Christian Times* 444, p. 10.

10 See Stephen Steinberg, 2016, 'The Myth of Ethnic Success: Old Wine in New Bottles', in Ronald Bayor (ed.), *The Oxford Handbook of American Immigration and Ethnicity*, Oxford: Oxford University Press, pp. 338–54.

11 Jean-Paul Sartre, 'Preface' to Fanon, *Les damnés de la terre*, in Constance Farrington, trans., 1963, *The Damned*, Paris: Présence africaine, p. 7.

12 See Robert Blauner, 1969, 'Internal Colonialism and Ghetto Revolt', *Social Problems* 16(4), pp. 393–408, and discussion of Frantz Fanon in E. J. R. David and Annie O. Derthick, 2014, 'What is Internalized Oppression, and So What?', in David and Derthick (eds), *Internalized Oppression: The Psychology of Marginalized Groups*, New York: Springer, pp. 1–30.

13 Homi Bhabha, 1994, 'Of Mimicry and Man: The Ambivalence of Colonial Discourse', in 2014, *The Location of Culture*, Routledge Classics Edition, Abingdon: Routledge, pp. 121–31, at 124–5; Ashcroft et al., 'Mimicry', in *Post-Colonial Studies: The Key Concepts*, pp. 124–5.

14 Sathnam Sanghera, 2021, *Empireland: How Imperialism has Shaped Modern Britain*, London: Viking, p. 166–7, with bibliographic citations at n. 1.

15 Rupert Wilkinson, 1964, *The Prefects: British Leadership and the Public School Tradition. A Comparative Study in the Making of Rulers*, London: Oxford University Press, pp. 9–10.

16 Mary Ann Perkins, 2004, *Christendom and European Identity: The Legacy of a Grand Narrative since 1789*, Berlin: Walter de Gruyter, pp. 46–7, quoting Matthew Arnold, 1869, *Culture and Anarchy: An Essay in Political and Social Criticism*, London: Smith, Elder & Co., p. 90.

17 Ingrid Storm, 2011, 'Ethnic Nominalism and Civic Religiosity: Christianity and National Identity in Britain', *The Sociological Review* 59(4).

18 Pierre Bourdieu, 1979, *La distinction: Critique sociale du jugement*, trans. Richard Nice, 2010, *Distinction: A Social Critique of the Judgement of Taste*, London: Routledge.

19 See Darren Sherkat, 2011, 'Immigrants, Migration, and Religion Economics', in Rachel McCleary (ed.), *The Oxford Handbook of the Economics of Religion*, Oxford: Oxford University Press, pp. 151–68, at 153 with references.

20 Andrew McKinnon, 2017, 'Religion and Social Class: Theory and Method after Bourdieu', *Sociological Research Online* 22(1) [online]. Available at: www.socresonline.org.uk/22/1/15.html (accessed 19.08.2021).

21 Section 7, 'God Calls a Bishop (does habitus choose them?)', in McKinnon, 'Religion and Social Class'.

22 Matthew Engelke, 2013, *God's Agents: Biblical Publicity in Contemporary England*, Berkeley, CA: University of California Press, p. 104. In the view of the Parliamentary Officer, the spiritual 'kingdom of God' should be emphasized, not temporal 'Christendom'.

23 Christian Smith, 2003, 'Theorizing Religious Effects among American Adolescents', *Journal for the Scientific Study of Religion* 42(1), pp. 17–30, at 24–5.

24 Alice Ross, 2019, 'The UK Boarding School Identity Crisis', *Financial Times*, 25 October [online]. Available at: www.ft.com/content/98ed81ac-f529-11e9-a79c-bc9acae3b654 (accessed 19.08.2021).

25 Yuan Ren, 2016, 'Importing the Gentleman: Our new elite is taking over the world, and we're modelling them on you', *Spectator*, 24 September [online]. Available at: www.spectator.co.uk/article/importing-the-gentleman (accessed 19.08.2021).

26 Bhabha, 'Of Mimicry and Man', p. 123.

27 See Chapter 1, 'Decolonizing the Map: Postcolonialism, Post-structuralism and the Cartographic Connection', in Graham Huggan, 2008, *Interdisciplinary Measures: Literature and the Future of Postcolonial Studies*, Liverpool: Liverpool University Press, pp. 21–33.

28 Map 1, 'The Apostles and Tradition', pp. 18–19; Map 27, 'Medieval Missions to the Mongol Empire and the East', pp. 81–82; Map 37, 'Protestant Settlers in North America: C17', pp. 104–5; Map 42, 'The Great Awakening in North America', pp. 116–17; Map 47, 'Christian Missions to India and South-East Asia', pp. 126–7, all in Tim Dowley, 2016, *Atlas of Christian History*, Oxford: Lion. Also 'Routes of Exploration' and 'The African Experience', in Henry Chadwick and G. R. Evans (eds), 1990, *Atlas of the Christian Church*, Oxford: Phaidon.

29 Dowley, *Atlas of Christian History*, p. 11, quoting Oliver Cromwell (1599–1658).

30 See, for example, D. Wood, 2003, 'Cartography is Dead (thank God!)', *Cartographic Perspectives* 45, pp. 4–7; J. W. Crampton and J. Krygier. 2006, 'An Introduction to Critical Cartography', *ACME: An International E-Journal for Critical Geographies* 4(1), pp. 11–33.

31 H. van Houtum, 2012, 'Remapping Borders', in T. M. Wilson and D. Hastings (eds), *Companion to Border Studies*, Chichester: John Wiley & Sons, pp. 405–18, at 409–11.

32 Rasmus Grønfeldt Winther, 2020, *When Maps become the World*, Chicago, IL: University of Chicago Press, chapter 7, pp. 180ff.

33 Winther, *When Maps become the World*, p. 182.

34 Carl T. Smith, 2005, *Chinese Christians: Élites, Middlemen, and the Church in Hong Kong*, Hong Kong: Hong Kong University Press, pp. 2–3.

35 Ien Ang, 2001, *On Not Speaking Chinese: Living between Asia and the West*, London: Routledge, p. 39.

36 Kwame Anthony Appiah, 2016, 'Mistaken Identities: Creed, Country, Color, Culture', Lecture 4: Culture [online], Reith Lectures 2016, *BBC Radio 4*. Transcript available at: https://fridayroom.files. wordpress.com/2017/01/2016_reith1-4_appiah_mistaken_identies.pdf (accessed 19.08.2021).

37 Appiah, 'Mistaken Identities'.

38 Houtum, 'Remapping Borders', p. 413.

39 Houtum, 'Remapping Borders', p. 414.

40 Edward Kamau Brathwaite, 1999, *ConVERSations with Nathaniel Mackey*, Staten Island, NY: We Press.

41 Elizabeth M. DeLoughrey, 2007, *Routes and Roots: Navigating Caribbean and Pacific Island Literatures*, Honolulu: University of Hawai'i Press, p. 2.

42 DeLoughrey, *Routes and Roots*, p. 2.

43 See Janet Wilson, 2010, Introduction to 'Section 1: Theoretical Reroutings: Cosmopolitanism, Transnationality and the Neo-liberal Subject', in Janet Wilson, Cristina Sandru and Sarah Lawson Welsh (eds), *Re-Routing the Postcolonial: New Directions for the New Millennium*, New York: Taylor and Francis, pp. 17–21.

44 Paul Youngquist, 2016, 'Introduction', in Paul Youngquist (ed.), *Race, Romanticism, and the Atlantic*, New York: Routledge, pp. 1–24, at 17, with reference to Édouard Glissant, 1997, *Poetics of Relation*, trans. Betsy Wing, Ann Arbor, MI: University of Michigan Press.

45 DeLoughrey, *Routes and Roots*, p. 22, quoting Derek Walcott, 1976, 'Names' (dedicated to Edward Brathwaite), in 1986, *Collected Poems 1948–1984*, New York: Farrar, Straus & Giroux, pp. 305–8.

46 Robert E. Johnson, 2010, *A Global Introduction to Baptist Churches*, Cambridge: Cambridge University Press, p. 53.

47 Smith, *Chinese Christians*, p. 3.

48 Baptist Press website [online, in Chinese]. Available at: www.bappress.org/about-us/ (accessed 19.08.2021).

49 Brathwaite, *ConVERSations with Nathaniel Mackey*, pp. 32–3, ellipses original.

50 Brathwaite, *ConVERSations with Nathaniel Mackey*, p. 34.

51 DeLoughrey, *From Routes and Roots*, pp. x–xi.

52 Antje Richter, 2015, 'Between Letter and Testament: Letters of Familial Admonition in Han and Six Dynasties China', in Antje Richter (ed.), *A History of Chinese Letters and Epistolary Culture*, Leiden: Brill, pp. 239–75, at 243.

53 中華周氏聯譜 – 廣東卷, *A Joint Genealogy of the Chow Family Name in China: Guangdong Volume*, 2012.

54 Marina Tan Harper, 2019, 'Shaping Philanthropy for Chinese Diaspora in Singapore and Beyond: Family, Ancestry, Identity, Social Norms', unpublished doctoral thesis, Indiana University, p. 116.

55 Carl T. Smith, 1971, 'The Emergence of a Chinese Elite in Hong Kong', *Journal of the Hong Kong Branch of the Royal Asiatic Society* 11, pp. 74–115, at 103. See also Smith, *Chinese Christians*.

56 Engelke, *God's Agents*, p. 110.

57 For example, famously, William Wilberforce, 1797, *A practical view of the prevailing religious system of professed Christians, in the higher and middle classes in this country, contrasted with real Christianity*, London: printed for T. Cadell. And Walter Lowrie, 1968, trans. of Søren Kierkegaard, *Kierkegaard's Attack upon Christendom 1854–1855*, Princeton, NJ: Princeton University Press.

58 Dana Roberts, 2009, *Christian Mission: How Christianity became a World Religion*, Oxford: Wiley-Blackwell, 'Postscript', pp. 176–7.

59 Frederick Harris, 2014, 'The Rise of Respectability Politics', *Dissent Magazine* [online]. Available at: www.dissentmagazine.org/article/the-rise-of-respectability-politics (accessed 19.08.2021).

60 Liu Xiaofeng, 1996, 'Die akademische Erforschung des Christentums im kulturellen System des Kommunismus', *China heute*, pp. 178–83, quoted in Roman Malek, 2015, 'Christendom and its Manifestations in China Today', in Max Deeg and Bernhard Scheid (eds), *Religion in China: Major Concepts and Minority Positions*, Vienna: Austrian Academy of Sciences Press, pp. 113–42 at 134.

61 Liu Xiaofeng, 'Die akademische Erforschung', p. 136.

Conclusion

Writing this book has been the process of coming to terms with my absence from the ancestral record, a fact that applies equally to my family heritage as to my religious. Having begun this project with the unquestioned assumption that I am a member of the Chow line, my heart sank as I turned to the last page of the genealogy book and discovered that, as far as the record is concerned, I do not exist because I am female. From a lineage that begins in 972 with the founding ancestor and proceeds through nearly 1,000 years, we arrive in the thirty-second generation at my father, who is recorded on the family tree as having only one child – my brother. When the genealogy is officially updated, the names of my brother's three sons will be added to this genealogy; neither I nor my own three children will appear anywhere in it. I wonder, do my uncles and distant uncles and male cousins with the Chow surname think I am foolish for taking such an interest in my ancestral history? What explains my enthusiasm for a genealogical record that so flagrantly bypasses my children and me?

'Ancestral feeling' is instinctual. Whether or not I benefit from recognition in the genealogical record, or from a formal inheritance of title or estate, ancestors ground my sense of identity, purpose and moral conduct. Merely mentioning the word 'ancestors' can induce feelings of humility, deference, hope and gratitude. And I find the presence of ancestors everywhere, not only on the official days set apart for honouring them but even more so in unexpected moments and mundane objects: a map, a street name, a piece of furniture, a pattern of fabric, a particular scent, a certain taste. Ancestors influence much of our daily existence even if we may not always realize it. As Uncle Roger instructs about making egg fried rice, and this is very true: 'Now we add soy sauce. Just use feeling. We put soy sauce in until our ancestors tell us is enough.'[1]

Many Christians apply this same 'ancestral feeling' to their faith. But Christian heritage often assumes a national character, like Wordsworth describing 'English hearts' possessed by the majesty of their spires, steeple-towers and ancient minsters. The history of Western Christianity is unavoidably central to the identity of Protestant and Catholic Christians all over the world, so why do we generally assume that it is only the white British who can speak with personal affection for it? Tom Holland's *Dominion: The Making of the Western Mind* and Peter Ackroyd's *Albion: The Origins of the English Imagination* once more galvanize our appreciation for Western Christian culture, but it's the failure to appreciate how much this spiritual kinship is shared with the non-white or non-English that stands out to me.[2] Some have quipped that being 'white British' does not automatically mean they have a 'Christian ancestry', because they are the first 'real Christians' in their family. I think they misunderstand the problem. For they live in a nation in which no dissonance exists between ethnic heritage and Christian heritage. They can add spiced currants into their pudding on Stir-up Sunday or flour in their pancake mix on Shrove Tuesday until their ancestors tell them it's enough – an action invoking at once their ethnic heritage and the religious heritage of their nation. As Tom Holland quotes of Pen Vogler, 'Christmas pudding isn't just a taste; it is a lifetime of personal memories; it is centuries worth of folk memories; it is almost unique in being a food and a cultural symbol of union across a nation.'[3] The problem here, I'd want to reply, is that the English went to Hong Kong and taught me to care about Christmas, but now I'm in England I'm told that Christmas pudding is only a symbol of your memories, not mine. With Roger Scruton's *Our Church: A Personal History of the Church of England*, I can emphasize this point further. Says Simon Jenkins of the spires, pinnacles, finials, Book of Common Prayer, Nine Lessons and Carols and church bells lovingly described by Scruton:

He surveys all this with an indulgent eye. He might be guiding us round a much loved ancestral home, patting the Chippendale here, pointing to a Gainsborough there, reminiscing about a dodgy uncle, quoting Milton, Bunyan, Auden, Larkin.[4]

But the truly revolutionary revelation is that, though a late-comer to Europe, I have as much right to assert this as *my* 'much loved ancestral home' too, such is the legacy of colonialism. By the fact of my confessional descent from the 'lineage' of Milton and Bunyan, they are *my* ancestors too. And so do I feel com-pelled to write a 'personal history of the Church of England', even if the task of finding my ancestors in this history demands that I develop a new sense of hearing and seeing. With Jeffrey Santa Ana, I understand that 'feeling ancestral' means engag-ing in the 'complex search for self-placement in history – a history intimately tied to the human consequences of globali-zation'. These twin poles – Wordsworth's English 'ancestral feeling' on the one hand, and Santa Ana's self-placement into the ancestral record on the other – have governed my argument and method in this book. I boast *ancestral feeling* in my West-ern Christian heritage, possessed by love and pious sentiment when I encounter minsters and steeples and towers; but this ancestral feeling can ever only represent oppression by Western hegemony unless it awakens the memory of my own ancestors.

Though fundamentally altered and shaped in mind, body and spirit by the legacies of imperial power and dominance, nevertheless I cannot agree with Foucault that ours should be an *anti*-genealogy, that we must reject a reverent, pious and grateful approach to the past, that we must be emancipated from 'heritage'. Christians of every colour have always received as a gift their 'goodly heritage': by faith we consider ourselves descendants of a long chain of faithful men and women who have expressed worship of God, experienced his good provi-dence, led a life of obedience, answered the call to preaching and evangelism, died in hope of a life that is to come. Via the creeds and Scripture, the faith of the apostles is 'handed down' by saints, martyrs, confessors, reformers, preachers, chaplains and the influential people in our lives: parents, siblings, aunts and uncles, neighbours, teachers, coaches, colleagues ... There is no other way to conceive of faith than as 'transmission' from one generation to another. So I stand and rise, 'bringing the gifts that my ancestors gave': this is what every Christian of faith affirms.[5]

This 'goodly heritage' – though instinctual – is not an easy reality for ethnic minority Christians: it raises uneasy questions and answers about where our inheritance comes from, and reminds us of our entangled roots, broken roots and missing roots. Thus, I have targeted my critique at historical thinking, because it is historical thinking that makes Europe (and England specifically in this book) inescapable. I wanted to find a way to think historically which fosters a more inclusive memory, one that allows my ethnic heritage to bear on my Western Christian heritage. Therefore, I argued that there are certain things we must unlearn in how we think about our Christian ancestry, components of the language of lineage which we need to discard as they keep ethnic minority Christians in a peripheral and marginal position vis-à-vis the centrality of Europe. A postcolonial reading of Christian history will notice: how the language of spiritual descent has been used to legitimize English nationalism and reinforce English exceptionalism; how explaining denominationalism and confessionalism by way of lineage makes Western European Christianity the central trunk and all other groups smaller and less significant branches; how our chronologies about the history of Christianity depend on epochal 'turning points' dictated by English Protestantism; how our definitions of Christian heritage reflect mostly the intellectual and artistic contributions, and tastes and values, of nineteenth-century English Romanticism; how our temporal and spatial visualizations make England the centre and reference point for the rest of the world; how our ways of thinking about metropole and provinces present the impossible choice between racial protest and racial betrayal.

Chapters 4–6 explored the use of family history to counteract the dominance of Western 'genealogical pedigrees', to bridge personal narrative with the grand narrative, writing a new lineage of belief for us who, though brought into a relationship with Western Christianity, are bypassed by its history. First, I tried to listen to the voice of my mother's adversity and aspiration in the English hymns from her school hymn book and contemplated how her deference to the Western canon constitutes an ancestral sphere of nurture. Next, I argued that the nostalgia which ecclesiastical heritage sites evokes should not be a monumental, nationalistic memory with authoritative interpretations, but should represent the memory-making activities of those whose connection to the site arises from colonialism and resultant fragmented identities. Finally, I proposed that our cartographic imaginations need to be adjusted in order to account for the limitless lineages which explain one's religious affiliations, and that we should acknowledge how Christian cultural heritage is associated with a family's intergenerational progress.

Ethnic minority Catholic and Protestant Christians are the invisible successors to the heritage of Western Christianity: its literary canon, ecclesiastical sites, sacred music, all of which are taught about in schools, displayed in museums, heard on radios and in concert halls as cultural achievements arising from the history of Europe, essential for understanding the last two millenia in the West, and often synonymous with English culture. In practical terms, my book registers the plea that we connect the personal family histories of ethnic minorities to the study of European historical subjects, and in this way increase belonging and widen participation in England's heritage sector. Promoting 'ancestor salience' so that the ethnic and religious no longer represent distinct circles of memory is one important postcolonial historiographical technique for countering continued hegemonies, what Jennings has called confronting 'the colonial fragments that have shattered our worlds and which we are constantly trying to unfold and piece together'.[6] Colonialism made heterogeneity and hybridity a positional reality for many. While many white British Christians may enjoy traditions that strengthen the coherence between religious memory, national memory and family memory, like attending choral Eucharist on Christmas morning, then enjoying a roast dinner, before watching the Royal Christmas Message, for me as an immigrant several times over, national religious holidays are disjointed experiences. My 'English'-themed Christmas (Mass followed by my best attempt at a Mrs Beeton Victorian Christmas dinner) and the 'ethnic'-themed one I grew up with (watching the choir of immigrants perform Messiah with heavy Cantonese accents at my Chinese Baptist church, followed by a 'hot pot' meal at a Chinese restaurant) produce angst in equal measure. Anxiously, I hover between embarrassment at my pathetic racial insecurities and disdain at the sight of my husband's fried noodle side dish adulterating my Christmas dinner. I am dissatisfied with platitudes about how to manage these 'specialized circles of memory'. Don't I realize how lucky I am, many say. Isn't it great, I am told, that I enjoy a 'fusion' tradition?

But the work of 'fusing' disparate horizons is hard. Colonized, diasporic, immigrant peoples have the particular task of reconstructing the link between what came before in global history and his or her own actual experience, to construct – using Hervieu-Léger's term – a 'chain of memory' which bridges the circles of nationality, ethnicity and religion rendered distinct by historic, global processes.[7] Bede, Benedictine monasticism, saints' shrines, Gothic cathedrals, Anselm, Thomas Cranmer, the King James Bible, the Toleration Act, William Wilberforce, and so on and so forth ... England's 'long and illustrious history' (to quote the official study guide, *Life in the United Kingdom*, for the settlement and citizenship examination) is filled with figures, movements and events whose importance cannot be undermined or replaced, even if we uncover other ones to represent our diversity, because they explain so much of Christian identity for so many Christians in the world.[8] So now, ethnic minority Christians must assert that these, too, are our heritage, because they do not exist in a historical bubble, untouched by the colonizations, migrations, fragmentations and hard-won assimilations and acculturations of today's Christians, not to mention their contributions to Christian life in Britain. Without doing so, 'our Christian heritage' will remain the domain of local interest societies composed of retired professionals in affluent villages with English Heritage stickers on their car windshields. Should it not be for my children that, having inherited the faith of their parents and *their* parents, they ought to feel that abbey ruins, the choral tradition, church bells – these things that Stanley Baldwin said make England what it is – ought to be *their* 'childish inheritance' and reflect something of *their* ancestral story too?[9] But declaring an intimate connection and personal stake in Western Christianity's literary and musical canon, heritage assets and cultural capital is a probing and taxing task, because these dimensions of Christian heritage relate to the hardships, aspirations and sacrifices of our parents, grandparents and great-grandparents, whose lives became entwined with global imperialism. Flippantly we may say that we are grateful for our Christian heritage, but, for me, I have found it an arduous undertaking to lay bare how the stories of poverty and aspiration in my family affect the way I sing an English hymn impregnated with medieval and medievalist imperial overtones, how family migrations colour and heighten my experience of nostalgia at a national heritage site, how the many possible lines of confluence and descent which explain the religious affiliations in my family mean that my adoption of Western cultural symbols is not a matter of racial betrayal. Bringing the fragments of my family history to the behemoth that is 'the history of Western Christendom' – to declare, in a land in which I am literally tripping over ecclesiastical history, that this is the inheritance left to me by my ancestors too – is uncomfortable, unseemly, even undignified. And, like my imagined encounter with Charlemagne in the Panthéon, I fear being ridiculed for it. But I would hope that Jennings is right when he says that 'This fragment work is a deeply Christian calling'.[10]

Western Christianity entered my family history and can therefore not be seen apart from 'the life which had produced me and nourished me and paid for me'.[11] The symbols of England's Christian heritage consequently arouse the memory of my ancestors. Walking beneath the breathtakingly beautiful fan-vaulted ceiling of a fourteenth-century cloister, I can bring to my mind the faces of my ancestors and remember that they, too, are central to my Christian inheritance. By the fact of England's presence in China and Hong Kong, the postcolonial reality is that England's Christian heritage is also the story of the faith, hope and love of my ancestors.

Notes

1 Uncle Roger, the persona adopted by comedian Nigel Ng [online]. Available at: www.youtube.com/watch?v=SGBP3sG3a9Y (accessed 19.08.2021).

2 Tom Holland, 2019, *Dominion: The Making of the Western Mind*, London: Little, Brown; Peter Ackroyd, 2002, *Albion: The Origins of the English Imagination*, London: Chatto & Windus.

3 Pen Vogler, 2020, *Scoff: A History of Food and Class in Britain*, London: Atlantic Books [electronic version accessed at the British Library], 303.7/979-305.0/979 (accessed 08.06.2021). Vogler's point here is that the meaning of Christmas pudding depends a lot on your age, and that for younger generations Christmas pudding may not be able to compete today with 'individualism, competition, the free market, and as much chocolate as you can eat'. But Tom Holland invokes this quotation on Twitter as a patriotic salute to Christmas pudding instead (27.04.2021).

4 Simon Jenkins, 2012, 'Nostalgic Nationalist Piety: Review of Scruton, *Our Church*', 10 November [online]. Available at: www.spectator.co.uk/article/nostalgic-nationalist-piety (accessed 19.08.2021).

5 Maya Angelou, 1986, 'Still I Rise', in *And Still I Rise*, London: Virago, pp. 41–2.

6 Willie James Jennings, 2020, *After Whiteness: An Education in Belonging*, Grand Rapids, MI: Eerdmans, p. 17.

7 The Jamaican cultural historian Stuart Hall remarked towards the end of his life that he was 'fated to mix memory with desire'. Patel reflects, 'Perhaps this is the inevitable longing that attends the lived experience of diaspora, in which the circumstances of the present and ancestral past begin to mix together, and the memories and motives operating beyond conscious retrieval begin to inhabit one's sense of the historical world.' Ian Sanjay Patel, 2021, *We're Here Because You Were There: Immigration and the End of Empire*, London: Verso, pp. 19–20, quoting Stuart Hall, 2018, *Familiar Stranger: A Life Between Two Islands*, London: Penguin, p. xiv, and with reference to pp. 198–9.

8 Home Office, 2013, *Life in the United Kingdom: A Guide for New Residents*, 3rd edn, Norwich: TSO, p. 14.

9 See Introduction, n. 63.

10 Jennings, *After Whiteness*, p. 37. He writes, 'Many people come

to theological education looking for help with the fragment, hoping that those who teach about their faith can help them reassemble what was shattered, help them gather together what remains' (p. 35). See all of pp. 35–44.

11 Raoul Peck (ed.), 2007, *James Baldwin: I Am Not Your Negro – A Companion Edition to the Documentary Film Directed by Raoul Peck*, New York: Vintage International, p. 13.

Afterword

This book was written mainly between the hours of 11 pm and 4 am owing to the extraordinary circumstances of a global pandemic and the attendant requirement to supervise the home learning of my three children. Meditating on my ancestral heritage at a time when I was literally barred from seeing my family overseas intensified the seriousness of the questions agitating me concerning my relationship with Europe. But during a time of crisis, I noticed how naturally we draw upon family tradition to survive. As I summoned the memory of my ancestors to make dumplings and a lion dance costume for our lockdown Lunar New Year, so too – in response to the closure of churches – did my children instinctively turn our bedsheet into an altar cloth, my dress into a chasuble, a shelf into a lectern, and suddenly set their iPad to play church music. Such things surely are not the monopoly of Western Christianity, yet for my family at least, and for the reasons I have outlined in this book, they represent inheritances that have come to us via Western Europe. Heritage, of course, depends on people feeling sufficient ownership over it to manifest and transmit it, and my children (still innocent enough to be unhampered by identitarian labels) showed me that it is possible to feel secure enough about one's inclusion in 'England's Christian heritage' to introduce its elements into our home. That my children can do so is the result of people in our lives who have refused to stifle us with the burden of 'English Christianity', but have instead affirmed our part in it, emboldened us to tell the complicated story of our connection to it, and urged us to apply our creative energies to shape it for the future.[1]

Notes

1 Here I acknowledge those without whom I would not have had the courage to write this book: Simon Cuff, Selina Stone, Lincoln Harvey, Peter Howarth, Mary Thorne and dear friends in the self-proclaimed 'Bloomsbury Social'. For efficient editorial work and production, I thank David Shervington, Hannah Ward, Rachel Geddes and Kate Hughes. The individuals who endorsed my book did so though I was a stranger: I thank them for their good will. Finally, I thank Nicholas, whose faithfulness, positivity and midnight snacks sustained me and secured the completion of this work.

Index